HUMAN RIGHTS AND INTERNATIONAL POLITICAL ECONOMY IN THIRD WORLD NATIONS

HUMAN RIGHTS AND INTERNATIONAL POLITICAL ECONOMY IN THIRD WORLD NATIONS

Multinational Corporations, Foreign Aid, and Repression

William H. Meyer

PRAEGER

Westport, Connecticut
London

HG5993
.M49
1998

Library of Congress Cataloging-in-Publication Data

Meyer, William H.
    Human rights and international political economy in third world
nations : multinational corporations, foreign aid, and repression /
William H. Meyer.
        p.   cm.
    Includes bibliographical references and index.
    ISBN 0–275–96172–9 (alk. paper). — ISBN 0–275–96280–6 (pbk. :
alk. paper)
    1. Investments, American—Moral and ethical aspects—Developing
countries. 2. International business enterprises—Developing
countries. 3. Human rights—Developing countries. I. Title.
HG5993.M49   1998
337'.09172'4—dc21   98–4940

British Library Cataloguing in Publication Data is available.

Library of Congress Catalog Card Number: 98–4940
ISBN: 0–275–96172–9
        0–275–96280–6 (pbk.)

First published in 1998

Praeger Publishers, 88 Post Road West, Westport, CT 06881
An imprint of Greenwood Publishing Group, Inc.

Printed in the United States of America

The paper used in this book complies with the
Permanent Paper Standard issued by the National
Information Standards Organization (Z39.48–1984).

10 9 8 7 6 5 4 3 2 1

Copyright Acknowledgments

The author and publisher gratefully acknowledge permission to reprint excerpts from the following:

William H. Meyer, "Toward a Global Culture: Human Rights, Groups Rights, and Cultural Relativism," *International Journal on Group Rights*, 3(3) (1995/1996): 169–95. Reprinted with kind permission from Kluwer Law International.

William H. Meyer, "Human Rights and MNCs: Theory Versus Quantitative Analysis," *Human Rights Quarterly*, 18(2) (May 1996): 368–97. Reprinted with permission from The Johns Hopkins University Press.

For my parents, Vince and Bobbie Meyer

Contents

Illustrations

Acknowledgments

I have many people to thank for assisting in the long process of producing this book. I am indebted to friends and colleagues at the University of Delaware who read and reacted to earlier versions of the writings presented here. Their suggestions were most helpful. I am especially grateful to Kurt Burch, Ken Campbell, Bob Denemark, and Jim Oliver. I also thank the many people who assisted in the research itself. At the risk of leaving someone out, I thank Becca Arenson, Lindsay Burt, Somaly Bun Chhun, April Clark, Alice Feldman, Kasey Fink, Alexa Hook, Yuko Kasuga, Tamara Neely, Jeff Neumann, and Kelly Whitman. I owe a special debt to Julie Mueller for her research on structural adjustment, Robbie O'Reilly for his work on Chile, Jane Winzer for her research on cultural relativism, and Ami Schiess for her work on the maquiladora zone in Mexico. Although this book would not have been possible without the help of these many friends, all errors and omissions that remain are mine alone.

Funding for this research was provided in part by a fellowship from the National Endowment for the Humanities and by a University of Delaware General Research Grant.

Abbreviations

AFP	Alliance for Progress
AI	Amnesty International
AID	Agency for International Development
AIP	Apparel Industry Partnership
ANC	African National Congress
ANCOM	Andean Common Market
BIP	Border Industrialization Program
BIT	Bilateral Investment Treaty
BJP	Bharatiya Janata Party
CAAA	Comprehensive Anti-Apartheid Act
CBI	Caribbean Basin Initiative
CE	Constructive Engagement
CEC	Commission on Environmental Cooperation
CIA	Central Intelligence Agency
CIDS	Corporate Internal Decision Structures
CJM	Coalition for Justice in the Maquiladoras
C/P	Civil and Political Rights
DA	Developmental Assistance
DFI	Direct Foreign Investment
EAI	Enterprise for the Americas Initiative
ECLA	Economic Commission for Latin America
EPZ	Export Processing Zones

FAA	Foreign Assistance Act
FERA	Foreign Exchange Regulation Act
FMF	Foreign Military Financing
FY	Fiscal Year
GAO	General Accounting Office
GE	General Electric Company
GM	General Motors Corporation
GNP	Gross National Product
GSP	Generalized System of Preferences
IBHR	International Bill of Human Rights
ILLIT	Illiteracy Rate of Adult Population
IMET	International Military Education and Training
IMF	International Monetary Fund
INFMOR	Infant Mortality per 1,000 Live Births
IPA	International Police Academy
IPE	International Political Economy
ISI	Import Substitution Industry
ITT	International Telephone and Telegraph Company
LDC	Less Developed Country
LIFEXP	Life Expectancy at Age One
LRFI	Law for Regulation of Foreign Investment
MFN	Most Favored Nation
MIC	Methyl Isocyanate
MNC	Multinational Corporation
NAAEC	North American Agreement on Environmental Cooperation
NAALC	North American Agreement on Labor Cooperation
NADB	North American Developmental Bank
NAFTA	North American Free Trade Agreement
NAO	National Administrative Office
NATO	North Atlantic Treaty Organization
NGO	Nongovernmental Organization
NIC	Newly Industrialized Country
OAS	Organization of American States
OECD	Organization for Economic Cooperation and Development
OPIC	Overseas Private Investment Corporation
OPS	Office of Public Safety
PQLI	Physical Quality of Life Index
PRC	People's Republic of China
RSA	Republic of South Africa

R^2	Variance Explained
SOE	State Owned Enterprise
UC	Union Carbide Corporation
UCI	Union Carbide of India
UDHR	Universal Declaration of Human Rights
UNCTAD	United Nations Conference on Trade and Development
WHO	World Health Organization

HUMAN RIGHTS AND INTERNATIONAL POLITICAL ECONOMY IN THIRD WORLD NATIONS

Introduction

In 1996 a new scandal caught the attention of the U.S. media and the U.S. public. Kathie Lee Gifford, hostess of a popular talk show, was accused of promoting sweatshops in Honduras through her work as a spokeswoman for clothing sold in Wal-Mart stores. Charges that Gifford was complicitous in the abuse of foreign workers led to tearful denials on her television program, and her husband, Frank Gifford, was even seen handing out cash to workers in New York City's garment district. The handouts were meant to show the Giffords' concern and compassion for textile workers around the world. The Kathie Lee sweatshop scandal also led the media to investigate whether other celebrities represent corporations that mistreat their overseas work force. Michael Jordan's ties to Nike and allegations of human rights abuses by Nike subcontractors in Indonesia and Vietnam are further cases in point. Nongovernmental human rights organizations, such as Amnesty International and Global Exchange, have used media attention to these cases as a way to further their own campaigns, putting pressure on corporations to improve working conditions for their labor forces in developing nations.

The Kathie Lee scandal, like most media events, came and went in a relatively short period of time.[1] However, the questions raised at that time remain relevant to this day. Do private corporations violate the rights of workers and other citizens in Third World nations? If so, what are the nature and extent of such violations? If not, where is the evidence to the contrary? Denials of worker abuse by Nike and other multinational corporations (MNCs) included a rejoinder that in fact these MNCs improve social and economic conditions in the Third World. If the MNC defense of their operations is valid, how can we be sure that private businesses have a positive impact on welfare in Third World nations?

This book seeks to establish the impact of U.S. economic actors on human rights in the Third World. The general approach taken here is to address human rights in developing nations as something that is influenced by international political economy (IPE). IPE focuses on linkages between global markets and other mechanisms that allocate political power or economic resources. IPE is particularly interested in the ties between global economic transactions and domestic and international political change. Although IPE is a relatively new approach to the study of rights in the Third World, it holds promise for sorting through the puzzling aspects of private and public economic activities, especially the impact these activities have upon political rights and social welfare in less developed countries (LDCs).

The chapters that follow investigate many dimensions of the IPE of human rights. Chapters 3, 4, and 5 present original research that seeks to break new ground in the study of human rights in LDCs. Prior to these studies, Chapters 1 and 2 provide a backgound in certain political, philosophical, cultural, and conceptual materials necessary to an understanding of rights in the Third World.

Chapter 1 defines the terms used in this study. Conceptual analysis of the terms "rights" and "human rights" can be found in the first chapter. Because this is a study of human rights in the Third World, special attention is also paid in Chapter 1 to the cultural debate over proper definitions of human rights. There is much disagreement between Western and non-Western societies over human rights priorities. A survey of this cultural debate about human rights serves to illuminate the research that follows.

Chapter 2 presents the political background necessary to understanding the connections between U.S. economic actors and human rights in the Third World. This chapter also discusses ties between economics and politics and theories of the proper role for personal ethics in the realm of politics. It contains a review of U.S. foreign policies on human rights and foreign policy related to MNC operations in LDCs.

Chapter 3 contains a quantitative study of the ties between U.S. businesses and human rights in Third World nations. Drawing on a data set that includes more than 50 LDCs, and with information from the 1980s and 1990s, Chapter 3 takes a macroscale view. It presents a description of how MNCs affect rights in LDCs by pointing to the broad international trends linking private corporations to different areas of rights. The quantitative information in Chapter 3 is presented in a way that is accessable to all students of human rights, regardless of their statistical acumen. The same applies for the data presented in Chapter 4.

Chapter 4 looks for connections between human rights and foreign aid. Foreign aid stands as a second significant economic input for LDCs, one that in some ways is inseparable from the presence of U.S. MNCs. Chapter 4 opens by discussing the connections between private investment by MNCs and public investment in the form of aid to the Third World. That chapter goes on to detail, through a second quantitative study, the relationships between economic aid, military aid, and human rights in LDCs. Chapter 4 identifies the overall trends linking different forms of aid to different types of rights. Chapters 3 and 4 stay at the same level of analysis. They employ aggregate and cross-national data to describe the IPE of human rights at the global level.

Chapter 5 moves to a lower level of analysis. It contains case studies of specific MNCs in certain Third World nations and describes the impact of MNCs on human rights in Chile, India, and Mexico. The case studies serve to articulate and elaborate on the larger trends tying MNCs to human rights in LDCs as well as to add texture and richness of detail to the descriptions of MNCs and human rights. Combining the cross-national data and the case study data produces an analysis of human rights that has multiple layers and greater validity.

The concluding chapter of this book pulls together the results from the various philosophical, quantitative, and case study analyses. Chapter 6 includes a description of alleged Third World sweatshops. Strategies used by nongovernmental organizations and by the Clinton administration to improve the behavior of MNCs are also analyzed. Chapter 6 ends with a discussion of international debate over human rights in the twenty-first century.

NOTE

1.   See Chapter 6 for more on sweatshops and recent U.S. policy to combat this form of worker abuse.

1

Universal Human Rights in a Cross-Cultural Context

As the world moves into the twenty-first century, global trends hold both promise and danger for international human rights. The collapse of communism and the demise of one-party states indicate an expansion of political rights in many regions. The dismantling of apartheid in South Africa points toward an end to this most egregious form of racial discrimination. The end of Cold War rivalries has stirred hopes that a peace dividend in the industrialized nations might be invested in ways that will promote global economic expansion. While communism recedes as an ideological and economic alternative to Western capitalist democracy, the developing nations of the South are looking more and more toward a liberal model of growth. Multinational corporations (MNCs) become the harbinger of jobs, investment, and production that might pull much of the world out of poverty.

These same trends, however, also contain the potential for serious violations of human rights. The centrifugal forces at work in the remnants of the Eastern bloc have exploded into widespread violence and acts of "ethnic cleansing." Post-apartheid factionalism in South Africa also threatens to undo a fledgling democracy because of ancient hatreds. Finally, those agents most likely to enhance rapid economic growth in developing nations — Western MNCs — also represent a potential threat to the rights of the people they ostensibly serve, for example: the residents of Bhopal,

India; or women laboring in the factories of Third World export processing zones (EPZs).

This chapter will set the context for an empirical study of MNCs, foreign aid, and human rights in developing nations.[1] The concept of universal human rights will be defined with special attention to human rights as they relate to Third World cultures. In Chapter 2, U.S. foreign policy on aid, corporate investment, and human rights will be analyzed. This conceptual, theoretical, and policy background will then serve as the basis for new research into human rights, U.S. businesses, and foreign assistance in the Third World.

TWO GENERATIONS OF RIGHTS

Any study of human rights must necessarily begin with a careful definition of the terms "rights" and "human rights." Any discussion of international human rights must come to grips with the cultural diversity of human existence. If human rights are truly universal as is often claimed, then they must apply to all people in all cultures.

This study is primarily interested in the relationship between MNCs and human rights in the Third World. Before addressing MNCs themselves, however, it is necessary to define our terms. One must also put the issue of MNCs and rights into the proper international political context. These considerations require a review of some of the philosophical and historical dimensions of human rights.

Human rights as a subject of international concern and the global campaign for legal recognition of universal human rights are largely post–World War II phenomena. Before World War II, how a government treated its own citizens was considered to be almost exclusively a domestic political or legal issue. Rights at that time were not generally subject to international law, international regulation, or international control. Now, attention to human rights as a subject of international political concern and as an area of international law is here to stay (Forsythe, 1989).

To trace the rise of the international human rights movement, one must begin with the origins of rights themselves. The earliest usages of the English word "right" as referring to a "standard of permitted [or] forbidden action within a certain sphere; law; a rule or canon" or as a "justifiable claim, on legal or moral grounds" can be traced back to the ninth and tenth centuries (*Oxford English Dictionary*, 1979: 669–70). Western conceptions of rights go back much further, however, to the classical days of Greece and Rome. The Greek system of rights as embodied in Athenian democracy established certain political rights for citizens. They had equality before the law, an equal right to speak in the forum, and the right to seek public office. Of course, these were rights for citizens only. To be a citizen one had to be an adult male with property (Cranston, 1973). Such rights did not apply to women, children, slaves, or the majority of the Athenian population.

The Roman system of rights that followed was developed largely by the Stoics, such as Cicero, Zeno, and Marcus Aurelius (Cranston, 1973; Pennock, 1981). In ancient Rome, rights were asserted for the first time to be universal. Roman law was the universal law governing nearly all of the known Western world from the British isles to the lands of the Mediterranean. Marcus Aurelius argued that all men (rights were still reserved for men only) had equal powers of reason. Hence, all men should enjoy equality before the law, regardless of nationality or station in life (Ebenstein, 1969: 163).

There was little or no development of rights theory in the Middle Ages, with the possible exception of just war theory as it applied to protection of combatants and noncombatants alike (Walzer, 1977). Then, during the early modern period of European history, there were rapid developments of new rights traditions, largely as a reaction to tyranny. Notable events included the Magna Carta of 1215. Forced upon King John I by the English barons, this document recognized special privileges for the aristocracy when it came to raising money in support of the monarchy. The Magna Carta also included a "primitive formulation of the right to a fair trial" (Robertson and Merrills, 1992: 4). The English Bill of Rights (1689) proclaimed the rights to freedom of speech, freedom from cruel and unusual punishment, and trial by jury. The U.S. Bill of Rights (1789) and the French Rights of Man (1789) asserted constitutional guarantees for free speech, a free press, equality before the law, and freedom of religion (among others).

These rights are often referred to as civil and political rights or as first generation rights. The Western (liberal) interpretation of these rights is that they guarantee freedoms for all, which rulers and governments cannot deny or abridge. First generation rights are designed to protect individuals from government tyranny. A critical interpretation of first generation rights advanced by Karl Marx is that these are rights only for the ruling class, or middle class rights. Such rights allegedly exist only for those with the economic resources to take advantage of them. Free speech, a free press, and economic opportunity were merely bourgeoise rights for Marx because they were available only for the enjoyment of the middle and upper classes. They could not be the rights of all people if the poorest classes have no way to enjoy them. If the dispossessed and disenfranchised are too busy trying to avoid hunger and starvation to exercise their nominal rights, then, for Marx, such rights were necessarily not universal (Marx and Engels, 1848). This Marxist critique of first generation rights closely parallels the current international debate over the relative importance of civil-political versus economic rights.

Human rights as a subject of international treaties first appeared in the late nineteenth and early twentieth centuries. Although the term "human rights" was not common in those days, precursors to more recent human rights treaties were developed at that time. The first international agreements to ban slavery and the slave trade and treaties to protect some religious minorities existed prior to World War I (see Robertson and Merrills, 1992: 14-19). After World War I, members of the League of Nations were obliged to promote the material and moral well-being and the social progress of their people (League of Nations Covenant, Articles XXII–XXIII). The League also worked to develop agreements to protect further some ethnic minorities (for example, Greeks living in Turkey).

With the advent of the Great Depression and the New Deal policies of Franklin Roosevelt, new government programs led to early talk of "welfare rights." Social security, unemployment insurance, and assistance for widows and orphans expanded the notion of rights into new social and economic areas. Such rights, so-called second generation social and economic rights, were added to a list that already contained first generation rights associated with the Bill of Rights.

"Human rights" is a term that comes into widespread usage and common currency only after World War II. International documents that speak of recognition and guarantees of human rights are exclusively post-1945. Reasons for the rapid growth of the postwar rights campaign have their origin in the war itself. The atrocities of the Holocaust; Hilter's "final solution" to the problem of removing those "unfit" for membership in the Third Reich (Jews, gypsies, homosexuals, the mentally ill); especially the horrors of the death camps; these were the events that provided the initial impetus to the international human rights movement. The call came for an international bill of human rights that would be adopted and upheld by all nations, hopefully making such genocide impossible in the future. The notion of "natural rights," a term used during the early postwar period as a synonym for human rights, was invoked repeatedly during the war crimes trials at Nuremburg. The protection of natural (human) rights was declared as justification for the international community of nations stepping in to punish a sovereign government for the way it treated its own people. Nazi leaders were condemned for their gross violations of human rights as being "crimes against humanity." This represented a revolutionary development in international relations (Forsythe, 1989). It was a radical change from the prewar belief that a government's treatment of its citizens was purely a domestic issue and of little or no concern to foreign powers.

The United Nations (UN) has played a key role in the global rights campaign. The United Nations has led the way in developing new human rights treaties. It has helped to turn attention to victims of human rights abuses. The United Nations has also helped to refine the methods of enforcing human rights compliance (monitoring, special reporters, economic and military sanctions). Article 55 of the UN Charter charges all members to "promote universal respect for and observance of human rights and fundamental freedoms." Each member must ratify the Charter prior to entering the United Nations. Therefore, all UN members are pledged to respect the basic rights of their people.

THE INTERNATIONAL BILL OF HUMAN RIGHTS

This study will use as its working definition of human rights those rights enumerated in the International Bill of Human Rights (IBHR). The IBHR can be divided into three parts: the Universal Declaration of Human Rights; the International Covenant on Civil and Political Rights; and the International Covenant on Economic, Social and Cultural Rights. Each of these documents is a product of the United Nations.

In 1946 the Economic and Social Council of the UN decided to begin work on an international bill of rights. The Economic and Social Council created a Commission on Human Rights. The first chair of the commission was Eleanor Roosevelt. The intentions of the commission were to produce a document that included the freedoms guaranteed by the U.S. Bill of Rights in addition to promoting certain welfare rights. Early work of the commission also echoed the four freedoms proclaimed by President Roosevelt in his 1941 State of the Union Address (see Chapter 2). Desires were expressed within the commission at the outset for creating a binding international agreement that UN bodies would have the power to enforce.

In 1947, the Commission decided on a three-part IBHR: first, a nonbinding declaration of rights; second, a binding treaty; finally, a mechanism by which the treaty could be enforced (Renteln, 1990). Part one, the Universal Declaration of Human Rights (UDHR), was drafted by the Commission and passed through the UN system in about one year. The UDHR was approved by the General Assembly on December 10, 1948, by a vote of 48–0. The UDHR represents a "common standard of achievement" toward which all members must strive. The UDHR is not normally recognized as a binding part of international law. It is merely a declaration or a pronouncement of principles.

The binding treaty that was to have been part two of the IBHR as originally conceived by the Human Rights Commission was much longer in coming. When finally finished, it also turned out to be two treaties rather than one. Early efforts to produce a single treaty on human rights failed. The General Assembly decided in 1952 to divide the labor into the drafting of two separate and distinct covenants. During the drafting, the United Nations more than doubled in size, and newly independent nations had their own rights agenda. The most important change from the UDHR to the two covenants was the expansion of the rights recognized. The UDHR contained primarily first generation rights. The covenants also include second generation economic and social rights. Third World nations tend to stress welfare rights as taking precedence over civil-political rights. The United States insisted that any document containing socioeconomic rights be separated from those that recognize civil-political rights. The U.S. tradition is to stress the latter over the former. Hence, the existence of two covenants rather than one is at least partially the result of international political differences dividing the northern and southern hemispheres.

Diplomatic disagreements also meant that the treaties, when finished, did not contain the type of strong measures for enforcement originally favored by the Human Rights Commission. Cold War politics got in the way of producing effective machinery to guarantee observance of human rights. The Soviet Union blocked attempts to make the covenants enforceable. In 1953, Secretary of State John Foster Dulles announced that the United States would not ratify the agreements under any circumstances. After that, the United States was not helpful in drafting the covenants and made no push to conclude an agreement. With the superpowers either dragging their feet or obstructing progress, it is no surprise that 18 years of work went into drafting the covenants. However, when completed, the two covenants did go well beyond the provisions of the UDHR, especially in regard to socioeconomic rights. Both covenants also contain provisions for enforcement, albeit weak ones.

Each covenant begins by recognizing the right of all peoples to self-determination. This right was not in the UDHR at all. It is, however, the only right included in both covenants, perhaps due to the high priority placed on self-determination by newly independent nations. Of the two treaties, the civil-political covenant is most like the UDHR in that it speaks of first-generation rights. Best known among these are the rights to free speech and a free press, freedom of religion, the right to political assembly, due process, the right to appeal, freedom of movement, and the right of privacy. First generation rights also include those relating to security of the person: the right to be free from torture and prohibitions against cruel and unusual punishment. These are the rights stressed most in the U.S. tradition. There have even been those leaders, such as President Reagan, who have argued that these are the only human rights, properly conceived (see Chapter 2).

Second generation rights found in the Covenant on Economic, Social and Cultural Rights include rights to employment, medical care, housing, education, labor strikes, retirement insurance, and to share in a cultural life. This treaty even goes so far as to call for an "equitable distribution of the world's food supplies according to need." Such areas are not recognized as rights under U.S. constitutional law. Although many administrations have proclaimed full employment and adequate housing as governmental goals, they are not constitutionally guaranteed rights as is, for example, a free press.

The two covenants were approved by the General Assembly on December 16, 1966. Although flawed in some respects, they set high standards for those states that ratify either or both treaties. They are much more than just a lowest common denominator of rights to which all states were willing to agree.

Beyond the two covenants, one now hears discussion of a possible third generation of human rights. Also referred to as solidarity rights, this third generation contains rights that must be enjoyed collectively; rights held jointly by all of humanity. No one enjoys these rights unless all enjoy them together. There are five third generation rights: a right to peace, to development, to a healthy environment, to humanitarian aid, and to share in the world's common cultural heritage. As noted by Forsythe (1989: 6) and others, these third generation rights are not generally recognized in global treaty law. However, the Rio Declaration, Agenda 21, and the other agreements that came out of the 1992 Earth Summit in Brazil could be viewed as taking the first steps in that direction, especially with regard to building a treaty regime covering the right to a clean environment.

The empirical research that begins in Chapter 3 uses the IBHR to provide an operational definition of human rights. My testing of theories that link MNCs to rights employs the distinction between first and second generation rights. Jack Donnelly has argued that "a more useful and precise classification [of rights] is possible" (1986: 606). Although a more precise typology of rights is certainly possible, this study will stick with the commonly accepted dichotomy between civil-political rights and socioeconomic rights. Such a simple (even oversimplified) categorization of rights is most useful for this study because this distinction is used in prior studies of human rights and development. That includes Donnelly's own seminal research into rights in the Third World (1989b). These prior studies will be reviewed in Chapter 3.

Using the IBHR as the basis for an operational definition of human rights could also be criticized on other grounds. Although the simple distinction between first and second generation rights admittedly lacks a high degree of precision, it also tends to beg a prior question. I have argued that we can define human rights simply by pointing to those rights enumerated in the IBHR. However, one might legitimately ask why the rights in the IBHR should be considered universal rights. In other words, a more philosophical approach might begin by asking what criteria a right must meet in order to be classified as a universal human right. Surely some rights are not universal; not all rights are necessarily human rights. To address concerns such as these, one must inquire into the questions of what rights are and which rights are properly considered to be universal human rights. I will attempt to answer these questions through a discussion of legal versus moral rights.

LEGAL VERSUS MORAL RIGHTS

A common distinction in much of the philosophical literature on rights is the one separating moral rights from legal rights. This dichotomy is often drawn in discussions of human rights as a way to point out that universal rights may fall under either or both headings. A legal right is simply any right protected by law. A moral right is any right that is claimed or justified by reference to some set of moral rules; rules that reflect conceptions of what is proper, what is just, or how we ought to live. When guaranteed by law, clearly rights identified in the IBHR would be legal rights in that context. However, even if not ensured by law in this way, human rights might still exist in the sense that they are moral rights, rights justified according to some moral code.

Roland Pennock (1981) defines a right as a "justifiable claim." Joel Feinberg (1973) defines a right as a "valid claim." In a widely cited work, Ronald Dworkin (1977) tells us that rights ought to be conceptualized as trumps. Clearly, the notion of rights is closely related to the notion of claiming; being able to claim some protection or some privilege as our right. Rights are trumps in the sense that they can be invoked to protect us against those who would unjustly deny us our due. These points are directly related to understanding both the nature of human rights and the extent to which human rights might be universal across all cultures. If we take a short but necessary detour into the philosophy of rights, we will find that claiming is but one dimension of those things we call rights.

Legal Rights

In his work on rights, Carl Wellman (1985) identifies a four-part distinction regarding rights. Following Wesley Hohfeld, Wellman divides the concept of rights into claims, privileges, powers, and immunities. X has a claim against Y if Y must do something for X. For example, a debt is a legal claim in the sense that Y must repay the debt to X. X enjoys a privilege in regard to Y if Y cannot stop X from performing some action. For example, X has the legal privilege to cut the grass in his or her yard, and neighbor Y has no legal means to prevent X's action. The right to make use of our own property is a legal privilege. Wellman later shifts to use of the term "liberty" as a synonym for privilege. These terms also have their Hohfeldian "jural opposites." If X has a claim against Y, then Y has a duty in regard to X. If X enjoys a privilege or liberty in regard to Y, then Y has a no-claim in regard to X.

Powers and immunities are also easily defined and they also entail their own jural opposites. X has a legal power over Y if X can do something to change Y's legal status. Judges have the power-right to marry, or to grant a divorce to, a man and woman (thereby changing the legal status of the couple). X has a legal immunity in regard to Y if Y is unable to perform any action that changes X's legal status. One person does not normally have the ability to sell another's property, or to terminate someone else's rights to personal property. We all enjoy the legal immunity that prevents others from disposing of our personal property. Hohfeld's jural opposites for powers and immunities are liabilities and disabilities, respectively.

According to Hohfeld, a legal right is equal to a legal claim, but common usage of the term also connotes liberties, powers and immunities (see Wellman, 1985: 35). For Hohfeld, "claim" is the most accurate legal translation of "right," because a right implies a duty, and duties are most closely associated with claims. Hohfeld, originator of these distinctions, argues that legal rights are legal claims, exclusively. Wellman goes beyond Hohfeld to argue that any particular right may accurately be said to exhibit the characteristics of any one of these four dimensions. Following Wellman, it seems to make sense to say that legal rights can be divided into four categories: claim-rights; liberty-rights; power-rights; and immunity-rights.

How do we know which type of right applies to a particular case? Wellman tells us to look at the context in which the right has been asserted. In some cases, perhaps even in the majority of cases, what has been asserted is a claim-right. In other cases, the right in question might be one of the other three forms. The type of right that is applicable is determined by the particulars of each situation: "what is distinctive and essential . . . is . . . a context in which the will of the right-holder might confront the will of some second party" (1985: 80). Wellman calls this an adversarial conception of rights. For Wellman, claims and powers are the "swords" of our rights. Liberties and immunities are our rights-based "shields." We need our rights to provide us with swords and shields because, in those cases where we must rely on rights talk, we are usually engaged in a legal or moral battle.

Why is it that rights are so closely associated with confrontation or conflict? Newton Garver has argued that rights are relevant only in situations of potential conflict because rights are always asserted against some individual, group, or institution.[2] Human rights are asserted when some individual, political group, or government seeks to deny our justifiable claims, liberties, powers, or immunities.

To support the position that rights are relevant only to confrontation, Garver refers us to the following passages from Simone Weil:

Rights are always asserted in a tone of contention; and when this tone is adopted, it must rely on force in the background, or else it will be laughed at . . . rights are dependent on force. . . . One cannot imagine St. Francis of Assisi talking about rights.
If you say to someone who has ears to hear: "What you are doing is not just," you may touch the spirit of attention and love. But it is not the same as with the words, "I have the right . . ." or "You have no right to . . ." They evoke a latent war and the spirit of contention. (Panichas, 1977: 323–26)

Rights rely on "force in the background" and rights are "dependent on force" because they are always asserted in a context of conflict. Rights are necessary only in an adversarial setting, hence the mere mention of rights, or to invoke defense of one's rights, will serve to "evoke a latent war and the spirit of contention." Garver and Weil raise these points because they want to go beyond rights talk to another form of human interaction that seeks justice via love and compassion. They want to "touch the spirit of attention and love" in the hearts of those who have "ears to hear" by avoiding talk of rights. I rely on these passages merely to highlight the valid point that rights are relevant to conflict. In nonconflictual situations, there is no need for recourse to talk of rights.

Moral Rights

Wellman indicates two ways to define moral rights. A common method is to point out that, just as legal rights are those rights that come from positive law, so are moral rights those rights that come from moral law. Alternatively, moral rights could be conceptualized as those rights that come from the specific status of an individual. I possess certain moral rights to love, respect, and courtesy by dint of my status as a husband, a father, and a teacher. Wellman suggests that human rights are moral rights that all humans possess regardless of status. Human rights are moral rights that require no special status. Human rights may be the only type of moral rights that are independent of status.

Wellman also briefly considers the debate between first and second generation human rights. Wellman holds that, contrary to Maurice Cranston and others, socioeconomic rights do exist as such. Economic, social, and cultural rights exist as "civic rights" for Wellman because they are "possessed by every citizen simply by virtue of belonging to this or that particular society" (1985: 181). He goes on to discuss the right to social security as an example, using his four-part Hohfeldian model of rights.

Following Wellman, one can unpack the concept of a right into a typology of rights: claim-rights, liberty-rights, power-rights, and immunity-rights. This typology can be applied to legal rights, moral rights, and human rights. Following Wellman, Garver, and Weil, we must further recognize the necessary conflictual nature of recourse to rights. One of Wellman's concluding observations points out that rights, thus defined, are not held by individuals alone. It also makes sense to speak of corporate rights. Corporate rights are those rights that are held by collectivities rather than by discrete individuals. Collective rights are granted to or claimed by corporate bodies (for example, MNCs) and (under the IBHR) ethnic or minority groups (Van Dyke, 1977). In the debate over the nature of universal human rights, these are often referred to as group rights. This discussion of Wellman's philosophy of rights has led us back to matters such as group rights; matters that are directly related to the connections between culture and human rights. I now turn to a review of three positions on the relationship between culture and rights.

CULTURE AND UNIVERSAL
RIGHTS: THREE VIEWS

Rights traditions that produced the two generations of rights discussed earlier originated in the context of Western civilization. The fact that many human rights emerged first in the West has led to a lively debate over the validity of extending Western notions of rights to non-Western societies. Are human rights as contained in the IBHR truly universal? Is there or can there be a single standard of human rights for all cultures? Is the international human rights movement one that transcends cultural differences, or is it a thinly veiled form of Western cultural imperialism? For human rights obligations to be relevant to MNCs operating in the Third World, the IBHR must apply to non-Western contexts.

There tend to be three views in the literature that address the proper relationship between rights and culture. One view, closely associated with the work of Donnelly, asserts that there is only one standard of human rights. This is a Western standard. All other competing views merely define standards of human dignity rather than standards of human rights. I will refer to this view as one of "normative hegemony." It is a view that claims suzerainty over international rights norms regardless of cultural differences.

A second view seeks to establish a more pluralistic approach to human rights standards by locating the functional equivalent of Western notions of human rights in those traits that are unique to non-Western societies. This second view, a view of "weak cultural relativism," holds that human rights are universal, however, different cultures may provide for those rights through different means.

A third view argues that the Western conception of human rights is not valid in non-Western societies and there can be no single standard of human rights. This position, one taken by those ascribing to a "strong cultural relativism," asserts that each culture defines for itself, in its own terms, what rights are. While the weak cultural relativists seek convergence with Western notions of rights, strong cultural relativists reject the need for convergence. They also reject the legitimacy of Western conceptions of rights in non-Western contexts (see Table 1.1).

Normative Hegemony

The view I refer to as normative hegemony is based on a belief that Western notions of rights take priority over non-Western notions when the two come into conflict. Western definitions of rights and human rights

TABLE 1.1
Relativism and Human Rights: Three Views

	Normative Hegemony	Weak Cultural Relativism	Strong Cultural Relativism
One standard of rights for all cultures	yes	yes	no
Role of culture in setting standards	priority to values of modern Western culture	culture interprets universal human rights standards	culture as source for independent human rights standards

reflect Western history and Western values. One of the most widely cited definitions of human rights is that offered by Cranston (1973: 65–67). Cranston applies three criteria that he argues constitute the defining elements of those rights that qualify as human rights. For a right to be a human right, according to Cranston, it must be of "paramount importance," it must be universalizable, and there must be practical methods (economic, legal, political) by which the right can be guaranteed. Cranston derives from these criteria a relatively short list of rights that qualify as human rights. Cranston explicitly excludes second generation rights, arguing that only civil and political rights should qualify as human rights.

Other authors, such as Donnelly and Rhoda Howard, tend to agree with Cranston that Western notions of human rights take priority, while at the same time disagreeing over the scope of the specific rights entailed. Donnelly criticizes Cranston for excluding second generation rights, but Donnelly, like Cranston, must be classified as one ascribing to the position of normative hegemony.

Western definitions of human rights reflect Western values. However, Western values are not equal to the sum total of all human values. Some non-Western societies hold values that compete or conflict with Western values. This is true of Islamic cultures, Oriental cultures, and many Third World cultures. In regard to human rights, this means that some non-Western cultures want to define human rights in ways that are not the same as Western definitions. Donnelly sorts through this confusion over international rights by positing a distinction between human rights and human dignity.

Donnelly defines human rights as "equal and inalienable rights held by all individuals against the state and society" (1989a: 2). For Donnelly, human rights are necessarily universal, and they reflect the norms of autonomy and equality. He also concedes that Western rights traditions tend to stress individualism, but argues that this is not a necessary product of the Western view. Donnelly finds room in the Western tradition for an interpretation that allows for socialism and economic rights (1989a: 47, 51–54). However, for Donnelly, any system of human rights must provide autonomy, equality, and universalizabilty.

Donnelly defines systems of human dignity as methods used to meet needs within a traditional social order; methods that are not equivalent to a system of human rights. These traditional means may be adequate (and even uniquely suited) to assuring a dignified life within traditional, communal societies. However, they cannot be properly considered systems of human rights because they do not guarantee the autonomy and equality that are the *sine qua non* of human rights for Donnelly.

Donnelly's argument is based on a definitional strategy that allows only certain values to serve as the basis for a system of human rights. These values, autonomy and equality, are part and parcel of the Western tradition of rights. Conflicting values may be part of a system of human dignity, but for Donnelly, they cannot properly be considered part of a system of human rights. When there is a conflict, when non-Western scholars advocate human rights norms, such as communitarianism instead of individual autonomy, the Western values and the Western definitions of human rights must reign supreme. Hence my use of the term "normative hegemony" to refer to this view:

[Communitarianism] is structurally, ideologically and philosophically incompatible with human rights. The view of human dignity found in all communitarian societies is that the individual realizes himself as a part of the group by unquestioningly filling his social role or being loyal to the state. This conception of human dignity is incompatible with human rights. At the core of this incompatibility is the denial of social value to personal autonomy and privacy. (Donnelly and Howard, 1986: 813)

Why are autonomy, equality, and privacy relevant to human rights while communitarianism is not? Donnelly and Howard argue this is due to the nature of modern society. They equate human rights with modernity and argue that non-Western systems of human dignity are relevant only to traditional societies. Therefore, human rights (properly defined) are universally applicable to all societies as they become modern, but traditional non-Western systems of human dignity are not (Donnelly, 1989a: 64–65; Howard, 1986: 27–34). "Why were there no human rights in traditional non-Western *and Western* societies? Because prior to the creation of capitalist market economies and modern nation states, the problems that human rights seek to address, the particular violations of human dignity which they seek to prevent, either did not exist or were not widely perceived to be central social problems" (Donnelly, 1989a: 64).

Donnelly and Howard both go on to argue that, because non-Western societies are all becoming modernized, they must adopt a modern approach to preservation of human dignity that is necessarily based on the Western approach to human rights.[3]

At times, the steps in arguments favoring Western normative hegemony come close to the following:

1. Human rights, properly defined, are equivalent to the Western definition of human rights.
2. Non-Western definitions of what some scholars claim to be human rights are more accurately understood as conceptions of human dignity.
3. When conflicts in values arise during international debates over human rights, Western definitions must displace or take priority over all others.

However, at other times Donnelly himself seems to back off from the third step in this hegemonic logic of rights. His more recent work seems to move to a more flexible position that allows for some limited cultural relativism. He argues that the substance of a particular human right must be fixed, although some variation in the form through which that right is implemented is acceptable. For example, all cultures must equally respect the substance of the "right of free and full consent of intending spouses" prior to marriage. However, Donnelly is willing to allow for variation in the divergent customs that "provide alternative [forms of] protection" for this right (1989a: 123). Allowing for variation between cultures at the level of forms of human rights implies a position at least partially consistent with a second view represented in the prior literatures on culture and human rights. This is the view of weak cultural relativism.[4]

Weak Cultural Relativism

Weak cultural relativism is the view that "argues in favor of universal human rights but acknowledges that some concession should be made to particular cultural differences or that cultural differences will affect the interpretation and implementation of the universal principles" (Forsythe, 1991: 5). Authors who take this position are usually engaged in the study of human rights in non-Western societies. They frequently seek to demonstrate that, although observance of basic rights may not be identical in non-Western as compared to Western contexts, there are functional equivalents that provide for human rights in non-Western cultures.

In R. Panikkar's terms, "we must search out the *homeomorphic equivalent* to the concept of Human Rights. . . . If, for instance, Human Rights are considered to be the basis for the exercise of and respect for human dignity, we should investigate how another culture satisfies the equivalent need" (1982: 77–78). Panikkar's aim is not the same as that of Donnelly, however. Donnelly distinguishes between systems of human rights and systems of human dignity in order to argue that the latter cannot substitute for the former. Panikkar uses the same distinction to construct an argument in favor of "cultural pluralism" as an approach to universal human rights. Panikkar thinks that if a system of human dignity provides for the same functional or homeomorphic equivalence as a system of human rights, then the two systems are equally valid. Panikkar's own work seeks to establish the notion of *dharma* from the Indian tradition as providing for a homeomorphic equivalent to human rights. Other authors have made similar attempts to reveal the functional equivalents to human rights in cultures from the Orient, in Africa, and under Islam.

Cultural relativism originated as a methodology in the discipline of anthropology. Franz Boas, Ruth Benedict, and Melville Herskovits were among the first to argue that evaluation of another culture necessarily required a relativist approach (Renteln, 1990: 63–65):

Cultural relativism emerged in its modern form in reaction to cultural evolutionism. The latter theory was a stage theory which held that human societies progressed from "primitive" or "savage" to "modern." Naturally, Western civilization ranked the highest on the scale because the standard for judging was based on Western values. . . . The core of [cultural relativism] is not just recognition of cultural differences in thought, value, and action. It is a theory about the way in which evaluations or judgements are made. . . . The theory calls attention not only to behavioral differences but to the perceptions of cultural phenomena. Culture is so powerful in the way that it shapes individuals' perception that understanding the way of life in other societies depends on gaining insight into what might be called inner cultural logic. (Renteln, 1990: 62)

In regard to human rights, this position holds that one must enter into the "inner cultural logic" of non-Western societies to seek out their functional (homeomorphic) equivalents to the legal, political, and social practices that are used to guarantee rights in the West. A good example comes from McLaren's discussion of the Japanese tradition of *kawaiso*. In the West, we have established elaborate legal codes and university guidelines to protect the rights of students. Such human rights safeguards do not always exist for students in Japan, but according to Ronald McLaren (1984), fair treatment of students is provided through the *kawaiso* tradition.

McLaren's example involves the need by a Japanese student at a Japanese university to use an English-Japanese dictionary during an exam. When the professor refused permission, an American student present protested by saying: "That's not fair." No doubt similar occurances have arisen at American universities over the years. With our rights traditions and litigious nature, such an event in an American university could easily lead to a hearing involving the nature of the student's rights under applicable laws and university regulations. According to McLaren, however, the Japanese culture would handle such an incident in an entirely different manner, perhaps with the same results.

In Japan this incident would not normally evoke charges of unfair treatment or claims that a student's rights had been violated. "It would not normally occur to a Japanese who wanted to make a plea on behalf of another in such a circumstance to view the issue as a matter of fairness [or rights] at all. The Japanese appeal, rather, would run something like, 'Oh, but he (the student) is so *kawaiso*.'" To say that someone in an inferior position is *kawaiso* is to say that they are deserving of sympathy or generosity from those in a position of authority. To use the Western rights-based approach and charge that the professor is unfair "offers him the choice of owning up to some kind of wrong or else defending his action or policy." To say that the student is so *kawaiso* offers the professor "an opportunity to display sympathy and generosity" while at the same time confirming the professor's position as superior; leaving his "position as superior unthreatened" (McLaren, 1984: 54–55).

McLaren's point is that, in a society based on feudal authority relationships, such as Japan, justice and fair treatment for students is better provided by the social tradition of *kawaiso* than it would be by American-style codes specifying student rights (including when the use of dictionaries may or must be allowed during testing). The Japanese tradition works best for them within their culture because it can be used to "rectify the subject's *kawaiso* condition without an admission that the superior had any part in the production of that condition. . . . It does not imply that the superior has wronged the *kawaiso* person" (1984: 55).

Another method common to those who ascribe to weak cultural relativism is to review a set of traditions as a system and then demonstrate
how the system is analogous to Western human rights. In a study of
Chinese culture, John Copper argues that Confucian, Buddhist, and Taoist
teachings in China have recently merged into a "total system that corre-
sponds closely to the foundations of modern human rights" (1985: 14).
Confucian scholars, such as Mencius, established the doctrine that political rule must be sanctioned by the "Mandate of Heaven." Because Heav-
en itself "does not speak," the only way one can know that the Mandate
has been granted is through the "people's acceptance" of the ruler's legitimacy. Copper argues that this is the Chinese analogue to the West's "popular mandate of democracy" (1985: 12–14). Copper goes on to argue that
other Chinese traditions provide analogous protections for "equality
before the law . . . safeguards [for] the rights of the weak, and social welfare" (1985: 14).

Claude Welch's work on African cultures and human rights takes a similar approach. Welch contrasts precolonial and postcolonial Africa to support the claim that "protection of human rights certainly existed in the
precolonial period . . . the web of kinship . . . provided the frameworks
within which individuals exercized their economic, political, and social
liberties and duties" (1984: 11). Welch goes to great lengths to demonstrate that precolonial African societies "recognized six major sets of
rights: the right to life, the right to education, the right to freedom of
movement, the right to receive justice, the right to work, and the right to
participate in the benefits and decision making of the community." Welch
notes that these same rights "existed within collective contexts, and were
frequently expressed in ways unfamiliar to Europeans. Ignorance of
African norms, and a firm belief in the superiority of European practices,
led colonial powers to abridge many rights that had been protected prior
to colonialism" (1984: 16). In a work that anticipates the arguments charg-
ing that normative hegemony is tantamount to cultural imperialism,
Welch blames colonialism for destroying, or attempting to destroy, non-
Western cultural traditions that legitimately sought to protect and promote
human rights.

A final tactic by scholars ascribing to a weak cultural relativism is to
dispute the historical claim that human rights traditions originated in the
West. Islamic authors have been especially concerned to show that observance of some basic rights, such as the protection of religious minorities,
first began outside of the context of Western civilization.

According to Kamal Aboulmagd, the first social contract was the Pact
of Medina. Aboulmagd compares the pact to the *Mayflower* compact,

arguing that these were "the only two instances in the history of mankind when bodies politic were created by an actual social contract" (1990: 5). Established by the Prophet Mohammed, the pact created the first Islamic state and represents "the first constitution in the history of mankind" (1990: 5). Hence Islamic scholars would lay claim to originating constitutional government. Aboulmagd also argues that Islamic societies were the first to provide legal, contractual protection to minority groups.

The Islamic term *dhimma* refers to a pre-Islamic Arab concept meaning a "covenant" or "agreement." The *dhimma* allowed an individual to join another tribe in order to obtain the rights and protection of the tribe. The rule that governs the substance of the *dhimma* is that the new members of the tribe must "enjoy our rights and fulfill identical obligations . . . they are equal" (Aboulmagd, 1990: 5).

This tradition carried over and was applied by the Prophet to non-Muslims when the first Islamic state was established. When Mohammed created his polity during a migration from Mecca to Medina, many Jewish tribes were included within its borders. Jews were "active citizens having equal rights within the Muslim state. . . . The Islamic state is not based exclusively on religion, and . . . non-Muslims enjoy an equal status" (Aboulmagd, 1990: 5).

After the Islamic conquest of the Middle East and beyond, Christians were also given protection by the Islamic state. Christians paid a special tax, the *jeziyah*, while Muslims paid a separate tax (or "dues") called the *zakkah*. The *jeziyah* was payment in exchange for "protection [of Christians] and their exemption from military service. In later periods, when the Muslims were unable to protect certain Christians . . . they were exempted from the tax" (Aboulmagd, 1990: 5).

Through this historical argument, Aboulmagd wants to disprove the common assumption that Islam is intolerant of other religions. He seeks to prove that Islam was the first civilization to provide human rights guarantees to minority religious groups.

Aboulmagd also lists freedom of thought among the human rights protected under the Islamic tradition. He even goes so far as to call it the "only absolute freedom" under Islam (1990: 4). Here we run into a good example of the apparent inconsistencies found in many of the writings upholding the weak cultural relativist view. Aboulmagd claims that Islam holds the freedom to choose a religion or faith as absolute, but he quickly qualifies this point by saying that this right can be restricted "within the limits of the law" (1990: 4). The limits of Islamic law often exclude the right of apostasy (renouncing one's faith) for Muslims. In fact, apostasy is often a capital crime for Muslims, punishable by death. When pushed to explain this apparent contradiction,[5] Aboulmagd has admitted that apostasy is allowed in only some Islamic states, and then only if done privately. Public pronouncements of apostasy are never tolerated. This example points to an inherent danger in nearly all weak cultural relativist positions. As Donnelly accurately notes, cultural relativism does not protect individual autonomy in all cases.

Consistent themes in the cultural relativism literatures are harmony, hierarchy, group rights, and duties to uphold traditional standards. Cultural relativists will be more likely than normative hegemonists to overlook violations of absolute equality and personal autonomy. Communitarianism is used to rationalize or partially justify restrictions on the rights of individuals. The crime of apostasy under Islam is but one example. The "web of kinship" (family, clan, tribe), defended by Welch (1984: 11) as a legitimate concept through which human rights must be defined in Africa, has been used by others in attempts to justify human rights violations as egregious as female circumcision. Female genital mutilation has been defended by some of the more radical cultural relativists as being consistent with traditional practices.

Panikkar's work on human rights in India also has a distinctively anti-egalitarian character. Panikkar asserts that the "structure of the universe is hierarchical" and that, because "the individual as such is an abstraction" this means that individuals "cannot be the ultimate subject of rights" (1982: 98). That which qualifies one as a rights holder, under this view, is determined according to one's status or station in life. Such a position seems to go against the very idea of human rights as universal rights. According to Donnelly and Wellman, that which qualifies one as a holder of human rights must be the same for all.

McLaren's example of the *kawaiso* tradition runs into similar difficulties. Under the Japanese tradition, *kawaiso* (sympathy or generosity) must be granted through the good nature and responsibile action of the professor (or those in a superior position). Just treatment for the student is dependent on the professor. Rights, in contrast, can be claimed or demanded by the student, regardless of the personal proclivities of the professor. This is especially important in the case of an unfair professor. Hence the rights-based approach to protection of the powerless seems to be stronger than the *kawaiso* tradition. Perhaps the feudal authority structures of Japan that the *kawaiso* tradition seeks to uphold are, at times, in need of questioning.

These are the types of human rights violations that the view of normative hegemony seeks to prevent. The Western liberal stress is on individual autonomy and equality. Human rights dangers inherent in the position of weak cultural relativism become even more pronounced when one moves to a strong cultural relativism. However, the Western liberal view also carries with it its own peculiar threats to universal rights. The dangers inherent in Western liberal normative hegemony, especially those apparent from a feminist perspective, will be discussed following a summary of strong cultural relativism.

Strong Cultural Relativism

David Forsythe defines strong cultural relativism as any view that is based on the argument that "all truth and goodness is relative to particular cultures" (1991: 3). He asserts that any such view necessarily stands "against universal human rights standards." Scholars and politicians who hold this position see the Western approach to human rights as a form of cultural imperialism. Forsythe cites President Daniel Arap Moi of Kenya as an example. Representatives from the People's Republic of China also expressed similar views at the 1993 World Conference on Human Rights in Vienna and at the 1995 World Conference on Women in Beijing. Scholarly arguments in favor of strong cultural relativism are best represented by the work of Josiah Cobbah.

Cobbah argues that Western rights traditions are fundamentally flawed and, in some important respects, inferior to rights traditions from Africa. Nearly all of Cobbah's examples of African culture are taken from the Akan of Uganda. Unlike the weak cultural relativists, Cobbah does not seek to demonstrate that universal standards of human rights can be interpreted through African culture. Rather, Cobbah wants to reject the notion of universal equal rights because it is derived from what he sees as a philosophically unsound view of human nature. Universal rights held equally by all is a "Lockean abstraction" that, according to Cobbah, denies the existence of culture (1987: 318). Cobbah also criticizes this view for failing to meet the needs of, and failing to provide dignity for, oppressed groups and individuals in Western and non-Western societies alike.

For Cobbah, the Western tradition creates an unnatural separation between humans and their cultures. This tradition is based on the early modern liberalism of Hobbes, Locke, and Rousseau. Cobbah refers to this as natural rights theory and summarizes it in terms of three fundamental postulates: the equality of all human beings, the inalienability of rights, and a stress on individualism (1987: 314). Cobbah argues that all three of these basic assumptions are unrealistic.

Citing Hegel, Cobbah rejects any approach that bases rights theory on a conception of humans in an abstract prepolitical state (the state of nature): "I suggest that a more solid foundation for modern human rights can be built on a conception of man in society rather than the Lockean abstraction of natural rights. While it is true that conceptualizing human beings in society may mean giving up the convenience of equality in nature, it is necessary that we deal with society in real terms in order to effectuate our desire as an international community to understand and affect matters of human dignity and human rights" (1987: 318).

Cobbah then cites the experiences of women and African-Americans in the United States as examples of those who have not been well served by a human rights regime that assumes an abstract equality of all individuals and that denies the reality of discrimination based on group identity (1987: 319). Thus Cobbah tries to show that the Western rights tradition based on Lockean abstraction not only denies the relevance of culture but also has failed to protect the rights of the less powerful.

Having (in his view) discredited the Western rights tradition, Cobbah seeks to replace it with an African counter-example as an international model for human rights. His African model is said to be more relevant to contemporary international politics because it can speak to the needs of the vast majority of the world's population, the needs of the developing nations. Cobbah believes that the African model is necessary for the promotion of second generation socioeconomic rights and third generation solidarity rights, especially the right to development. "African communitarianism has ingredients that should aid in the formulation of cross-cultural human rights norms. . . . Westerners may indeed have a lot to learn from Africans" (1987: 310). Cobbah's African model stresses communalism, duties, and hierarchy: "Within the organization of African social life one can discern various organizing principles. As a people, Africans emphasize groupness, sameness, and commonality. Rather than the survival of the fittest and control over nature, the African worldview is tempered with the general guiding principle of the survival of the entire community and a sense of cooperation, interdependence, and collective responsibility. . . . Although African society is communal, it is [also] hierarchical" (1987: 320–21).

At one point, Cobbah writes that this African model of human rights is "as valid as the European theories of individualism and the social contract" (1987: 323). However, the thrust of his work is not to offer the European and African models as being equally valid (as a weak cultural relativist might argue). Rather, Cobbah ultimately seeks to go beyond, or to deny the legitimacy of, any claim that there is a basic commensurability between the African and Western views. He wants to argue that the African view is superior where it really counts, and hence his position entails rejection of the Western tradition in a fundamental way.

For example, Cobbah blames human rights violations by African governments on the colonial heritage of Western concepts of rights imposed upon Africa and the resulting "dysfunction that plagues the imposition of Western liberalism over communal African lifestyles" (1987: 326). African states carry the colonial baggage of Western liberalism. African constitutions are based on the Western model; being, in Cobbah's words, "everything but African" (1987: 328). These facts allegedly explain human rights violations in Africa, rather than serving as means for the protection of human rights.

The Feminist Critique

A final body of literature critiques all three of the above views on culture and rights — the views of normative hegemony, weak cultural relativism, and strong cultural relativism. This more recent feminist critique takes all three views to task for their alleged androcentric biases and for a susequent lack of attention to women's rights (Brems, 1997). Women's concerns regarding human rights, especially those pertaining to human rights abuses, are not always the same as the concerns of men.

Spike Peterson has constructed a feminist critique of what she calls the "givens" in human rights discourse (1990). Her characterization of the discourse posits the mainstream view as being similar to what I have termed normative hegemony. This discourse has three defining elements or givens. These include the Western element, the element of liberalism, and the element of individualism.

The Western element contains certain assumptions about politics and society. The state is normally characterized as something from which we must be protected. This assumption leads to a heavy emphasis on first generation civil and political rights in the mainstream discourse. Here Peterson echoes some of the views expressed by the schools of weak and strong cultural relativism. However, a feminist perspective would be quick to point out that cultural relativism can also allow for its own forms of women's rights violations. The burning of wives in Asia often goes unpunished under the tenets of traditional values. Women in Islam are frequently stripped of their rights at the time of marriage or divorce.[6] Female genital mutilation remains routine and widespread in large parts of eastern Africa due to local cultural values.

Peterson's second given is liberalism. The liberal element makes assumptions about human nature. All humans are presumed to have equal powers of reason. The laws of nature and morality are said to be understood through these powers of reason. Therefore, individual autonomy becomes paramount. If we all have the same fundamental rationality, we must each be given the same freedom to conduct our own affairs. The closely-related third given, the element of individualism, makes assumptions about the philosophy of rights. Individuals are characterized as atomistic. The individual is said to be prior to all groups. Groups are inherently unstable and epiphenominal according to mainstream human rights discourse. Rights, therefore, are for individuals and must stress the protection of individual interests. Rights are not for groups as such, or for the protection of group interests.

Having thus summarized the three givens, Peterson proceeds to a post-positivist feminist critique of these elements. She charges that the Western element is based on male perspectives, male priorities, and male realities. At its root is the distinction between the public and the private spheres. We are to be protected from the state in the public sphere, and the state is supposed to leave us alone in our private spheres. The public sphere is a realm of male-domination and the primary focus of rights discourse. The private sphere, also male dominated, contains a largely excluded women's sphere. Women's views, perspectives, priorities, and realities become marginalized or ignored. This is, for Peterson, a thoroughly androcentric view that is based on a false dichotomy between the public and private spheres. A well-known credo of feminist activism is that "the personal is political." That which happens in the private sphere, for example, battered wives, is of concern for feminist theorists, and it should be the concern of public policy.

The liberal element is criticized by Peterson for giving priority to the abstract and to political rights. A feminist perspective prefers to stress the concrete and the primacy of economic rights. Liberalism constructs rights as a way to protect the interests of self-interested autonomous actors. Peterson echoes Cobbah's critique of liberalism; both authors compare the mainstream view to non-Western alternatives. Both critical views (feminist and cultural relativist) stress the communal realities of human existence (Brems, 1997: 157). Peterson points to research that shows knowledge, language, and identity are all developed within the context of social groups (1990: 312, 324–25).

Finally, Peterson decries individualism as a masculine viewpoint. Individualism stresses the abstract, separation, apartness. The woman's view is said to be based on the concrete, connectedness, the group; it is more relational and organic.

A second useful feminist critique, one that is much less philosophical and much more political, has been offered by Charlotte Bunch (1990). Bunch begins her discussion with attention to the grim realities of abuses of women's rights. Women are "routinely subject to torture, starvation, terrorism, humiliation, mutilation, and even murder simply because they are female . . . women are discriminated against and abused on the basis of gender" (1990: 486). In spite of this, women's rights are still not routinely classified as fundamental human rights. Human rights documents and international human rights regimes tend to neglect gender-based abuse. Feminists, therefore, are seeking to "redefine human rights abuses to include the degradation and violation of women" (1990: 487). Recent efforts in this regard were prominent at the 1993 World Conference on Human Rights in Vienna.

Narrow definitions of human rights in the West conceptualize rights solely as a matter of state violation of civil and political rights. This is a view that "impedes consideration of women's rights" (Bunch, 1990: 488). Violations of women's rights include violations of their civil liberties, but often (and perhaps more importantly) such violations go beyond first generation rights to the "larger socioeconomic web that entraps women" (1990: 488). Hence Bunch and Peterson both stress the fact that second generation socioeconomic rights must receive increased attention if we are to address women's concerns.

Women are also especially fearful of domestic violence, rape, and being battered within the so-called private sphere. Ellen Goodman cites Bunch's later work, in connection with the 1993 conference in Vienna, showing that when you ask women: "what is the form of inhuman and degrading treatment that they are most afraid will happen to them . . . it's that they will be raped or battered" (Goodman, 1993). Bunch's earlier work (1990) contains a long listing of such abuses: wife battery, incest, rape, dowry deaths, genital mutilation, and sex selection for males that leads to aborting female fetuses.

Abuse of women had not been a top priority in the post–World War II campaign for human rights. However, it has become increasingly so in recent years. Altogether, some 124 nations presented petitions at the human rights conference in Vienna during 1993 demanding that "gender violence . . . be recognized as a violation of human rights" (Goodman, 1993). In the words of Judge Elizabeth Odio of Costa Rica, "We must make sure the absurd division between public and private spheres disappears" (Goodman, 1993: 11). This is a campaign that has been opposed by the People's Republic of China and other nations that want human rights to be defined by means of strong cultural relativism.

Women's rights have also been addressed by the World Health Organization (WHO). In 1993 the WHO targeted female genital mutilation for elimination, cultural arguments notwithstanding. Once defended by some as consistent with traditional African values, these practices include "cuts in the clitoris to complete removal of the labia, and sewing up of most of the vagina." The WHO estimates that 80 million women have been maimed by these customs (Nullis, 1993). Once rationalized as a means to ensure chastity and to protect against rape, parents sometimes fear that unless they observe such customs their daughters will not find husbands. Nearly all women in Somalia, Ethiopia, and Sudan are still subjected to genital mutilation. The practice is also widespread in Kenya, Uganda, and Tanzania (Nullis, 1993). The 185 nations at the WHO Assembly in 1993 unanimously approved a charge to Director General Hiroshi Nakajima for preparation of a report that would include new steps for eliminating female mutilation. The 1995 World Conference on Women also produced a Platform for Action that explicitly targeted elimination of genital mutilation (Brems, 1997: 153).

Bunch has also called for new initiatives on all fronts to move women's rights to center stage in international human rights arenas. She wants increased attention to civil and political rights violations, socioeconomic subordination and inequalities, and new national and international laws protecting women's rights (1990: 493–97). Bunch also calls for a "feminist transformation" of human rights. Such a transformation would take greater account of women's lives and would change our human rights concepts to become more responsive to women. For example, violence against women would be considered a hate crime as is violence against homosexuals, Jews, and other minorities. The Vienna Conference produced a Declaration and Programme of Action designed to combat violence against women (Brems, 1997: 151).

Attention to the impact of MNCs must also inform our transformation to a newer and deeper understanding of human rights. Once again, feminist research has helped to lead the way by broadening our understanding of human rights abuses to include those committed by both governments and private actors (for example, MNCs). This is largely due to their focus on the lot of women, especially women in the Third World: "Feminism challenges the values of this society: progress, accumulation, industrialization. . . . Central to change is the response of women to the activities of multinational corporations, for which they are the crucial labor source and whose failures they can evaluate on the basis of women's particular concern for social conditions" (Black, 1989: 169).

Naomi Black's basic point in the above passage is that women are especially well situated to evaluate the failures of MNCs, including their failures to promote and protect human rights. Black and Cynthia Enloe both have stressed the indispensible nature of female labor for international corporations. Black and Enloe also agree that harm inflicted by MNCs on developing nations falls disproportionately on women. Enloe's work (1990) includes case studies of the roles that women play in international agriculture, banking, diplomacy, the military, national liberation fronts, and tourism. A telling example pertaining to women's rights comes from her studies of international banking and related modes of economic production in less-developed countries (LDCs).

Enloe begins with an assertion that international political economy and international banking are masculinized areas (1990: 158). To say that banking is masculinized is to say that it is heavily reliant on international risk taking. This penchant for risk taking led international bankers to make questionable loans to LDCs, especially during the late 1970s and early 1980s. These unsound loans led, in turn, to the Third World's debt crisis of the late 1980s and the 1990s. The debt crisis then led to a heavy emphasis on crash programs to increase LDC exports as part of the lending and aid programs associated with austerity or structural adjustment (see Chapter 2). Export enhancement has been achieved in most cases by Third World nations creating EPZs consistent with the dictates of the Western-controlled World Bank. EPZs represent the connection between masculinized banking, the debt crisis, and exploitation of women's labor.

In the EPZ, governments set aside territory and provide economic incentives specifically for factories producing goods for the international market. "Most attractive . . . is the governments' offer of cheap labor. Women's labor has been the easiest to cheapen, so it shouldn't be surprising that in most Export Processing Zones at least 70 per cent of the workers are women, especially young women" (Enloe, 1990: 159). If Enloe is correct, masculinized banking created the Third World debt crisis. Policies designed to correct the crisis are based on creating EPZs to attract Western MNCs. MNC production, in turn, is dependent on exploitation of women's labor. Minimum wage laws, safety regulations, and environmental protections are often waived within the EPZs. Therefore, MNC production entails the diminution of labor rights and other socioeconomic rights for women in the EPZs. Enloe, and others, would also argue that the whole system requires repressive Third World regimes in order to perpetuate itself (1990: 160; see also the discussion of Stephen Hymer's work in Chapter 3). Hence, violations of civil and political rights are also part and parcel of the system.

CORPORATIONS, CULTURES, AND HUMAN RIGHTS

What does a review of different types of human rights tell us about research into MNCs and rights? What does a survey of different views on the relationship between culture and rights suggest about the proper way to conceptualize connections between MNCs and rights in LDCs? A discussion of different categories and different definitions of rights suggests that research into rights in the Third World must be based on a multifaceted understanding of human rights. Such study must address all three generations of rights. Attention to civil-political rights, such as protection from government repression, must complement — but not supercede or displace — attention to second generation rights (for example, human welfare) and third generation rights (for example, development, environment).

Philosophers of rights would caution us not to overlook either the legal or the moral dimensions of MNC activities in the Third World. Research into the human rights impact of MNCs must be cognizant of rights and obligations that apply to corporations in both a legal and a moral sense. One must also be attentive to local cultural values and priorities when analyzing human rights across Third World nations (particularly when doing case studies). Finally, the gender-based critiques of mainstream human rights discourse counsel in favor of scrutinizing the impact of multinationals in both the public and private spheres. Women's rights, children's rights, and the rights required by other similarly dispossesed or disenfranchised segments of society should be of special concern.

Returning to the three views on culture and rights, as we move from normative hegemony to weak cultural relativism and to strong cultural relativism, concern for the impact of nonstate actors (for example, MNCs) increases. Western normative hegemony contains little or no attention to private actors as potential violators of human rights. Donnelly argues that human rights are "held by all individuals against the state and society," but does not consider rights violations by MNCs (1989a: 2). Weak and strong cultural relativists, by contrast, have greater concern for human rights actors other than states. Why the enhanced attention to nonstate actors on the part of the relativists? This is largely because non-Western

philosophies of rights place greater reliance on intermediate social, political, and economic organizations.

Western, liberal philosophy (normative hegemony) stresses the protection of individuals from the state (that is, civil and political rights). My
review of the two generations of rights revealed the historical origins for
this Western bias. First generation rights were established at a time in
Western civilization when protection from tyranny was of paramount concern. Individuals had to be shielded from the abuse of the all-powerful,
Hobbesian state. Universal rights held the promise of protecting isolated
individuals from the state.

Within the non-Western context, on the other hand, intermediate groups
that stand between the individual and the state serve crucial economic,
social, and political functions. Ethnic groups often serve as the primary
basis for political association (for example, political parties). Language
and socialization are governed by group membership. Employment,
patronage, and social welfare are also frequently a function of group
membership. Donnelly and Howard correctly point out that these intermediate associations largely define the individual in terms of proper
behavior, thought, and sociopolitical norms: the "individual realizes himself as a part of the group" (1986: 813).

Western individualism and Western rights traditions helped to overcome the tendency for group membership to restrict individual autonomy
in Western societies. Normative hegemony seeks to deny the tyranny of
the majority as it also protects individuals from state tyranny. Membership
in medieval guilds and other positions within the feudal hierarchies once
determined the futures of individuals in the West. Acceptable behavior,
correct political thinking, and religious orthodoxy were dictated to individuals by medieval authorities such as the church and the crown.
Philosophers of the Enlightenment wanted to break these Rousseauen
chains and liberate individuals from the constraints imposed by intermediate associations. Therefore, in the West, since the advent of the modern
age, individual freedoms are taken to be absolute. The tendency is to dis-
count and even denigrate group membership when determining fundamental rights claims. Normative hegemony is based on the position that
human rights begin and end with individuals. For cultural relativism, there
is still more to the story. Cultural relativists argue that we must consider
groups and group membership in regard to rights that are held individually and collectively.

Perhaps a combination of the basic elements of these views is possible.
A synthesis of normative hegemony and weak cultural relativism would
stress the absolute equality of individuals as our starting point. Individual

rights would be granted a certain prima facie legitimacy. Unlike pure normative hegemony, the compromise position would hold open the possibility that group membership may affect the protection of rights for individuals. Affirmative action programs for minorities would be a case in point (Van Dyke, 1977). Affirmative action is granted to individuals who belong to groups that have been subjected to a history of unjust discrimination, even if the individuals who benefit from affirmative action were not themselves the victims of such discrimination. These individuals qualify for inclusion in affirmative action simply by their membership in the oppressed goup. For the rights of these individuals to be fully protected, we must necessarily take into account their group membership.

The synthesis of normative hegemony and weak cultural relativism would also start with an overriding concern for the impact of states on human rights. However, it would not stop there. The Western stress on state actors may be largely justified due to the relative impact that governments have had on human rights. Nation-states are the most influential actors when it comes to protecting rights. They are also the most significant actors when it comes to violating rights. Again, we must be open to the possibility that nonstate actors, such as MNCs, also have a direct impact on human rights. Therefore, MNCs should be an additional focus of our research, our activism, and our methods of regulation when it comes to the philosophy, the laws, and the politics of human rights.

NOTES

1. Joan Spero defines an MNC as "a firm with foreign subsidiaries that extend the firm's production and marketing beyond the boundaries of any one country" (1990: 104). In other words, an MNC is a corporation with production and marketing operations in more than one nation. I will use Spero's definition of MNCs as my working definition of this term for the purposes of this book.

2. Garver made these comments at a seminar in 1992. The seminar was sponsored by the National Endowment for the Humanities and was held at the State University of New York in Buffalo. This author was a participant in that seminar on "Human Rights in Theory and Practice." The seminar was directed by Garver and Welch.

3. A feminist critique of this view will be summarized later in this chapter.

4. In his textbook on human rights, Donnelly classifies himself as an advocate of weak cultural relativism (1993: 36).

5. Aboulmagd made a presentation on these views at the Salzburg Seminar, Session 273: "Human Rights across Cultures and Political Systems" (Salzburg, 1989). This author was a student at that seminar.

6. Women are said to have an equal right to divorce under the laws of Islam, but will be taken to a mullah and told to swear off this right prior to marriage. This telling example was offered by William Butler at the Salzburg Seminar in 1989.

2

Foreign Policy and Human Rights

POLITICS AND ECONOMICS

Multinational corporations (MNCs) and other foreign economic actors could have a positive or a negative influence on rights in developing nations. To understand the impact on human rights from international economic inputs flowing into the Third World, one must first understand the political context. All international economic actors, including U.S. MNCs, operate within a political framework established by the major powers. To understand the relationship between human rights and MNCs, one must first be familiar with official government policies. Political factors partially determine economic outcomes at several different levels of analysis.

According to Joan Spero (1990), the operations of international economic actors (for example, MNCs) are to a great extent determined by the actions and policies of international political actors (for example, nation-states). To support her claim that an understanding of international politics is a prerequisite to any analysis of international economic interactions, Spero gives a brief history of international political economy. In each historical period, the international political system shapes the international economic system, and governments establish the political parameters within which private economic actors must operate. The economic system of mercantilism from the fifteenth to eighteenth centuries was shaped by its central political features: the rise of modern nation-states, an equal distribution of power between these states, and limits to competition (because of a shared political culture, small armies, and limited military objectives). These political factors produced the mercantilist economic competition of the same period that took the forms of tariffs, quotas, subsidies, monopolies, and colonies to make the metropoles more self-sufficient. Thus, Spero points out, the "emerging state . . . determined economic interaction" (1990: 5). When the international political structure changed, the economic system changed with it.

In the early nineteenth century international military and political dominance was established by Britain. This created an economic system of free trade centered on Britain. The British regime removed mercantilist tariffs and established navigation laws that guaranteed access to the high seas. However, by the end of the nineteenth century the primary political determinant of free trade (British military and political dominance) had disappeared. Political changes once again brought about the creation of a new economic system, this time one based on imperialist competition. New political factors included rivals to Britain's power and modern nationalism. These new political factors in turn produced a new economic resultant; the "action and reaction dynamic of imperial competition . . . [was] the basis for a new international economic system" (Spero, 1990: 6). In the imperial era, political domination over a given territory led to economic domination of the same area for any major power.

The imperial system in turn collapsed because of World Wars I and II and was replaced by the bipolar political balance between the United States and the Soviet Union. The bipolar political system was mirrored by a bipolar economic system. In the West, U.S. military-political dominance was "matched by U.S. economic dominance." In the East, the Soviets decided "for political reasons" to create a "socialist commonwealth economically dependent" on the Soviet Union (Spero, 1990: 7).

More recently the end of the Cold War and a relative decline in U.S. economic power have led to a new order at the end of the twentieth century. The post–Cold War setting has brought about yet another overhaul in global political factors (see Chapter 4 for a discussion of political changes in the post–Cold War era). However, these most recent changes do not alter the basic fact that policy by nation-states partially determines the activities of private economic actors. At the level of the international system, politics establishes the foundation for economic interaction.[1] Politics also helps to determine economics at the national level. For example, in 1987 the U.S. Congress prohibited all new investment by U.S. corporations into the Republic of South Africa (RSA); a prohibition on investment imposed because of human rights violations in the RSA associated with the system of apartheid. The ban on investment was not lifted until 1991, after the RSA had begun the long process of dismantling apartheid. This is but one of many possible examples that shows how governments can still set limits and guidelines within which economic actors must operate.

The chapters that follow will discuss how U.S. corporations and U.S. foreign aid affect human rights in the Third World. Before moving on to those topics, however, the political context must be set. Just as Chapter 1 provided the philosophical, conceptual, and cultural dimensions necessary for any study of human rights in developing nations, so this chapter will review certain international political information that is necessary before analyzing MNCs themselves. I will provide this background material by presenting a history of U.S. foreign policies on human rights.

ETHICS AND FOREIGN POLICY

Opinions on the proper role played by ethics in U.S. foreign policy cover a wide spectrum. Some analysts and practitioners argue that private standards of morality cannot be the basis for international policy. Others take an opposing view, positing private ethical standards as the ultimate foundation for any workable foreign policy. This wide range of opinions can best be understood by means of two ideal types. At the extremes are the theoretical stances of realism and utopianism. These are ideal types in the sense that they represent alternative conceptual frameworks for linking ethics to foreign policy. The view of any particular individual would tend to lean more toward one side or the other (realism versus utopianism), and most authorities on foreign policy use language that partakes of both positions. However, discussing realism and utopianism in their purest forms will facilitate the detailed look at actual policies on human rights that follows.

Early twentieth-century views on ethics and foreign policy were akin to the ideal type of utopianism. Popular among politicians and intellectuals in the 1920s and 1930s, utopianism became almost synonomous with Wilsonianism because of its congruence with the foreign policies of President Wilson. Utopianism contains four basic elements:

Utopianism was the dominant view during the interwar period (between World Wars I and II).

Utopianism is optimistic. It emphasizes how national leaders *ought* to behave. Utopianism argues that behavior can be morally improved. Utopianism also tends to see human nature as something that can be molded and guided through ethical instruction and education.

Utopianism stresses the importance of international law and international organizations. Utopians seek to create new laws that will limit and regulate the behavior of nations. They also favor the creation of international organizations as a way to manage and prevent interstate conflict.

Utopianism seeks to establish a widely shared set of international norms. These moral rules and ethical principles are to serve as the proper basis for international laws, international relations, and foreign policies. (See Dougherty and Pfaltzgraff, 1990: 81–83)

The utopian nature of this view is most evident in its desire to make the world a better place. Utopians look to private ethical standards as a way to create a morally defensible world order. Interwar utopians were optimistic enough to believe that they could effectively outlaw war. The Kellogg-Briand Pact of 1928 claimed to do just that. This was a moralistic declaration that purported to prohibit war between nations.

Utopianism in the United States found its impetus in U.S. reactions against the horrors of World War I. A war that was different in kind from all prior conflicts, the Great War of 1914–18 exhibited a barbarity and wrought destruction on a scale the world had never seen. New techniques of mass destruction were introduced (aerial bombardment, gas warfare, the machine gun). Trench warfare and tactical maneuvers designed with expected casualty rates of 50 percent or more led to the decimation of entire armies for little or no military gain. Led by President Wilson, many Americans expressed desires after the war for a more moral and peaceful world order. They argued that European power politics had been the cause of World War I. Wilson's design for the League of Nations after the war was an attempt to transcend power politics. Wilson's hopes for a new world order based on the League were a concrete manifestation of utopianism in post–World War I U.S. foreign policy.

Utopians like Wilson tend to disdain the use of military force. They will try to avoid the turn to military options in foreign policy if at all possible. Utopians prefer the use of other means: diplomacy, treaty obligations, economic sanctions. Utopians will also tend to resort to force only when that military pressure is applied in a collective fashion, and by a multilateral alliance that has been sanctioned under an international organization (for example, the League of Nations, or more recently, the UN Security Council).

The most common criticism of utopianism is that it lacks any effective enforcement mechanisms. Collective security as demonstrated by the

League failed to stop fascist aggression in the 1930s. The Kellogg-Briand Pact had no way to enforce its moralistic prohibition against war. A more recent example can be found in the foreign policy of President Carter. Carter sounded very much like a utopian in 1979 when he announced that the United States would not employ force or the threat of force to rescue U.S. hostages in Iran. One of Carter's first actions during the Iranian hostage crisis was to declare publicly that he would not resort to military force as a way to free the hostages (Calvocoressi, 1987: 282). His subsequent efforts to end the crisis through diplomacy and economic sanctions largely failed. Carter therefore seemed powerless to do anything that would effectively end the crisis.

The failure of the League to prevent aggression in the 1930s helped to bring about World War II. After the war, the Cold War came to dominate U.S. foreign policy. The Cold War led to the demise of utopianism. Cold War politics were guided by realism and the tenets of realpolitik. As we shall see, realism is the dominant view in U.S. policy to this day. Although the intellectual history of realism dates back to ancient Greece, the four basic elements of realism as an ideal type in U.S. foreign policy begin with its post–World War II character:

Realism is the dominant view in the post–World War II era (during both the Cold War and post–Cold War periods).

Realism is a pessimistic view of politics and human nature. It is suspicious of political idealism and emphasizes how leaders and nations do behave (rather than how they ought to behave). It emphasizes the evil elements of basic human nature.

Realism focuses on power and the balance of power. Power, not law or organizations, is used as the means to regulate behavior.

Realism makes a distinction between private morality and public morality. Realism argues that private moral standards are not directly applicable to the actions of nations.

Textbook treatments of realism (see Dougherty and Pfaltzgraff, 1990: 90 ff.) trace its origins back to the Greek philosopher Thucydides and to the early modern works of Machiavelli and Hobbes. The intellectual staying power of realist arguments has helped political realism to remain the mainstream view throughout the Cold War and post–Cold War eras. Perhaps the best defense of these arguments is still to be found in the writings of Machiavelli. Of all classical realists, Machiavelli has been the most influential among modern day followers of this view.

Realists believe that utopian goals and crusades to make the world a better place can only lead to ruin. Utopianism tends to distort national policy, according to this view, and inhibits effective leadership. Although often misinterpreted as an amoral or even an immoral position, realism is better understood as that view that holds utopian idealism to be simply counterproductive. In the words of Machiavelli:

To go to the real truth of the matter . . . how we live is so far removed from how we ought to live, that he who abandons what is done for what ought to be done, will rather learn to bring about his own ruin than his preservation. A man who wishes to make a profession of goodness in everything must necessarily come to grief among so many who are not good. Therefore it is necessary for a prince, who wishes to maintain himself, to learn how not to be good, and to use this knowledge and not use it, according to the necessity of the case. (1952: chap. 15)

Machiavelli's book *The Prince* is the first realist handbook. This realist text contains extensive reflections on the nature of power. Realists study power, rather than law or international organization, as their preferred means for protecting national interests and managing conflict. Acquisition of power, maintainance and expansion of power, displays of power, the use of force and diplomacy backed by the threats of force, these are the tools of realist foreign policy. Realists argue that only the study of power politics and history can instruct us on the ways to prevent war. Only power and balances of power can guide or alter the behavior of nations. Law and political institutions cannot effectively restrain the actions of nations, but force and diplomacy backed by military force can. Machiavelli's handbook on power has often been referred to as the first political science textbook.

Machiavelli also gives us the most succinct and definitive statement on the differences between public and private morality: "It must be understood that a prince . . . cannot observe all those things which are considered good in men, being often obliged, in order to maintain the state, to act against faith, against charity, against humanity, and against religion . . . in the actions of men, and especially of princes . . . the end justifies the means. Let a prince therefore aim at conquering and maintaining the state, and the means will always be judged honourable and praised by every one" (1952: chap. 18).

Realists believe that the moral standards applicable to the public actions of national leaders are not necessarily the same as those that we apply to our private activities. Again, often misinterpreted as a view that argues for amoral or even immoral behavior, realism instead seeks to present a distinct moral calculus for public actions. The supreme moral obligation for any leader, according to realism, is the preservation of the state. Beyond that, leaders are also obligated to do their best to protect the interests of their people. These moral requirements of leadership may oblige a president or a prime minister to take public actions that are contrary to private or religious moral standards. Nevertheless, realists since Machiavelli have argued that a national leader must do what is necessary to protect national interests, even if that means learning "how not to be good." History shows that leaders often behave badly, and one must learn how not to be good or risk losing power and security altogether.

Realists criticize utopians for being misled by their preoccupation with private standards of morality. Pre–World War II utopians in the League were condemned for their unwillingness and inability to use force to stop aggression by Germany, Italy, and Japan (Carr, 1939). To avoid war, realists argue that U.S. foreign policy must concentrate on a stable international balance of power. This was the basic logic behind Cold War policies of containment against the Soviet bloc. Realists like George Kennan and Henry Kissinger constructed policies in which force was met with military force. Realists fear that a preoccupation with morality for morality's sake will lead to distraction, muddle one's thinking, and result in campaigns to change the world that must necessarily fail. The end product, according to this logic, would be the failure to protect the United States, Americans, and U.S. national interests.

On the other hand, realism is not devoid of morality. Every leader has the supreme moral duty to provide for national security and the physical safety of the citizenry. According to Kissinger, "peace is the fundamental moral imperative" (Forsythe, 1989: 3). Realists concentrate on balance of power politics because they believe that, without a balance of power, without international order, without stability and security, then no moral behavior of any kind is possible in the international arena. When once asked to compare the relative importance of order versus justice, Kissinger quoted Goethe: "If I had to choose between justice and disorder, on the one hand, and injustice and order on the other, I would always choose the latter" (LaFeber, 1997: 258). Without order, the result is often the kind of state-of-nature war of all against all witnessed in Lebanon during the 1970s or in the Balkans during the 1990s. In a world of anarchy and rampant disorder, no one is safe, anything goes. Events in Liberia, Rwanda, and Somalia in the 1990s are additional cases in point.

Realism heavily influenced U.S. foreign policy during the Cold War. As we shall see, even after the end of the Cold War, realpolitik remains the dominant view. However, one cannot push the distinction between realism and utopianism too far. Utopians such as Wilson and Carter were not ignorant when it came to power politics, nor were they averse to the use of force when they deemed it absolutely necessary. Wilson took the United States into World War I in order to make the world safe for democracy. He also deployed more than 10,000 troops into Russia after the war as part of an unsuccessful attempt by the Allies to overthrow Lenin (LaFeber, 1997: 3). Carter attempted an unsuccessful military rescue of the hostages in Iran, after having sworn publicly against just such an action (a sequence of events as Machiavellian as anything undertaken by any realist). Utopians can and do use force, only perhaps not as often or as quickly as would a realist. Realists, at least the more sophisticated realists, also understand the importance of international law and international morality when it comes to national security. A sophisticated realist acknowledges that protection of national interests can depend at least in part on ethical considerations and the ethical consequences of foreign policy. In the view of some, the so-called late Kissinger moved to such a position when he argued during the Ford administration that the United States must take international human rights more seriously.

It is in the area of human rights policy that the tension between utopianism and realism becomes most readily apparent. It is also in regard to international human rights that the need for a synthesis of these two views becomes most necessary. Alan Tonelson (1982) has argued that ignoring human rights abuses by pro-U.S. dictatorships often backfires on the United States and leads in the long run to endangering U.S. national interests. Donnelly (1993: 32–34) reminds us that, despite the realists' definitions of national interests in terms of power and security, human rights and "other moral concerns" might well constitute necessary additional elements of the national interest. In the long term, utopian concerns, such as human rights, and realist concern for national security may ultimately converge. Before this can become apparent, however, a review of the particulars of U.S. foreign policies on human rights is needed. Although they have their limitations as ideal types, the conceptual categories of realism and utopianism will inform a historical review of human rights policies. Human rights, as such, have been a factor relevant to the study of foreign policy only since World War II. However, there are certain important precedents that date back to the United States' earliest days as a sovereign nation.

FROM INDEPENDENCE TO THE FOUR FREEDOMS

Since the birth of the United States, ideas about rights and public policies on rights have been inextricably intertwined with its evolution as an international actor. When Jefferson wrote the Declaration of Independence, he spoke of the "inalienable rights" to "life, liberty and the pursuit of happiness." Violations of these rights by the British government constituted the moral and philosophical grounds on which Jefferson argued in favor of a right to independence (self-determination) for the 13 colonies. Following Jefferson, and throughout the nineteenth century, U.S. leaders based their foreign policies on notions of morality and self-images that were widely shared across the country.

Separated from the old world by the Atlantic and lacking the overseas colonies that were prized by European powers, Americans saw themselves as politically and morally unique. They eschewed standing armies as a symbol of European autocracy. U.S. leaders extolled the virtues of democracy, written constitutions containing a bill of rights, and free enterprise. However, U.S. foreign policies during this period were also decidedly isolationist. The United States made no efforts to remake the world in its own image during the 1800s. Its role in the world was to stand as a moral example that other nations could emulate, if they so wished. The United States was the shining city on the hill that other nations could and should try to copy. U.S. exceptionalism, especially in terms of active foreign policies, meant that its leaders would be content to tend their own garden. The rest of the world would have to find its own way, largely without the direct help or intervention of the United States.

The first halting steps away from U.S. isolationism were taken by Wilson after World War I. Wilson's foreign policies might appear to be a clear break from the isolationist past. However, they were also essentially consistent with nineteenth-century policies in that, at their core, these new policies were likewise based on a vision of the moral role that the United States should play in the world. Wilson's Fourteen Points (1918) were to become the basis of a new world order; a global order that would make the world safe for democracy; and a global order that would for the first time declare certain inalienable rights at the international level. Among the rights expressed in the Fourteen Points was the right of self-determination for nations that were under a "colonial claim." The "sovereignty" and "interests" of the colonized peoples were to be given "equal weight" as compared to the claims and demands of the colonizers (Point V). "[M]utual guarantees" of "political independence and territorial integrity" were to be given by all states to all other "great and small states alike" (Point XIV) (see Vasquez, 1987: 18–19).

The aggression that led to World War II, along with the coincident failure of the League of Nations to prevent such aggression, meant that Wilson's new order was not to be achieved. However, this did not prevent a subsequent U.S. president from offering his own vision of the proper moral basis for a just world order. In his State of the Union Address of 1941, President Roosevelt declared the "Four Freedoms." These freedoms were to be universal. Roosevelt argued that they should be enjoyed by all peoples everywhere. They are: freedom of speech, freedom of religion, freedom from want, and freedom from fear (Kinder and Hilgemann, 1978: 187). Roosevelt declared the Four Freedoms prior to U.S. entry into World War II. However, the wars that were already raging in Asia and Europe were clearly on the President's mind when he declared these freedoms to be the ethical minimum that all people had a right to expect from their own governments. The implication was that fascist governments, by definition, did not ensure such liberties.

FROM THE UNIVERSAL DECLARATION THROUGH THE EARLY COLD WAR

The historical connection between World War II and the international human rights movement is definitive. The horrors of the Holocaust and the various war crimes committed by fascist governments led to two immediate results at the war's end. First, war crimes tribunals were established to punish the guilty. Second, in the newly formed United Nations, a Commission on Human Rights was established. The first chair of this commission was Eleanor Roosevelt. The commission was charged with drafting an international bill of human rights (IBHR). The first element of the IBHR became the Universal Declaration of Human Rights (UDHR), adopted by the UN General Assembly on December 10, 1948. The tenth of December is commemorated each year as international Human Rights Day.

During this early post–World War II period, the United States was at the forefront of the international human rights campaign. U.S. leadership, most notably the work of Mrs. Roosevelt, helped to push the UDHR through the United Nations. Written largely by Roosevelt and one of her top aides, the UDHR is a nonbinding standard of achievement. U.S. leadership regarding international human rights quickly dissipated, however, with the advent of the Cold War. Foreign policy in the 1950s was dominated by desires to contain communism and to prevent Soviet expansion.

Presidents Truman and Eisenhower showed little interest in promoting human rights as such. Their top concerns were to establish a string of military alliances, anchored by the North Atlantic Treaty Organization (NATO), and to enforce the Truman Doctrine, which promised U.S. aid to any nation fighting against communist aggression. U.S. foreign policy in the 1950s exhibited a narrow focus on realism. The only rhetoric used during this period on human rights was in regard to the need to protect the "free world" (America's allies) from the Soviet bloc. Eisenhower gave in to congressional critics of the United Nations, led by Senator John Bricker of Ohio, who opposed all treaties on human rights. The United Nations drafted binding covenants on rights as a follow-up to the Universal Declaration. These binding treaties were largely completed by 1954 (Forsythe, 1991: 61). However, the opposition led by Bricker forced Eisenhower's administration to announce that the United States would not be a party to any rights treaties produced by the United Nations. To this day, congressional opposition to human rights documents is still referred to as Brickerism (Forsythe, 1991: 122).

Bricker made three kinds of arguments against ratification of human rights treaties (Van Dyke, 1970). First he argued that rights and protections of rights are domestic political issues, and therefore not proper subjects for international treaties. Because, in his view, the U.S. Constitution always takes precedence over any treaty, and because international law does not apply directly to U.S. citizens (in Bricker's opinion), rights are not subject to foreign treaties. In this instance, Bricker was simply restating the position that had been the dominant view on rights prior to World War II. A second set of arguments from Bricker involved Cold War politics. Bricker characterized the UN General Assembly as a forum dominated by America's enemies, specifically the Soviet Union and its allies in Third World socialist nations. Because most human rights treaties are a product of General Assembly resolutions, Bricker saw them as threats to U.S. national interests. Finally, Bricker expressed the opinion that human rights documents represent "socialism by treaty," a charge that one still hears to the present day from such members of Congress as Jesse Helms of North Carolina. Treaties on second generation rights — specifically the Covenant on Economic, Social and Cultural Rights — posit jobs, housing, and medical care (among others) as areas that are to be promoted through the provision of rights. Because such things are not recognized as rights under the U.S. Constitution, becoming a party to this treaty would allegedly bring socialism into the U.S. political system through the back door.

Bricker's ultimate goal was a constitutional amendment prohibiting the United States from joining any international treaties on rights. Bricker failed in his attempt to amend the Constitution. He succeeded, however, in preventing U.S. foreign policy from supporting any international human rights obligations throughout the early Cold War era.

POSITIVE AND NEGATIVE
DEVELOPMENTS IN THE 1960s

When President Kennedy redesigned U.S. foreign policy in the 1960s, he gave increased attention to international issues other than the Soviet threat. Development in the Third World, especially within Latin America, was elevated in importance to become a primary objective of U.S. policy. There was a markedly more generous approach to foreign aid. New assistance programs were set up under the Peace Corps and the Alliance for Progress (AFP). President Johnson followed up on these policies and expanded the Food for Peace program that had been established in 1954. This was also the age of the domestic civil rights movement capped by the Civil Rights Act (1964), signed by Johnson. All of these policies were designed to promote equality at home and abroad and to help people everywhere better meet their basic human needs. The United Nations finished the two international covenants on human rights in 1966: the Covenant on Civil and Political Rights; and the Covenant on Economic, Social and Cultural Rights (see Chapter 1). The covenants are binding treaties for those nations that ratify them. The two covenants and the Universal Declaration make up the three parts of the IBHR. Richard Falk (1981: 13) describes the Kennedy-Johnson years as a period of "expansive international liberalism," and paints a rosy picture of Kennedy in particular as "an idealistic force in international society." A more balanced history of the period however, such as the one given by Lars Schoultz (1981), reveals a darker side to U.S. foreign policy.

The Alliance for Progress was economic aid directed toward Latin America. The hope was that economic development would reduce the likelihood of more Castroite revolutions. The AFP would enhance growth and defuse some of the economic tensions that might result in political unrest. The other side of this coin was the Office of Public Safety (OPS), also created by the Kennedy administration. While the AFP was bringing economic growth to Latin America, the OPS was designed to keep the lid on communist insurgencies. The latter program provided arms, training, and technical know-how for fighting guerilla wars waged by national liberation fronts. The OPS created an International Police Academy (IPA) that trained forces from 52 nations (Schoultz, 1981: 179). Most of this training was for internal security. The targets of OPS-IPA programs were leftists of various sorts. Critics charged that the IPA was teaching torture and other forms of repression. Similar charges have been made in regard to the International Military Education and Training program, a successor to the IPA (see Chapter 4 for more on the International Military Education and Training program). Schoultz cites a congressional report from 1971 that detailed the kinds of training provided to Latin American security forces through these programs:

Courses were offered in riot control, intelligence, psychological warfare, counterguerilla operations . . . censorship . . . defoliation, electronic intelligence, the use of informants, insurgency intelligence, counterintelligence, subversion, countersubversion, espionage, counterespionage, interrogation of prisoners and suspects, handling mass rallies and meetings, intelligence photography, polygraphs, populace and resources control, psychological operations, raids and searches, riots, special warfare, surveillence, terror, and undercover operations. (Schoultz, 1981: 232)

The OPS was also implicated in violations of rights in South Vietnam during the same period. The OPS itself was part of the larger Agency for International Development (AID) (see Chapter 4 for a detailed discussion of AID). The OPS was intimately linked to the South Vietnamese police forces, and AID provided the funding for the notorious "tiger cages" on Con Sol Island, cages used by the South Vietnamese security forces for interrogation and torture of suspected Viet Cong rebels. A congressional aide named Tom Harkin photographed the tiger cages and published the photos in *Life* magazine in 1970. Prisoners were bolted to the floor of the cages in such a way that they could not stand, sit, or recline for weeks, even months, at a time. Congresssional testimony about the effects of this form of torture showed "severe nutritional deficiency coupled with prolonged immobilization. Each man had spent months or years without interruption in leg shackles while subsisting on a diet of three handfuls of milled white rice and three swallows of water per day. This combination of prolonged immobilization and starvation has . . . never occurred before on such a scale" (Schoultz, 1981: 181). The Air Force doctor who gave this testimony concluded by noting that, "Their paralysis together with the causative conditions are unique in the history of modern warfare, and the U.S. bears a heavy burden of complicity" (1981: 181).

The legacy of the Kennedy-Johnson years and the programs initiated by these presidents thus leaves a checkered balance sheet regarding U.S. foreign policy and human rights. The admirable goals and the good works of the Peace Corps and the AFP were offset by the repression enhanced by the OPS and the IPA. When these Democratic administrations were succeeded by Republican presidents, the stage was set for a battle between the White House and Congress for control of foreign policy, especially policy in regard to human rights.

KISSINGER VERSUS THE CONGRESS

Kissinger was the principal architect of U.S. foreign policy in the Nixon and Ford administrations. Well known for his scholarship and practice of political realism, Kissinger aided Nixon in the creation of détente during the 1970s. Détente was an effort to promote peaceful coexistence while containing communism through new means. Kissinger pursued nuclear arms control, negotiations on trade with the Soviets, and policy in Vietnam. The Nixon administration escalated the war in Vietnam before negotiating a withdrawal of U.S. forces. Kissinger was awarded the Nobel Peace Prize in 1973 for his achievement at the Paris peace talks with North Vietnam. Although famous for détente, Kissinger also has received considerable attention from those who study the history of U.S. policy on human rights.

Falk claims that Kissinger was "openly scornful of introducing human rights concerns into serious diplomacy" (1981: 13). As a realist, Kissinger argued that inserting human rights matters into policy would interfere with more important issues, such as maintaining a stable balance of power and limiting nuclear weapons. Stressing human rights violations, even those in the Soviet Union, was set aside by Kissinger to pursue détente. Kissinger would not broach the subject of rights in his dealings with the Soviets. He wanted to avoid embarassing the Soviet Union in any way that might increase tensions between the superpowers and thereby endanger détente.

Schoultz describes Kissinger as a man who had a change of heart on human rights. Schoultz details what he calls the "early" as opposed to the "late" Kissinger. The early Kissinger was a dyed-in-the-wool realist. The early Kissinger saw only two options for U.S. policy when it came to human rights violations: "In our bilateral dealings we will follow a pragmatic policy of degree. If the infringement on human rights is not so offensive that we cannot live with it, we will seek to work out what we can with the country involved in order to increase our influence. If the infringement is so offensive that we cannot live with it, we will avoid dealing with the offending country" (Schoultz, 1981: 110).

For the early Kissinger there were only two choices. Either the United States could turn a blind eye toward human rights violations, ignoring abuses and conducting business as usual in its foreign policy, or it could cut all ties with the repressive regime when rights violations became too egregious. Reducing the policy options to these two extremes, in effect, stacks the deck in favor of turning a blind eye toward rights violations. Kissinger, in both his early and late periods, never advocated cutting ties to any regime because of its human rights violations. Kissinger also opposed using aid as leverage. Leverage is the reduction or suspension of foreign aid to a government as punishment for human rights abuses. Kissinger argued that linking foreign aid to human rights was too utopian, it was part of a misguided "temptation to crusade," and he said cuts in aid would damage national security (Schoultz, 1981: 191). Instead of leverage, Kissinger preferred quiet diplomacy as his means to improve human rights.

The late Kissinger described by Schoultz experienced a change of heart regarding human rights, a change allegedly reflected in his 1976 speech before the Organization of American States (OAS). Present at this speech were representatives from the government of Chile. Headed by General Pinochet, Chile's military junta had become notorious by 1976 for its human rights atrocities. Speaking before the OAS, Kissinger said: "One of the most compelling issues of our time, and one which calls for the concerted action of all responsible peoples and nations, is the necessity to protect and extend the fundamental rights of humanity" (Schoultz, 1981: 111). In the same speech, Kissinger referred to human rights as "the very essence of a meaningful life" (Forsythe, 1989: 108).

There are at least three ways to interpret Kissinger's 1976 conversion on human rights. One interpretation would be simply that he was sincere in his change of heart. Perhaps the great statesman decided during his last year in the State Department that his prior realism had to be tempered with a greater concern for international morality and human rights. Schoultz seems to lean toward this view on Kissinger (1981: 112). A second interpretation is that Kissinger lied when speaking before the OAS. His speech may have been a cynical use of rhetoric to fool the U.S. public into believing that he had experienced a change of heart. Forsythe seems to lean toward this view when he says of the 1976 speech that "Kissinger was nothing if not duplicitous" (1989: 109).

A third interpretation of Kissinger's talk before the OAS would see the speech as something designed primarily for domestic consumption in the United States. After all, 1976 was an election year. A Democrat running for president, Jimmy Carter of Georgia, was using the rhetoric of human rights to garner national attention for his campaign. Kissinger had also been under pressure from Congress for years to make human rights leverage a part of official government policy (something Kissinger consistently resisted). Kissinger himself may have recognized the political value of human rights rhetoric; he may simply have been trying to steal Carter's thunder while defusing the human rights movement within Congress.

While Kissinger was orchestrating White House policy, congressional leaders initiated a countertrend that sought to reduce or remove U.S. support for right-wing governments that abused human rights. Congress was bothered by the moral complicity of the United States in regard to the Vietnamese tiger cages and training by the OPS at the IPA (Bedau, 1979: 40; MacLean, 1979: 98). Concerns by Congress led to a series of legislation that required the White House to integrate new human rights policies into its agenda. Human rights strings were attached by Congress to economic aid and military aid.

In 1974, Congress amended Section 502B of the Foreign Assistance Act to apply human rights leverage to foreign military aid. As amended, this law states that "no security assistance may be provided to any country the government of which engages in a consistent pattern of gross violations of internationally recognized human rights . . . unless the President certifies in writing . . . that extraordinary circumstances exist warranting provision of such assitance" (see Brown and MacLean, 1979: xi). Hence, under Section 502B military aid cannot be extended to governments that consistently violate human rights standards. However, the "extraordinary circumstances" clause is a national security loophole that allows repressive regimes to receive military aid if a president argues that such aid is necessary for U.S. national interests. At different times in the past, this loophole has been invoked to ensure continued military aid to nations such as Iran, the Philippines, and South Korea.

In 1975 Congress moved to attach the same conditions to economic aid. The OPS was also shut down by a separate act of Congress in 1975. Economic aid was made subject to human rights leverage under the provisions of an amendment to Section 116 of the Foreign Assistance Act. Also referred to as the Harkin Amendment in honor of its author, Tom Harkin of Iowa (onetime congressional aide who photographed the tiger cages, later a member of Congress), this law is a "cornerstone of human rights legislation" (Schoultz, 1981: 195). As amended, Section 116 denies economic aid "to the government of any country which engages in a consistent pattern of gross violations of internationally recognized human rights, including torture or cruel, inhuman, or degrading treatment or punishment, prolonged detention without charges, or other flagrant denial of the right to life, liberty, and the security of the person, unless such assistance will directly benefit the needy people in such country" (see Brown and MacLean, 1979: xiii–xiv). The Harkin Amendment goes on to require of the White House "annual presentation materials" certifying that nations that receive U.S. economic assistance do indeed uphold international standards of human rights. The "needy people" loophole of the Harkin

Amendment allows economic aid to be granted to a nation that displays gross human rights violations if that aid goes to the direct benefit of the most needy. Haiti is an example of a country for which the needy people loophole has been invoked as a way to ensure continued aid. On such occasions, however, Congress will further require that the aid be channeled through nongovernmental organizations, such as the Red Cross. Use of nongovernmental organizations under these circumstances is a way to see that needy people are not penalized for crimes committed by their government. At the same time, corrupt officials in a repressive regime have no direct access to the aid themselves.

The Harkin Amendment also has had a lasting impact on U.S. foreign policy because it has institutionalized the processes of human rights reporting by the State Department and certification of human rights compliance by the Congress. This act led to annual publications on human rights conditions around the world from the State Department. Released in February of each year, the country reports on human rights from the State Department have become an increasingly important source of information for Congress and the public alike. Once subject to politicalization, the reports have become progressively more objective over time.

Section 502B and the Harkin Amendment stand as the key pieces of human rights legislation governing military and economic aid, respectively. Both acts were vigorously opposed by Kissinger and the White House when originally drafted. Presidents Nixon and Ford resisted the human rights leverage on foreign policy that these acts represented. President Carter, on the other hand, came into the White House very much in favor of such legislation and of increasing the role that human rights would play in his administration.

THREE CHARACTERISTICS
OF THE CARTER POLICY

President Carter came into office promising a change from the old way of doing things under Nixon and Kissinger. He promised a change from the immorality of the Watergate scandal and the dirty tricks of the Nixon White House (G. Donaldson, 1996: 123). Carter ran for the presidency as an outsider. A former governor from Georgia, Carter was unconnected to the old boy network of Washington. He ran against the idea of politics as usual. His campaign stressed Carter as an idealist, and he spoke of himself as a former Sunday school teacher. A man who focused on his moral beliefs, Carter even confessed in a published interview to the weakness of having "lusted in his heart" after women other than his wife, but he quickly added that he would never act on such feelings. He wore his heart on his sleeve and displayed morality as his badge of courage.

Carter's early foreign policies were consciously constructed on utopian grounds. He said he wanted to make the U.S. government as good as the American people. He believed that morality had to be the basis of international policy. This meant no more turning a blind eye toward human rights violations by allied governments. Carter sought to distance the United States from right-wing dictatorships, especially those in Latin America. He came into office very much in favor of using aid leverage to exert pressure on rights abusers.

Carter promised to make human rights the moral focus of his foreign policy. He said that his administration's commitment to rights would be absolute. Upon taking office, Carter moved quickly to display his devotion to the cause of human rights. He signed the American Convention on Human Rights, which is a regional rights treaty from the OAS. He signed the two UN covenants on human rights, both the civil-political covenant and the covenant on socioeconomic rights.[2] Within the State Department, Carter created the Bureau of Human Rights and Humanitarian Affairs, headed by an Assistant Secretary of State for Human Rights. The president elevated the preexisting office of human rights within the State Department to the assistant-secretary level. The first assistant secretary for human rights was Patricia Derian, a diplomat who became famous for scolding Chile's General Pinochet and others for their use of torture. Carter took all of these actions within his first year in office as a way to show the high priority he placed on human rights as a key element of foreign policy.

Carter's approach to human rights is best summarized according to three principal features:

A single standard. Carter vowed to have a single standard of human rights for all nations, friend and foe alike.

Publicity. Carter chose to use public criticism of human rights abusers. He wanted to publicly denounce the worst abusers of rights.

Leverage. Carter promised to cut off aid to violators of human rights.

The single standard employed by Carter promised to bring an evenhanded approach to human rights policy. Tonelson criticizes Carter for adopting the "pipe dream" of evenhandedness and then failing to live up to his own goals (1982: 53–54). Forsythe also makes much of the differences between the rhetoric of Carter's declared policy on rights and the reality of Carter's actual policies (1989: 110ff.). In theory at least, the single standard was going to apply the same rights criteria to the behavior of both pro-U.S. and anti-U.S. regimes. Communist dictatorships and right-wing juntas that violated rights were to be treated equally, regardless of their strategic relationship to the United States.

The single standard was based on three areas of human rights, ranked in order of importance to the Carter administration. Secretary of State Cyrus Vance articulated the elements of the single standard in a speech to the University of Georgia's law school in 1977. First and foremost were rights involving the security of the person (for example, the right to be free from torture). Second in importance were social and economic rights to the things that help fill basic human needs. These include the rights to food, health care, and shelter. Carter's was the first and still the only U.S. administration to formally recognize the existence of some second generation socioeconomic rights. Finally, civil and political liberties, such as free speech and freedom of religion, were ranked third in order of importance by Carter and Vance (Vance, 1977).

Carter's use of publicity and criticism of rights abusers in the mass media replaced the Nixon-Kissinger preference for quiet diplomacy. Publicity and the media spotlight were used to denounce major violations of rights. Carter was vocal in his condemnation of the Somoza dictatorship in Nicaragua. Carter also led the international criticism of the Republic of South Africa when anti-apartheid activist Stephen Biko was beaten to death by security officers in 1977. In practice, the White House seemed to direct its harshest attacks against governments that sided with the U.S. in the Cold War, bringing into question the evenhanded principles that Carter had espoused.

The consistency of Carter's human rights policies was also brought into question by his use of aid leverage. Carter came into office in favor of the Harkin Amendment, Section 502B, and additional legislation that applied human rights leverage to other assistance programs. The Carter administration ended aid to Paraguay, Uruguay, and the Somoza regime in Nicaragua. Aid was reduced to the Shah of Iran and Pinochet's Chile. Aid was redesigned to go directly to the most needy in Guatamala and Haiti (Schoultz, 1981: 205). However, Carter did not cut aid to the Marcos dictatorship in the Philippines, nor did he use aid as leverage against South Korea, even though both governments were widely known for their repression. Furthermore, Carter reduced aid to Chile during a time when private investment into Chile's economy and private lending to Chile's government were booming (Lippman, 1985: 256–59; Tonelson, 1982: 63). Increases in private funds flowing into Chile offset and vastly surpassed the cuts in public assistance imposed by Carter. The example of Chile points to the importance of tracking both public aid and private investment into the Third World when trying to establish the impact of U.S. economic transactions on human rights (see Chapters 3 and 4).

Carter's public criticism and use of leverage tended to focus primarily on America's allies. Right-wing, anticommunist regimes were much more likely than leftist regimes to feel the sting of Carter's rhetorical barbs. Thus, the adminstration seemed to undermine in practice the evenhanded single standard that they proclaimed in principle. There is a logical reason for this to be the case. As Tonelson points out in his critique of the Carter approach:

America can withold aid only from aid recipients, deny weapons only to arms clients, embargo trade only to trading partners. Thus any peaceful human rights policy involving deeds must fall most heavily on countries linked most closely to the United States. Every concession to this reality, no matter how well explained, sabotages the claim of evenhandedness and compromises the credibility of U.S. policy the way each leak compromises the credibility of a dam. (1982: 55)

Despite the lack of rigid consistency in the Carter approach, U.S. policy did experience some notable successes in the late 1970s in terms of improving human rights around the world. Thousands of political prisoners were released in Asia and Latin America during Carter's tenure (Falk, 1981: 23; Tonelson, 1982: 63). No doubt at least some of the credit for the release of these prisoners of conscience goes to Carter's use of aid leverage and public criticism. Some of those released even thanked Carter for their freedom.[3] Leverage imposed by Carter undermined the political strength of military dictators who relied heavily on U.S. security assistance to stay in power. The Carter staff would claim credit for starting a trend toward replacing dictatorships with democracies in Latin America, a trend that came to fruition only after Carter had left office.

Carter's use of public pressure also helped to bring deaths in confinement in South Africa almost to a halt. In the two years before Carter made the murder of black leaders held in South African prisons a major issue in bilateral relations, 27 suspicious deaths were recorded (during 1976 and 1977). This number includes Stephen Biko's death by torture on September 12, 1977. After Carter helped to publicize the brutal death of Biko, the killing of black leaders dropped to approximately one per year for the remainder of Carter's term in office. Deaths of blacks in RSA jails escalated dramatically once again after Carter left office and while the Reagan administration replaced Carter's use of public pressure with their preference for quiet diplomacy.[4]

Carter also used the power and prestige of the U.S. presidency to bring the issue of human rights to center stage in world politics. He did what perhaps only a U.S. president can do. He took an international issue that had received only token attention and moved it higher up on the agenda of global political priorities. Evidence of this fact is most readily observable in the area of presidential politics. Although no president before Carter articulated a policy on human rights qua human rights, every president since Carter has felt obliged to develop a specific set of policies that addresses human rights as such. No president since Carter has ascribed to all three of Carter's principles on rights (single standard, publicity, and leverage), but each president has taken the time and effort to work out a detailed set of policies on human rights. This is perhaps the most important legacy of the Carter administration when it comes to human rights.

Carter also had his notable failures in the area of foreign policy. Although his failures were not in the area of human rights policy itself, Carter's critics were quick to point out that, in their opinion, his preoccupation with international rights led him into foreign policy blunders in other areas.

His most notable foreign policy failures were the hostage crisis in Iran and the Soviet invasion of Afghanistan. Carter often gave the appearance of being too soft on the Soviets and other enemies of U.S. interests. Revolutionary governments came to power in both Iran and Nicaragua and then developed anti-U.S. ideologies. During his last 18 months in office, Carter wavered in his support for human rights as the guiding principle of U.S. foreign policy. Tensions developed between his human rights ideals and the geopolitical necessities determined by an international balance of power. Vance resigned as Carter's Secretary of State to protest the unsuccessful use of force to try to free the hostages. Vance (a utopian) was replaced as Carter's top foreign policy advisor by Zbigniew Brzezinski. The latter was clearly a political realist. Carter then proceded on more of a case-by-case basis in his bilateral dealings, in essence giving up on the single standard.

Ronald Reagan defeated Carter in the 1980 election in part because of Carter's weaknesses in foreign policy. Reagan charged many times during the campaign that Carter's preoccupation with human rights had allowed the United States' enemies to take advantage of its interests. Reagan believed that Carter's approach to human rights had punished America's allies and abetted its enemies. Because he was too much of a utopian purist, Carter's single-minded devotion to human rights had been counterproductive to U.S. strategic interests, according to the Reagan critique (Carleton and Stohl, 1985).

Carter succeeded in bringing the issue of human rights to center stage in international relations. This was perhaps his broadest and most lasting contribution as president.[5] However, in so doing, Carter "raised the stakes" involved in supporting human rights as a key element of foreign policy (Falk, 1981: 30). Falk has argued that Carter raised the stakes by investing so much energy, so much of his own prestige, and so much political capital in the area of human rights. Then, when Carter seemed to fail in his foreign policies in other areas, the results did indirect harm to the international human rights campaign. Carter's failures (the hostages, Afghanistan) became associated with the failure of a human rights agenda as the guiding light for U.S. foreign policy. Carter's floundering led to a realist-oriented backlash in U.S. politics, a backlash against the failures ascribed to Carter's utopian views.

Reagan capitalized on this pro-realist backlash in the 1980 campaign. Upon taking office, Reagan made good on his promises to redirect U.S. foreign policy and to once again stress power politics (a realist approach). Reagan also redirected policy on human rights in such a way as to make it a tool in the resurgent Cold War of the 1980s.

The swing toward realpolitik in foreign policy helped Reagan to unseat Carter. This is a trend that is still very much with us after the end of the Cold War. The trend away from utopianism and toward realism also translates into a greatly diminished probability that the U.S. public will support human rights policies in the future that are akin to those of the early Carter years (Holsti, 1996).

THREE ELEMENTS OF THE REAGAN POLICY

The focus of President Reagan's foreign policies was on power, especially military power. Reagan was concerned foremost with the international balance of power between the West and the Soviet Union. Reagan oversaw a huge buildup in U.S. military forces. Total military expenditures under Presidents Reagan and Bush exceeded $3 trillion (FY 1982–93). There was much less attention paid by the White House to human rights as such, both in comparison to the previous administration and in comparison to the Reagan administration's affinity for power politics. As had been the case in the early 1970s, major human rights policies during the Reagan years were pushed by Congress, often with stiff opposition from the White House. The most important piece of human rights legislation of the 1980s, the Comprehensive Anti-Apartheid Act (CAAA) of 1987, had to be passed over Reagan's veto. Human rights issues did play a part in Reagan's foreign policy, but in most cases primarily as a strategy for pursuing Cold War campaigns against the Soviets.

The Reagan administration's early rights emphasis was to concentrate on violations of rights in communist nations: the Soviet Union, the People's Republic of China (PRC), the Sandinista regime in Nicaragua, and Cambodia. They also tended to downplay violations in allied states: the Republic of South Africa, El Salvador, the Philippines, and South Korea. Reagan was very much a realist, but, unlike Kissinger before him who refused to criticize the Soviets for fear of endangering détente, Reagan was willing and eager to denounce Soviet transgressions.

The particular rights that Reagan focused on were first generation civil and political rights. Especially important were freedom of the press and regularly scheduled, honest elections. Emphasizing these rights brought international pressure to bear on the Soviets and the Sandinistas. The first annual human rights report out of the Reagan State Department in 1982 included a special introduction declaring that there are no such things as economic and social rights. The Reagan administration also defined international terrorism as a human rights violation. In fact, terrorist acts were identified as entailing the most egregious forms of rights violations. Of course this tactic also had its residual Cold War utility. Because Reagan believed that almost all terrorism was traceable to Soviet instigation or to Soviet proxies, focusing the human rights debate on terrorism would help the White House in its diplomatic battles against the Soviet Union.

A sharp contrast between Reagan's human rights policies and Carter's policy emerges from comparing three principles of the Reagan approach to the prior Carter matrix:

A double standard. The Reagan administration had two distinct sets of criteria for evaluating a nation's record on rights. One standard was applied to authoritarian regimes, and a separate standard was applied to totalitarian regimes.

No public criticism of allies. Reagan preferred to deal with violations of rights in friendly states by means of quiet diplomacy.

No leverage against allies. Reagan opposed denying aid to pro-U.S. regimes because of violations of rights.

The rationale for the double standard was laid out by Reagan's ambassador to the United Nations, Jeane Kirkpatrick. In an article entitled "Dictators and Double Standards," Kirkpatrick (1979) argued that major violators of human rights come in two types: authoritarian versus totalitarian regimes. The Kirkpatrick Doctrine holds that Carter's single standard was hopelessly flawed because it did not take into account the differences in kind between left-wing regimes and right-wing regimes. Public criticism of allies and denials of aid based on Carter's utopian approach only served to undermine allies and endanger U.S. security interests (Kirkpatrick, 1981). Instead, the Reagan policy would be based on a more realistic understanding of rights and politics. According to this view, both authoritarian and totalitarian regimes violate rights. However, authoritarian regimes tend to be rightist and pro-U.S., while totalitarians are almost always leftist and anti-U.S. Futhermore, according to Kirkpatrick, authoritarians are usually content to control the political system, imposing dictatorships and one-party rule, but allowing considerable latitude and relative freedom in nonpolitical areas. Authoritarians are more likely than totalitarians to permit a capitalist economy, private property, and at least some religious and cultural liberties. There is allegedly a "far greater likelihood of progressive liberalization and democratization" in authoritarian regimes, as compared to totalitarian ones, because there are more freedoms in nonpolitical spheres on which to base a campaign for political liberalization (1979: 44).

According to the Kirkpatrick Doctrine, totalitarians will never transform themselves into a more liberal polity. Precisely because they seek to control the totality of human existence, left-wing communist totalitarian states "claim jurisdiction over the whole life of society" (Kirkpatrick, 1979: 44). Hence, there is no economic, cultural, or religious space within a totalitarian state in which the roots of liberal reforms can take hold and spread.[6] Policy implications follow from Kirkpatrick's distinction between the two types of human rights violators. The United States should maintain its ties to the authoritarian regimes, including provision of official assistance. Because authoritarian regimes are uniformly anticommunist, aid from the United States serves not only as a force for change from within, it also serves to bolster strategic interests. Conversely, the policy best suited to totalitarian regimes is one that "tightens all screws" by putting as much formal and informal pressure on them as is possible.

The other two elements of the Reagan approach follow logically from the first premise of the double standard. There was to be no public criticism of allied states for their lapses in human rights protection. Rather, this adminstration preferred to work behind the scenes, applying pressure informally and off the record. The Reagan White House returned to the quiet diplomacy option toward allies used previously by Kissinger. A notable difference between Kissinger's and Reagan's realism, however, was the latter's public criticism of the Soviet Union. Kissinger had eschewed human rights agendas vis-à-vis the Soviets in deference to his détente initiatives. Reagan, by contrast, took advantage of every opportunity to denounce violations of rights in Russia during both his first and second terms.

The Reagan adminstration did agree with Kissinger when it came to opposing the use of aid as leverage against friendly governments. Reagan worked very hard to get legislation through Congress in 1985 that eliminated special human rights restrictions on aid to El Salvador.[7] Reagan also tried to prevent passage of the economic sanctions against the RSA contained in the Comprehensive Anti-Apartheid Act. The Reagan administration did impose economic leverage in one case. It was directed against totalitarians in Poland for their crackdown on the Solidarity labor movement in December of 1981. A prior policy of preferential terms for trade and loans to Poland was suspended by Reagan.[8]

The lack of public criticism and the refusal to use leverage against pro-U.S. regimes was exemplified by the policy of constructive engagement toward South Africa. Constructive engagement (CE) was the term coined to describe policies developed by Chester Crocker, Reagan's assistant secretary of state for African affairs. CE was a set of incentives rather than sanctions that were aimed at promoting reform in South Africa. CE offered increased aid, increased trade, and other incentives to the RSA as a way to lessen the pressure felt by the white minority regime. The hope was that, if the whites felt less pressure, then they would be more likely to allow increased political and economic freedom to the nonwhite majority. Liberal reforms might then lead to the dismantling of apartheid. However, during the period of CE as official U.S. policy, repression in South Africa increased. A state of emergency was imposed by the white minority regime (Donnelly, 1993: 73), and deaths of black anti-aparthied leaders in confinement skyrocketed (see note 4 in this chapter). By 1985, the Reagan adminstration had to admit that constructive engagement had failed.

Meanwhile, a countermovement in Congress had grown, demanding the imposition of tough economic sanctions against the RSA as a way to help bring down apartheid. Reagan tried to defuse the congressional movement toward sanctions by imposing token economic pressure through presidential decree. In 1985, Reagan suspended importation of gold Kruggerands (coins minted by the RSA government), ended sales of high-tech equipment (such as computers) to the RSA security forces, and allowed public loans to the RSA government only if those funds were to be used for the benefit of the nonwhite majority (for example, new housing).[9] These were token sanctions in the sense that they seemed designed to have little or no impact on the economic position of the whites.

Rather than placating Congress, the weak nature of the 1985 presidential sanctions stimulated even greater desires on Capitol Hill for a general trade embargo against South Africa. This took the form of the Comprehensive Anti-Apartheid Act of 1987. The CAAA was first vetoed by Reagan and then became law by a vote of Congress overriding that veto. The CAAA prohibited importation into the United States of most RSA exports, outlawed exportation of petroleum products to the RSA, and denied all public loans to the RSA government (regardless of purpose). Perhaps the harshest economic blow to the RSA, however, was the CAAA ban on all new investment into South Africa's economy. Direct foreign investment from the United States to the RSA had run at a level of about $2 billion per year prior to 1987. All such new investment was halted by the CAAA.

A notable loophole in the CAAA was the provision allowing continued importation of strategic minerals from South Africa. Strategic minerals, such as manganese and vadium, are necessary to U.S. defense industries. They are key components for making alloys with high tensile strength used in the production of armored vehicles and fighter aircraft. Given existing technologies, many of these strategic minerals could be exported in quantity only by South Africa and the Soviet Union. Hence the Congress deemed it in the national interest to allow trade in strategic minerals to continue throughout the period of economic sanctions against South Africa.

Although the presidential sanctions of 1985 had little or no economic impact within South Africa, the CAAA combined with sanctions imposed by the European Union had a major effect. A report released within the RSA two years after the CAAA went into effect summarized the impact of foreign economic sanctions.[10] According to Bankorp, sanctions against the RSA cost that nation $40 billion in economic output, reduced the economic growth rate by 10 percent, and cost South Africa 500,000 jobs. Such economic pressure, combined with the internal resistance to apartheid led by the African National Congress (ANC), was too much for the white regime to bear. In 1990 Nelson Mandela, the leader of the ANC, was released after 26 years in prison. The ANC was also legalized at that time, ending a political ban dating back to 1963. Mandela's release and the legalization of the ANC quickly led to new political talks that established a democratic constitution and the first fully free elections in South Africa's history. By 1991, most of the laws of apartheid had been stricken from the books. In 1994, Mandela was elected president of South Africa.

The success associated with the use of economic pressure against the RSA, however, came in the face of White House opposition to these congressionally mandated sanctions.[11] Reagan, like Carter, had both notable failures and important successes in the area of human rights and foreign policy. The most notable failure of the Reagan years was the complete inefficacy of constructive engagement toward South Africa (Unger and Vale, 1985). By contrast, policies of quiet diplomacy did help to further the cause of rights in South Korea and the Philippines. When Corazon Aquino led a popular uprising against the Marcos dictatorship in the Philippines in 1986, the Reagan administration did not try to prop up Marcos but instead used behind-the-scenes pressure to convince Marcos to abdicate power.[12] A quiet diplomacy approach also seemed to have an effect on the military-backed government in South Korea in 1988. Demonstrations and riots preceded the scheduled opening of the Seoul Summer Olympics of 1988. The Reagan White House once again pursued a strategy of quiet diplomacy and convinced the South Korean leaders to hold competitive elections prior to the games (something the government had sworn in early 1988 that they would not do). A wave of democratization in Latin America also came to a head from 1982 to 1989 (Boyd, 1990: 217). As noted earlier, the Carter administration believed its policies of public criticism and aid leverage were behind the eventual fall of military dictatorships in South America. However, because these juntas were voted out in most cases during the Reagan years, Carter's successor also claimed credit for that international trend.

Finally, a review of the Reagan years would not be complete without mentioning the end of the Cold War and the fall of communism in Eastern Europe. The heady days of the communist collapse began with the fall of the Berlin Wall and the election of the first noncommunist governments in the former Soviet bloc, both of which came in 1989. Although these events took place after Reagan left office, officials in the Bush administration and the Republican Party accorded most of the credit for this breakthrough to Reagan himself. The most common explanation for the fall of communism and the end of the Cold War (although not necessarily the most valid explanation) is that the military buildup of the 1980s under Reagan bankrupted the Soviet system. This account views Soviet efforts to keep up militarily as the single most important factor leading to communism's demise in Europe.[13]

The end of the Cold War or the spread of democracy in Europe and the Americas has many possible explanations. It would be overestimating the power of U.S. foreign policy to assume that either trend was due largely to the actions of one or more U.S. presidents. The internal politics of communist regimes and Latin American dictatorships may be affected to some extent by U.S. policy. However, it would be a gross oversimplification to give the credit for these trends to U.S. leaders. There is also some question as to whether any president has ever adopted a set of human rights principles and then consistently stuck to those principles. The changes in Carter's policy on rights during his last year in office have already been discussed. At least one author has argued that Reagan's foreign policy on rights also experienced fundamental changes. Forsythe believes that Reagan's policies during his second term were actually more akin to those of Carter than they were to Reagan's own policies during his first term (1989: 120–21). He cites as an example the increased willingness by the Reagan adminstration in its second term to criticize authoritarians as well as totalitarians. Forsythe also argues that "the Soviet Union and its allies were no longer special targets of U.S. public criticism" during Reagan's second term (1989: 120). This slant on the Reagan years tends to overlook what the president himself said. During his last year in office, President Reagan gave a speech in Chicago honoring the fortieth anniversary of the Universal Declaration.[14] During his last major address on rights, Reagan took a position that was essentially the same one he had espoused when he first took office almost eight years earlier. Reagan counseled Americans concerned about human rights in 1988 to focus their attention primarily on the Soviet Union. Reagan argued that if one wants to criticize human rights violations or promote respect for human rights internationally, then one should start with the human rights problems within the Soviet Union. Furthermore, according to Reagan, one should keep one's attention and human rights pressure fixed mainly on the Soviets. In this crucial respect, Reagan's approach to human rights stood in stark contrast to that of Carter or even Kissinger. Regarding his emphasis on rights in the Soviet Union, Reagan was consistent throughout his years in the White House.

TEST CASES DURING THE BUSH YEARS

President Bush's administration expressed a view on human rights that, at least on the surface, appeared to be a synthesis of the Carter and Reagan policies. In theory, Bush claimed to be willing to use public criticism of violations wherever they might occur. These claims reflected the themes of publicity and evenhandedness expressed by Carter. In practice, however, Bush's policy was much closer to that of Reagan, as one would expect.

Bush's policy was a continuation of the Reagan approach in several important respects. They shared the same general definition of human rights. Bush, like Reagan, restricted the denotation of rights to only civil and political rights. According to the Bush adminstration, what some call economic and social rights require active promotion and affirmative steps by governments, therefore they are not rights as such. Rather, economic and social welfare (jobs, medical care, shelter) should be left to the work of private enterprise and market forces; they should not be the subjects of guarantees or promotion by the public sector (Schifter, 1988: 70–71). The first annual human rights report out of the Bush adminstration (1990) tried to sort out some of the alleged confusion that leads others to speak mistakenly of socioeconomic rights. The same report also detailed the Bush policies for addressing international rights.

The 1990 report by the State Department set two ends and two means for Bush's policies on rights (Schifter, 1990: 4). The ends were to oppose specific human rights violations "wherever they occur" and to work to strengthen democracy around the world. The first goal was stated in such a way as to recall Carter's single standard. The second goal, bolstering democracy, was to become especially important because Bush was the first U.S. president required to develop post–Cold War foreign policies. The means for pursuit of these goals were to be "traditional" (quiet) diplomacy as a first option and "public statements" as a fallback position if the first option was unsuccessful (1990: 4). The first means, quiet diplomacy, was to become almost the exclusive tool for Bush, while the second means, public pressure, once again harkened back to the Carter days but was almost never utilized by Bush. A series of test cases served to take the Bush approach to task.

Lithuania

The first test case for the Bush approach to human rights and a key case also in regard to the end of the Cold War was Lithuania. Lithuania was one of the 15 republics that made up the Soviet Union. Like its Baltic neighbors, Latvia and Estonia, Lithuania had experienced political independence between the World Wars, only to be forceably annexed into the Soviet Union by Stalin in 1940. During the Cold War, the United States did not officially recognize the Baltic states as part of the Soviet Union. However, at least since 1975, U.S. policy had been not to recognize the Baltics as fully independent either.[15]

In March 1990 Lithuania unilaterally declared its independence. Gorbachev, despite his rhetoric in favor of glasnost (openness), responded to Lithuania's declaration of independence with force.[16] The Red Army conducted new military maneuvers inside Lithuania. Printing presses were seized. Radio and television broadcasting in Lithuania, claimed by both the local government and the regime in Moscow, were taken over at Gorbachev's orders. Control of government buildings was seized by Soviet "black berets" (special forces). Gorbachev also imposed an economic embargo against Lithuania, cutting off badly needed goods, especially oil.

The Bush response to Gorbachev's repression in Lithuania was limited. The president refused to support demands by the Baltics for independence. Bush also refused requests from Congress to deny most favored nation (MFN) trading status to the Soviets as a way to punish Moscow for its crackdown on Lithuania. Temporary MFN status was first granted to the Soviet Union in 1990, a status that was made permanent in 1991. Trade with the Soviets took precedence in the Bush White House over the right of self-determination for the Baltic republics. There was little or no pressure by Bush on the Soviets to grant non-Russian republics their freedom. He even made public statements to the contrary (LaFeber, 1997: 344).[17]

With the thaw in the Cold War stimulated by the fall of the Berlin Wall in 1989, Bush was keen to promote a new era of détente between the superpowers. Like Kissinger before him, Bush did not want tensions over human rights to stand in the way of increased trade with the Soviets (for example, MFN status). Kissinger and Bush were both more concerned with trade and arms control than with human rights violations inside the Soviet system.[18]

The dissolution of the Soviet Union in December of 1991 brought the demands for independence by Lithuania and the other non-Russian republics to a successful conclusion. The fact remains, however, that their demands found no support within the Bush administration. The president put a realist's emphasis on the necessities of international stability, and stability within the Soviet Union, ahead of the requests of the Lithuanian people.

China

Most favored nation status for a communist dictatorship became a key test of the Bush policies on rights in a second case as well, that of the PRC. Repression inside the PRC peaked during the massacre in Tiananmen Square in June of 1989, forcing the Bush administration to deal with violence committed by another communist regime. The events leading up to the 1989 massacre found their origins in a 1987 movement for student democracy.

Students in the PRC demonstrated in 1987, asking for political rights. Specifically, student leaders wanted the right to form their own political parties independent of the Chinese Communist Party and to run candidates for office in student governmental organizations. Hu Youbang, a top party official, refused to use force against the student protests and was ousted from the party's inner circle by Deng Xiaoping, the unquestioned ruler of the party.[19] Hu was succeeded as China's second in command by Zhao Ziyang, and Hu later died in 1989.

Students marched in early 1989 to honor Hu Youbang on his death. Their activities quickly coalesced into a renewed democracy movement. Students gathered in Tiananmen Square in the heart of Beijing to demand freedom of speech and the right to assemble. By all indications, Deng Xiaoping and Zhao Ziyang disagreed on how to respond to the student's demands. Zhao, like Hu before him, did not want to use force against the students.[20] Deng subsequently ousted Zhao from the ruling elite in favor of Li Peng. Deng and Premier Li Peng then declared martial law and ordered army units to clear the square on June 4, 1989. The subsequent massacre of unarmed protesters produced hundreds, perhaps thousands, of casualties.

The Bush response to the egregious violations of the Tiananmen massacre was once again limited. China's MFN status, enjoyed throughout the 1980s, was defended by Bush. Bush announced that all high level diplomatic contacts would be suspended as a result of the massacre, but he also consistently supported continued MFN trading arrangements. Furthermore, in December of 1989, Bush's National Security Advisor, Brent Scowcroft, was seen in Beijing toasting Deng Xiaoping at a state dinner.[21]

Bush's arguments in favor of MFN status for China held that economic sanctions against the PRC would be counterproductive. Bush stated many times that he thought it would be a mistake to isolate China in response to the violence at Tiananmen. He argued that U.S. businesses in China could serve as a force for economic liberalization from within. In a variation on the Kirkpatrick Doctrine, Bush believed that political reform in the totalitarian PRC would be more likely if U.S. economic ties were expanded rather than restricted. Because Deng had already allowed limited capitalism in the PRC, despite the political repression, continued trade with the United States was the best hope for promoting reform, in Bush's view. MFN status was extended to the PRC throughout the remainder of the Bush administration. Bush did impose an annual review of human rights conditions in the PRC before agreeing to renewal of MFN status every year, and Bush threatened to suspend MFN status unless there was consistent improvement in rights. However, despite his critics' wishes to the contrary, Bush never moved to make good on those threats.

El Salvador

A third case that tested the Bush administration's commitment to human rights was El Salvador. Politically motivated murders by so-called death squads in El Salvador became a contentious issue in bilateral relations with the United States during the 1980s. Death squads are right-wing private armies of the night that target leftist politicians, labor leaders, and church activists for assassination. Research has also shown that most of these death squads are made up of off-duty military personnel who receive support from the military-backed government of El Salvador (Hadar, 1981; Human Rights Watch, 1991). The United States extended heavy military aid to El Salvador during the Reagan and Bush administrations ($40–$50 million per year). A civil war between the right-wing government and the leftist guerillas produced more than 75,000 deaths between 1979 and 1992.

The key test for the Bush administration came with the killing of six priests by uniformed military personnel in 1989. Members of the Jesuit order, and suspected by the government of being communists or communist sympathizers, the priests were killed along with two of their housekeepers. Bush publicly condemned the killings, and Secretary of State Baker called the killings a "turning point" in U.S.-Salvadoran relations. However, Bush also argued against ending military aid to El Salvador's government in response to the killings.[22] Congress voted to freeze $42 million in aid to El Salvador until the priests' killers were tried. The president wanted the aid released by Congress as soon as possible. A long trial eventually led to the conviction in 1992 of two military officers for ordering the killings (including the former head of the National Military Academy in El Salvador). This opened the way for a renewal of military aid, something Bush had long favored. In the case of El Salvador, Bush once again employed a realist approach when it came to human rights violations. He consistently opposed use of leverage against the Salvadoran regime despite death squad activities and the murder of priests by the military. A campaign against Marxist revolution was given priority over the human rights abuses of the allied government waging that campaign.

South Africa

A final case from the Bush years was U.S. policy toward the Republic of South Africa. As Reagan's vice president, Bush had opposed the economic sanctions against the RSA contained in the Comprehensive Anti-Apartheid Act. In July 1991 President Bush announced that, in his opinion, enough progress had been made within South Africa to allow the suspension of CAAA sanctions.[23] By this time, Mandela had been freed, the African National Congress had been legalized as a political party, and most of the official statutes of apartheid had been striken from the books. Talks were also underway in 1991 to establish a new democratic constitution and free elections in the RSA. All of these conditions had been stipulated within the CAAA itself as necessary preconditions to ending U.S. economic sanctions.

Based on this progress, Bush announced that he was ending economic sanctions by executive order. Some members of Congress protested, arguing that Bush's actions were premature. Bush's critics were supported in their position by Mandela himself, who thought that Bush should wait until all political prisoners had been released. Mandela also argued that international sanctions should remain in place until the new constitution was in place, guaranteeing political rights to the black majority.[24] Despite these sentiments to the contrary, CAAA sanctions ended under the Bush administration in 1991.

CLINTON: A SYNTHESIS OF
REALISM AND UTOPIANISM?

As the United States moves into the twenty-first century, a possible synthesis of realist and utopian views on human rights and foreign policy seems to be in the making. The outlines of such a policy are evident in the way that President Clinton addressed human rights crises during his administration.

The issue of human rights surfaced in the 1992 presidential campaign. During televised debates, candidate Clinton criticized Bush for being soft on China. Clinton implied that, if elected, he would take a harder line in regard to violations of rights in the PRC.[25] Once in office, however, Clinton did no more than to continue the Bush approach of reviewing human rights in the PRC before agreeing to renew MFN status in 1993. Furthermore, in 1994, Clinton went so far as to drop the annual review of rights. Clinton dropped all connection between rights and trade with China during his second year in the White House. He argued that it was not fair to U.S. businesses to have to fear the annual rights review or possible suspension of special trade ties between the United States and the PRC.[26]

The Clinton approach to human rights did inject one relatively new element. Clinton seemed to be more willing than his predecessors to employ military force and humanitarian intervention as a means to ensure protection and promotion of human rights. Clinton's justifications for intervention employed a Carter-like rhetoric of utopian motives. A closer look, however, reveals that military intervention by the Clinton administration was driven primarily by realism. Four cases in point show both the utopian nature of Clinton's declared policy, as well as the realpolitik of the actual policy behind the rhetoric. Somalia and Rwanda are negative examples of the Clinton policy; these are cases in which humanitarian intevention was either not employed (Rwanda), or where intervention was terminated when it became too costly (Somalia). Haiti and Bosnia stand as positive examples of the Clinton approach; cases in which intervention was pursued for reasons that were justified in terms of utopianism but which were better understood as realist policy. Military actions in Bosnia and Haiti were primarily motivated by national interests and domestic political dynamics.

Somalian intervention was a policy Clinton inherited from Bush. Bush ordered the intervention in December 1992 with the objectives of feeding the starving victims of the Somali civil war and then turning the peacekeeping mission over to the United Nations once security had been established.[27] Humanitarian efforts to feed the Somali people were successful, but subsequent plans for disarming the warlords and for nation-building that would produce a permanent peace failed miserably. Then, when 18 U.S. servicemen were killed during a fight with the militia loyal to Mohamed Aidid on October 3, 1993, Clinton moved quickly to arrange a phased withdrawal of U.S. forces. Clinton canceled efforts to disarm the Somali factions and ended a search for General Aidid (Access, 1994).

The lesson of Somalia for U.S. foreign policy was that humanitarian intervention would not be pursued if it posed too great of a risk to military personnel. Protection of American lives was given priority over the more idealistic goals of the original intervention mandate set down by Bush in 1992.

Having been burned during the Somalian incursion, Clinton adjusted his intervention policies accordingly in the cases that followed. In both Haiti and Bosnia, Clinton justified intervention in terms of utopian goals for protecting human rights. However, in these cases troops were dispatched because of a combination of domestic political considerations and perceptions of U.S. national interests. In those crucial respects (domestic politics, perceptions, national interests), U.S. actions in Haiti and Bosnia were not significantly different from Cold War campaigns such as Vietnam.

When Clinton dispatched troops to Haiti in 1994 and to Bosnia in 1995, he defended his decisions in terms akin to the utopian project of preventing further abuses of human rights. The Haitian intervention was needed, according to the president, because of the massive rights violations commited by General Cedras and his regime.[28] Likewise in Bosnia, U.S. troops were needed to put an end to the form of genocide known as ethnic cleansing. The president even compared ethnic cleansing in Bosnia to the genocide of the Holocaust.[29] In both Haiti and Bosnia, the stated policy was one that pointed to a utopian concern for humanitarian action compelled by abuses of rights. However, upon closer examination, the actual policy in both cases was one of realpolitik.[30]

In the case of Haiti, Clinton was forced to act by a wave of refugees spilling out of the island nation toward Florida. Domestic political interests opposed to absorbing these immigrants pressured the president to take action (Zolberg and Smith, 1996: 28–29). National interests defined as the inability (or unwillingness) to relocate the Haitian masses were more of a motivating factor than the concomitant desire to end the suffering of Haitians trapped inside that country. If desires to stop the bloodshed had been the primary reason for intervention, Clinton would have taken action much sooner in both Haiti and Bosnia. Instead, he delayed the military option as long as there was no perception of a threat to the national interest (Jentleson, 1997: 54); this was classic realist calculation.

In the case of Bosnia, 250,000 people died and an estimated 20,000 rapes occured before the United States became militarily involved. Once again, Clinton used the utopian rhetoric of protecting the innocent and preserving rights to justify sending in troops.[31] Once again, however, it was a realist desire to protect U.S. interests that compelled Clinton to act when he did. Utopian desires to protect human rights would have been relevant to any intervention following the first acts of ethnic cleansing in Bosnia beginning in 1992. The Clinton administration waited until 1995 to dispatch troops because of a realist calculus that disputed the existence of a threat to any vital U.S. interest before that time.[32] The UN Security Council, the World Court, and the UN Commission on Human Rights declared ethnic cleansing in Bosnia to be acts of genocide long before Clinton took military action (Human Rights Watch, 1995: 3). Clinton was able to overlook the abuses and failed to invoke human rights violations as a justification for intervention until after U.S. global leadership and credibility were squarely on the line (leadership and credibility, once again, being considerations relevant to realist policy — such as in Vietnam — but not necessarily linked in any direct way to utopian concerns for protecting rights).

By the time the United States finally did intervene in Bosnia, the United States had been thrust into a leadership role for seeking a settlement because of the repeated diplomatic failures of the United Nations and the European Union. There was also a widely shared realist perception that events in Bosnia, if left unchecked, could "disrupt irreparably" NATO and other U.S. security commitments (Woodward, 1995: 2). The immediate task given to U.S. and other NATO forces was the enforcement of the 1995 Dayton agreements brokered by U.S. negotiators. Military intervention was structured so as to ensure disengagement of the warring factions behind the cease-fire lines established at Dayton. The forces were explicitly not given the charge of locating and arresting those individuals indicted for war crimes by the international tribunal established through the Security Council. U.S. troops were told to apprehend war criminals if they came across them in the course of their other duties, but the task of directly seeking them out was too utopian and too dangerous, especially in the context established by the debacle in Somalia.

The pattern thus established during the Clinton years was not to act when human rights atrocities occured, unless those abuses were also related in a direct way to U.S. interests defined in terms of power, prestige, credibility, and domestic political concerns. Rwanda was the case that most clearly demonstrated the fact that massive violations alone would not be sufficient to move the United States to action. Genocide on the scale of 500,000 dead in Rwanda during 1994 did not result in humanitarian intervention by the United States.

By contrast, when intervention because of realist policies of protecting national interests has been used in the post–Cold War era, the consistent rhetoric has been one of idealism spurred on by violations of human rights. The 1990s rhetoric of humanitarian concerns and motivations is yet another example of the long-term legacy of the Carter administration when it comes to presidential politics. Carter, who has maintained an active role by negotiating the departure of a dictator in Haiti and by acting as an international observer of human rights conditions in Bosnia, still stands as the patron saint for rights as a part of U.S. foreign policy. Clinton's refusal to intervene unless realpolitik dictated the need to protect interests, however, shows that recent U.S. policy has remained essentially consistent with the kinds of calculations that drove foreign policy during the prior Cold War. In both ages, U.S. foreign policy has been one typified by realism, first and foremost.

CONCLUSION: FOREIGN POLICY AND MULTINATIONAL CORPORATIONS

One last dimension of the political context will serve to inform the chapters that follow. The original research presented in Chapters 3, 4, and 5 will specify the many connections between foreign aid, foreign investment, MNCs, and human rights in the Third World. A summary of major U.S. foreign policies related to U.S.-based MNCs will add to the political context established by the more detailed review of policies on rights.

There was no U.S. foreign policy on MNCs prior to World War II because MNCs did not exist in the size or to the extent that the world has known since World War II. Even after the war, MNC expansion was not immediate or robust. Both the Truman and Eisenhower administrations had to "persuade hesitant U.S. corporations to expand their operations abroad" (Bergsten, Horst, and Moran, 1978: 310). Corporations were reluctant to expand operations beyond the borders of the United States unless they had assurances that their assets would be protected from foreign economic and political threats. Especially crucial in this regard was policy to protect direct foreign investment (DFI) made by MNCs into overseas plants and operations. The most important foreign policies for MNCs are those that seek to restrict, to protect, or to promote direct foreign investment.[33]

U.S. foreign policies governing U.S. MNCs that produce and sell outside the United States focus almost exclusively on protection and promotion of investment. There is very little policy that imposes restrictive regulations on MNC activities abroad. Promotion and protection of direct foreign investment by MNCs became a top priority after World War II because of the broad consensus among politicans that: "Free capital flows were integral to the vision of a liberal world order that would allocate resources efficiently and prevent a repetition of the global and domestic economic depression and political fragmentation of the 1930s. Indeed, restoration of an open multilateral economic system ranked alongside 'no more Munichs' as a cornerstone of postwar U.S. foreign policy" (Bergsten, Horst, and Moran, 1978: 309–10).

An open environment for investment would enhance the growth of U.S. MNCs. The same efforts to facilitate foreign investment would also promote U.S. national interests by bringing in raw materials, enhancing U.S. exports, and securing political allies via economic interdependence. This continues to be the basic logic behind policies on MNCs and foreign investment in the post–Cold War era as well.

U.S. policies on MNCs and DFI are designed to create an open door to the world's markets for these economic interests. To discourage foreign regulations that would impede MNC activities, the United States "supports only guidelines or codes regulating MNCs that are voluntary."[34] Insistence on voluntary codes of conduct rather than binding regulation for MNCs is only one element of U.S. open door policy for DFI going into the Third World. The principles of national treatment and protection of investors' property rights also support the open door policy. National treatment means that international investors should be treated by foreign governments the same as domestic enterprises. Protection of investors' property means that "financial, physical, and intellectual property" can be expropriated by foreign governments only when nationalization "is accompanied by prompt, adequate, and effective compensation."[35] Use of voluntary codes, national treatment, and protection of investor property rights are broad policy guidelines that seek to ensure an open door for U.S. MNCs operating in the Third Wold. The areas of restrictions, protections, and promotions of DFI provide useful categories for summarizing the more specific U.S. policies on U.S. MNCs that operate in the Third World.

Restrictive Regulations

Federal policies that restrict what MNCs can do while operating in the Third World are rare. The general feeling in the White House and on Capitol Hill has always been that minimal government interference is the best policy in regard to foreign investment by U.S. businesses (Cohen, 1994). Non-U.S. MNCs that operate within the United States find an investment environment that is largely unrestricted (Reich, 1989).[36] For U.S. MNCs that operate abroad, a similar approach is favored. U.S. policy seeks to minimize the political constraints on U.S. corporations doing business in other countries. In general, this has led to a free hand for U.S. MNCs as to where and how they invest. Of course, there are exceptions to this general trend.

Cold War restrictions against trade with communist countries banned DFI in Cuba, Vietnam, and elsewhere. Post–Cold War changes have eliminated such bans in most cases (although a trade embargo against Cuba remains in effect). A separate, temporary ban on new investment into South Africa while the CAAA was in effect was noted in the review of human rights policy. These comprehensive restrictions on investment into selected countries are very rare, however, and are often circumvented by MNCs. In 1996 the Antiterrorism Act imposed a new ban on direct investment into states that support international terrorism. This ban was quickly waived by Clinton in regard to Sudan, however, to allow a U.S. oil corporation to negotiate with the Khartoum government.[37]

Congress has had occasion to impose additional restrictions on DFI in years past when international scandals or embarassment have compelled them to act. Congress passed regulations requiring increased disclosure of information about foreign operations after MNCs, such as International Telephone and Telegraph (ITT), were accused of aiding and abetting the destabilization of an elected government in Chile and supporting Pinochet's 1973 coup (United States Senate, 1979). Hearings before the Senate Subcommittee on Multinationals into the ITT-Chile affair led to subsequent legislation that required U.S. MNCs to make fuller disclosure of their economic transactions within Third World nations. A second series of scandals involved U.S. corporations doing business in the Middle East during the 1970s and 1980s. Firms such as the Bechtel group allegedly were using bribes to government officials in these foreign countries to help secure lucrative government contracts (McCartney, 1988). The bribery scandals led to legislation discouraging the use of such payments by U.S. businesses operating abroad.

Prohibitions against DFI going into communist countries or into South Africa and regulations requiring increased financial disclosure or precluding bribery are the exceptions that prove the rule. Because such policies are so rare, and because when they are invoked they are few and far between, it is safe to say that restrictive regulation of U.S. MNCs in the Third World is consistently avoided by both presidents and members of Congress alike.

Protection of Direct Foreign Investment

U.S. foreign policy has been more likely to seek ways of facilitating and protecting foreign investment than to establish restrictions on that investment. The Overseas Private Investment Corporation (OPIC) is a federal agency charged with providing protections for U.S. investors overseas. Established in 1971, OPIC provides investment insurance, direct loans, and loan guarantees for U.S. corporations that invest abroad. OPIC exists to reduce the risks of international investing. For example, it covers part of the loss suffered when a foreign government nationalizes ownership of a U.S. business without providing full market compensation. OPIC also insures U.S. MNCs against the political risks of war, revolutions, and civil strife abroad. It promotes private investment through financing of foreign ventures. Direct loans run from $1–$6 million and loan guarantees are available for amounts of $6–$50 million. OPIC financial backing provides as much as 50 percent of total project costs for a new venture and up to 75 percent of total cost for expansion of existing projects (Overseas Private Investment Corporation, 1996).

Congress has also been very active in policy to help protect DFI. The Johnson-Bridges Amendment to the Mutual Security Act of 1959 required the United States to end (within six months) foreign aid for any government that nationalized a U.S. business without compensation (Conteh-Morgan, 1990: 26). The more well-known Hickenlooper Amendment of 1962 was even tougher. Hickenlooper imposed a mandatory and immediate suspension of aid to any nation that took over a U.S.-owned corporation without compensation. Although the Hickenlooper Amendment was later modified to end the mandatory retaliation clause, even this change in 1973 had the support of MNCs (Cingranelli, 1993: 157). Experts disagree about the number of times that Hickenlooper was invoked,[38] and its effectiveness is impossible to gauge because we have no way of knowing how many nationalizations might have been enacted if the Hickenlooper Amendment had not been on the books.[39]

Earl Conteh-Morgan (1990: 26–27) provides two more examples of the congressional approach to protecting foreign investment. The Pelly Amendment of 1968 ended military aid (sales, credits, and so forth) to any nation that seized U.S. fishing vessels more than 12 miles off their coast. The Gonzales Amendment of 1972 promised that the United States would oppose loans from international financial institutions (the International Monetary Fund [IMF], the World Bank, or the various regional development banks) if these loans were requested by a government that had disrupted U.S. international investment efforts.

The OPIC and these various acts of Congress are good examples of how the U.S. government seeks to protect DFI that is already overseas. A final approach, and one that has been much more common in the 1980s and 1990s, is to initiate policies that expand investment opportunities abroad for MNCs.

Promotion of New Direct Foreign Investment

The most recent policy option in regard to DFI has been to use political and economic pressure against less developed countries (LDCs) as a way to open up new opportunities for DFI by MNCs. The Caribbean Basin Initiative (CBI) under Presidents Reagan and Bush is a good example. The CBI was proposed by Reagan in 1982 and eventually produced \$14 billion in special assistance to states in that region (Conteh-Morgan, 1990: 166). CBI funds were designed to promote growth and development in the Caribbean while enhancing U.S. security. The CBI also had the direct effect of opening up the region to expanded MNC investment.

Caribbean nations were offered duty-free access for most of their exports to the U.S., tax incentives that would promote business tourism, and aid for balance-of-payments problems.[40] In return, participating Caribbean governments had to agree to exchanges of information regarding taxes and banking. Furthermore, DFI restrictions had to be dropped to participate in the CBI. Reagan pressured LDCs to guarantee nondiscrimination in their treatment of U.S. MNCs and to sign bilateral investment treaties (BITs) if they wanted into the CBI (Page, 1987: 35). By their very nature, BITs would make it easier for MNCs to find new areas of investment in the region. LDCs in Africa, Asia, and South America have been the primary targets of subsequent BIT initiatives.

Bush extended the CBI during his administration and followed up with an even more ambitious program he called the Enterprise for the Americas Initiative (EAI). The EAI had the same overall approach as the CBI, but expanded these policies to include all of Latin America. A key consistency between the CBI and the EAI was their shared emphasis on DFI. In order to qualify for trade incentives offered under the EAI, foreign governments had to, once again, expand investment opportunities for U.S.-owned MNCs. One of the pillars of the EAI, according to the State Department, was "Promoting investment in the region and helping countries compete for capital by eliminating policies that discouraged private investment."[41]

The CBI, BITs, and the EAI were each linked to privatization of LDC economies. This trend is further enhanced by structural adjustment policies imposed on LDC governments by the World Bank and the IMF in the 1980s and 1990s. Structural adjustment of LDC political economies, a trend that has strong bipartisan support in Washington, requires macroeconomic reforms as a prerequisite for LDCs to qualify for international loans and debt relief. Governments must reduce budget deficits, lower inflation rates, eliminate subsidies, and enact monetary reforms as part of the structural adjustment guidelines. Structural reforms, especially those favored by U.S. policy, must also include privatization of the economy and liberalization of policy on foreign investment. Structural adjustment requires developing countries to sell off state-owned enterprises and to eliminate policies that "inhibit investment."[42] Structural adjustment requires privatization, and privatization necessarily enhances investment opportunites for MNCs. Transnational corporations are the primary beneficiaries of the new investments that open up as a result of structural adjustment.

U.S. policies to deal with the Third World's debt crisis in the 1980s and 1990s have also been based on requirements for new structural adjustments. The Baker Plan and the Brady Plan from the Reagan and Bush administrations, respectively, offered new monies to help LDCs reduce their debts and to reestablish growth in their economies. However, to qualify for access to these new funds, developing nations had to put themselves under IMF and World Bank supervised austerity programs (Sachs, 1989; Whitehead, 1988). One of the options given to investors by these programs was the debt-equity swap. Foreign investors could purchase delinquent LDC loans at a discounted rate and then swap those notes for equity in developing country enterprises. Hence, even U.S. policy to reduce debt in the Third World was designed in such a way as to lead directly to new DFI opportunities for private corporations.

Critics of structural adjustment have often pointed to the alleged diminutions of rights and the escalation of repression that they see as an indirect result of the imposition of such policies (Skogly, 1993, 1994). Structural adjustment is said to have the negative results of reducing public expenditures on welfare programs, driving down wages, reducing standards of living, and eventually leading to an escalation of social and political unrest. Structural adjustment also enhances economic inequalities in the Third World (Zolberg and Smith, 1996: 22). If these claims are accurate, then there is support for the further charge that structural adjustment has the long-term effect of producing repression when Third World governments crack down on popular opposition to austerity measures (Sachs, 1989). Government repression endangers first generation civil-political rights, and erosion in standards of living threatens second generation socioeconomic rights.

If true, the critical view identifies a connection between policies that expand investment by MNCs and a concomitant deterioration of human rights in the Third World (see Chapter 3 for a test). The CBI, BITs, the EAI, structural adjustment programs, the Baker Plan, and the Brady Plan were all designed to open up LDC economies for an expansion of DFI and a larger MNC presence. These same economic policies have the potential to produce long-term and indirect reductions in levels of both civil-political and socioeconomic rights. The policies reviewed in this chapter have thus brought us full circle, back to the connections between politics and economics with which we started. The possible connections between human rights, MNCs, repression, and public welfare in the Third World are the subjects of new empirical research presented in Chapter 3.

NOTES

1. Nation-states write the rules for international trade and finance. States create and govern the international organizations or regimes that regulate trade and finance (the General Agreement on Tariffs and Trade system, the IMF, the World Bank, and the World Trade Organization). Transnational corporations and other economic actors must tailor their activities to conform to the rules and norms set down by these international political organizations.

2. The final drafts of the two covenants were approved by a vote of the General Assembly in 1966. The treaties were then offered to all members for signing and ratification. No president before Carter was willing to sign the treaties. Carter signed the treaties in 1977 and turned them over to the Senate for ratification. Carter promised to lobby Congress in favor of ratification of both treaties, but failed to carry through on this promise (Forsythe, 1989: 111). The treaties remained on a congressional back burner until the Civil and Political Covenant was finally ratified by the Senate in 1992. The International Covenant on Economic, Social, and Cultural Rights remains unratifed by the United States, and there is little chance that this will change in the forseeable future.

3. Jacobo Timerman, newspaper publisher and noted dissident in Argentina, was arrested in 1977 by the military junta there, tortured, and imprisoned until September 1979. After his release, he publicly thanked President Carter and gave Carter much of the credit for forcing the generals to let him go. For more on this case, see Timerman, 1981.

4. During 1976 and 1977, 27 black leaders died in South African jails of suspected torture. This number includes Biko's death in 1977. After the evidence proving Biko's murder was smuggled out of the RSA, and after Carter began applying public pressure, deaths of black leaders in RSA jails dropped to a total of 4 between 1978 and 1980 (the remainder of Carter's tenure). During the Reagan adminstration's policies of constructive engagement toward South Africa (for example, a return to quiet diplomacy and no public criticism), deaths of blacks in confinement escalated to a total of 28 in 6 years (1981–86). All of this is documented in the film about the life and death of Biko, "Cry Freedom" (Universal Studios, 1988). Details on each case and on the numbers of deaths per year are listed at the film's conclusion.

5. Of course, Carter is also honored for the achievement of the Camp David accords that resulted in a lasting peace between Egypt and Israel.

6. Kirkpatrick came under much post hoc criticism in academic circles after the fall of the Soviet Union and the democratization of Eastern Europe. These were events that her 1979 article seemed to hold as impossibilities. Despite the unprecedented turn of events and the scholarly critiques, Kirkpatrick refused to recant her earlier assertions.

7.   In the early 1980s Congress had subjected El Salvador to a human rights review every six months, rather than once a year as was the case with other aid recipients. Reagan and his advisors successfully removed these additional human rights strings on aid to El Salvador by persuading Congress to eliminate them after 1985.

8.   "Further U.S. Help Is in Abeyance Until Polish Situation Is Clarified," *New York Times*, December 15, 1981.

9.   "Reagan, In Reversal, Orders Sanctions on South Africa," *New York Times*, September 10, 1985.

10.   This study was released by Bankorp of Cape Town in December 1989.

11.   Vice President Bush, speaking on behalf of the Reagan administration, restated their opposition to the imposition of tough CAAA sanctions when Congress passed them over the President's veto. Bush, however, also pledged that the White House would faithfully carry out its duties to impose the CAAA sanctions.

12.   The Reagan administration also gave indirect support to the Aquino faction by allowing pilots who were defecting from the Marcos regime to land their aircraft at Clark Air Base in the Philippines.

13.   Although I have no desire to debate the many possible reasons for the end of the Cold War here, suffice it to say that, in the opinion of this author, Reagan's military budgets were only one of the contributing factors, and perhaps not even the most important one at that. Other causes for the end of the Cold War in 1989 would involve the impending merger of the economies of the European Union in 1992 and the very complicated internal dynamics in the political economies and party elites of both Poland and the Soviet Union. The mass exodus in 1989 from East Germany through Hungary (the first communist nation to open its borders with the West in 1989) and into West Germany was another crucial triggering factor for the fall of the Berlin Wall and the delegitimization of communist leaderships. Hence, the end of the Cold War is a classic case of an international event that is overdetermined. A number of contributing causal factors (such as economics, military spending, changes in leadership, migration, and so forth) interacted at a key time in history to bring about a reshaping of the political landscape in Europe.

14.   Reagan gave this speech in Chicago on May 4, 1988.

15.   In 1975, the United States and 34 other parties to the Helsinki Accords, including the Soviet Union, agreed to recognize the existing borders in all of Europe. At that time, existing European borders placed the Baltic states de facto within the Soviet Union. The United States therefore at least implicitly acknowledged the Baltics as part of the Soviet state. The Helsinki Accords themselves were part of 1970s détente policy.

16.   "Moscow Putting Added Pressure On Lithuanians," *New York Times*, March 20, 1990.

17.   In 1991, Bush traveled in the Soviet Union and advised the Ukrainians and others against seceding from the Union. See: "Bush, in Ukraine, Walks Fine Line on Sovereignty," *New York Times*, August 2, 1991.

18. Kissinger negotiated the SALT I treaty of 1972. Bush negotiated and signed the START I treaty of 1991, and START II of January 1993. SALT was a strategic arms limitation treaty; START I and II were strategic arms reduction treaties.

19. "Leader of Party in China Is Ousted for His 'Mistakes'," *New York Times*, January 17, 1987.

20. "U.S. Voices Regret at Events in China," *New York Times*, May 20, 1989.

21. "2 U.S. Officials Went to Beijing Secretly in July," *New York Times*, December 19, 1989.

22. "6 Priests Killed in a Campus Raid in San Salvador," *New York Times*, November 17, 1989.

23. "Bush Lifts a Ban on Economic Ties to South Africa," *New York Times*, July 11, 1991.

24. "Mandela Group Votes to Retain Curbs," *New York Times*, July 7, 1991.

25. "Candidates Stick Mostly to Facts, but Disputes Arise over China," *Washington Post*, October 12, 1992.

26. "Trade Privileges for China's Goods: A Policy Reversal," *New York Times*, May 27, 1994.

27. "Bush's Talk on Somalia," *New York Times*, December 5, 1992.

28. "Showdown in Haiti," *New York Times*, September 19, 1994.

29. "Excerpts from Clinton News Conference: 'The U.S. Should Lead' on Bosnia," *New York Times*, April 24, 1993.

30. For more on the realist nature of Clinton's policies for Bosnia see: "Blank on Bosnia," *New York Times*, October 16, 1996; "Plan to Limit U.S. Forces Stay in Bosnia Has Disintegrated," *Philadelphia Inquirer*, October 29, 1996.

31. "Balkan Accord; Clinton's Words on Mission to Bosnia," *New York Times*, November 28, 1995.

32. "Backing Away Again, Christopher Says Bosnia Is Not a Vital Interest," *New York Times*, June 4, 1993.

33. The close connection between MNCs and direct foreign investment will be explained in detail in the next chapter.

34. "Multinational Corporations," *Gist* (Department of State), March 1986.

35. "International Investment Policy," *Gist* (Department of State), June 1989.

36. The only area that has been guarded against foreign investment coming into the United States is national security, narrowly defined. There are a few restrictions on investment coming into the United States, if the industry in question is perceived to be related to national defense, but even those restrictions are almost never invoked (see Tolchin and Tolchin, 1992: 45–47).

37. "Sudan Was Exempted from Terrorism Act," *Wilmington News Journal* (Wilmington, Delaware), January 23, 1997.

38.   Conteh-Morgan (1990) lists sanctions under Hickenlooper against Cuba, the Dominican Republic, and Chile. Cingranelli (1993) writes that Hickenlooper was invoked on only one occasion and that was against Ceylon.

39.   Cingranelli is of the opinion that Hickenlooper was never effective (1993: 157).

40.   "Caribbean Basin Initiative," *Gist* (Department of State), April 1990.

41.   "Enterprise for the Americas Initiative," *Gist* (Department of State), September 21, 1990.

42.   "Structural Adjustment and Economic Performance," *Gist* (Department of State), June 1989.

3

Human Rights and Multinational Corporations: Investing in Repression?

It is widely accepted that multinational corporations (MNCs) have a massive economic impact on Third World nations. Often overlooked, however, is the potential impact of MNCs on human rights in less developed countries (LDCs). International documents on human rights rarely mention MNCs in any specific way. Theories and empirical studies of human rights stop short of considering the MNC as a causal factor. These facts point to the need for new research on rights, businesses, and development in the Third World.

A NEED FOR NEW RESEARCH

Political Factors

Issues involving the promotion of human rights and investigations into human rights violations have revolved around nation-states. The politics of rights, legal protection of rights, and most philosophical treatments of human rights all posit nations as the primary actor. Although voluntary codes of conduct have been developed for MNCs by the United Nations (UN) and by Amnesty International, international documents on human rights limit liability for violations to "state parties" (Lippman, 1985: 252). The relatively weak provisions for international regulation of MNCs that do exist focus on the economic impact of these enterprises, while only briefly or indirectly speaking of the corporate impact on rights. Again, these are primarily voluntary codes with little or no binding legal authority.

The UN Centre on Transnational Corporations has called on multinationals to respect human rights; abstain from involvement in and subversion of domestic politics in host nations; practice nondiscrimination; and respect host government priorities on employment, the environment, and socioeconomic policy (see Lippmann, 1985, for a more detailed summary). These are only recommendations. Binding international legal obligations do not exist to require that MNCs promote and respect fundamental rights. A growing body of literature, however, argues that corporations do have specific moral obligations regarding human rights. Hence, any empirical study of MNCs and human rights is forced to deal with the philosophical distinction between legal rights and moral rights. There are basically no binding legal obligations on MNCs to promote or to protect human rights. Human rights obligations for transnationals as a function of legal rights is a null set. There are none.

However, this is not to say that MNCs have no moral obligations or responsibilities when it comes to the protection and promotion of human rights. MNCs may indeed have clear human rights responsibilities based on moral claims and moral rights. To discuss the possible human rights obligations that accrue to businesses as a function of moral rights requires that we review arguments as to whether corporations are properly considered to be moral actors.

Philosophical Factors

It has become common for philosophers (like politicians) to argue that rights obligations fall only upon governments. Rex Martin's views (1980) are a typical example. Martin, like many others, argues that human rights constitute claims against governments alone. According to this view, practices for recognizing and maintaining rights are purely within the domain of public (state) actors (1980: 79). Martin disputes Cranston's well-known position that human rights represent claims against "all men" (1980: 79-80). Martin points out that the documents themselves identify governments as parties to the various human rights agreements. States are responsible for establishing mechanisms to provide for the rights of due process, fair trials, nondiscrimination, and so forth. At most, Martin argues, human rights may be "double-barrelled" rights (Feinberg, 1973) in that they create specific obligations for governments and more general obligations for society at large. The most significant responsibilities, however, remain those required of states (Martin 1980: 80).

Martin and Cranston do not consider the possibility that human rights claims might create obligations for corporations as well (see also Donnelly, 1982: 306, for another typical example of this view). Recent innovations in the philosophy of rights and in economic theory, however, tend to stress the moral and social dimensions of MNCs (T. Donaldson, 1982; French, 1984; May, 1987; Thurow, 1992). Perhaps the best of these treatments is that by Peter French. He argues that moral claims and responsibilities are as legitimate in regard to corporations as to individuals and governments (see also Wellman, 1985: 145). In fact, French believes that the changing nature of postmodern politics and the socioeconomic influence of large corporations often make them more important than states when it comes to impacting upon our day-to-day lives. Corporate entities "define and maintain human existence within the industrialized world" (French, 1984: viii).

French bases his analysis of corporations as moral agents on their ability to act according to corporate intentions. This is a point on which French and Thomas Donaldson disagree (see French, 1984: 166; Donaldson, 1982: 22). For French, a "moral person" has the following characteristics: it is the subject of a right, has a capacity for accountability, and possesses intentionality (1984: 38). French takes for granted the facts that corporations possess rights and accountability. Therefore, the crucial factor becomes intentionality. A corporation must have intentions to be considered as a "moral person" and to hold moral responsibilities.

Corporate intentions are not the same thing as the sum total of the individual intentions of its directors, executives, and managers. This is a common misconception that French refers to as the fallacy of methodological individualism (1984: 35). Rather, corporate intentions are those regarding the "general policy" or the "basic beliefs of the corporation" (1984: 43). Corporate intentions are produced by a process French terms corporate internal decision structures (CIDS). The CIDS vary from firm to firm, and they establish corporate intentions that are distinct from those of its members. When these basic beliefs (corporate intentions) are not followed, or when they are violated by agents of the corporation (for example, an executive acting as a loose cannon), then those actions are "no longer the policy of that company. . . . Similarly when the corporate act is consistent with . . . established corporate policy, then it is proper to describe it as having been done for corporate reasons, as having been caused by a corporate desire . . . in other words, as corporate intentional" (1984: 43–44).

Union Carbide's operation in Bhopal, India is a good case in point. French does not discuss the Bhopal tragedy in his work on corporate responsibility. His examples come primarily from the airline industry. However, his work can serve as a basis for similar investigations into corporate culpability in cases like that of Bhopal. In December 1984, more than 2,000 people died as a direct result of the disaster in Bhopal. A toxic cloud was released over Bhopal from Union Carbide's pesticide production facility.

The plant in Bhopal is part of Union Carbide of India (UCI), a majority-owned subsidiary of Union Carbide (UC). UC owns 51 percent of UCI. UC designed the plant, including the design of safety and backup systems. UC trained UCI personnel to run the plant. The corporate structures of UC and UCI were integrated to the extent of sharing common members on their boards of directors (Bogard, 1989). A CIDS analysis of UC and UCI, employing French's approach, would point out that it was the corporate intention of UC that the plant in Bhopal be constructed with a design that lacked certain safety standards built into a similar plant in the United States (in Institute, West Virginia). Lack of those safety features increased the severity of the 1984 disaster in India. Under a CIDS approach, it makes sense to say that UC intended to train employees in Bhopal in such a way that the unanticipated result was worker inability to cope with a series of failures in the containment system, failures that led to the disaster of 1984. Therefore, a CIDS analysis would argue that UC, the parent company, is responsible for the disaster at Bhopal, despite UC's initial claims that they had no direct control over the plant or its operations (thereby allegedly negating any responsibility on UC's part).

Donaldson (1982) and Larry May (1987) construct moral arguments on collective and corporate responsibility that are similar in some respects to the work of French. However, these other authors base their analyses on philosophical grounds different from those of French's intentionality. Donaldson is primarily interested in applying social contract theory to corporate relations between workers, managers, and consumers. Regardless of the differences among these views, they all conclude that corporations qua corporations are moral agents and therefore must accept obligations and responsibilities. Paramount among these obligations must be promotion of and respect for fundamental human rights.

My discussion of morality and corporations has undertaken no critical assessment of these arguments. One might inquire into the legitimacy of the criteria offered by French and others for establishing corporate responsibility. One might ask whether there are other criteria that are more relevant. One might even argue that no form of moral philosophy is applicable to corporations, because they are merely economic actors that calculate efficiencies, not moral actors that calculate values. The relationship between moral obligations and legal obligations also remains problematic.

According to French, legal status and moral status are not directly related. Legal personhood is a matter of institutional rules, while moral personhood is metaphysical (1984: chap. 13). Therefore, even if we accept French's position on the moral obligations of corporations, firms might still have no specific legal obligation to uphold human rights. Extant international law is consistent with such a claim. French goes on to point out that in criminal law there is a close association between moral personhood and legal liability. Therefore, if French and others are right about the moral dimensions of corporations, this would point to the need for new international legal instruments to exact such liabilities. Furthermore, even if there were no moral or legal obligations applicable to corporate entities, an empirical analysis of MNC impact on human rights would still be necessary. In fact, empirical analysis may well be a necessary step prior to any further development of moral philosophy and legal codes in these areas. Empirical analysis will illuminate moral and legal studies of MNCs.

Systemic Factors

The evolving nature of the international politicoeconomic system also indicates a need for new research into rights and multinationals. As the globe becomes more interdependent; as the low politics of transnational issues like trade and investment displace the high politics of war and national security; as nonstate actors (MNCs) eclipse the income and power of nation-states; as all of these global transformations advance, multinationals move to center stage in the international arena.

Lester Thurow believes that the omnipresent nature of MNCs in the post–World War II system is largely explained by their ability to satisfy deep human needs. Individuals have a psychological need to produce. They also desire conquest. Humans are "social builders who want to belong to empires that expand. . . . Belonging, esteem, power, building, winning, and conquering are all human goals just as important as maximizing consumption and leisure" (1992: 118). Thurow goes on to argue that membership in a large corporation may be the only way for most individuals to actualize their will to power in the contemporary age: "In the modern world, corporations offer the best opportunities for empire building. The nation-state forbids making war on the neighboring clan, the days of colonial empires are over, expanding one's national boundaries by conquest is rare, and nuclear weapons make conquering the world a goal not worth pursuing. Even the family now offers fewer opportunities to exercise leadership and power" (1992: 120).

Thurow's purpose is to expose these aspects of corporations as a way to improve America's competitiveness, especially vis-à-vis Japan. "The Japanese secret is to be found in the fact that they have tapped a universal desire to build, to belong to an empire, to conquer neighboring empires" (1992: 118). This is the basis of Japanese "producer economics" and "communitarian capitalism" that now outperform the "consumer economics" of the United States in "head to head" competition.

Thurow's insightful analysis helps to explain the rapid rise and spread of postmodern MNCs. His work also reveals some of the ethical and power-wielding dimensions of this form of organization. His explanation for the existence of MNCs is analogous to Morgenthau's explanation for popular support of governments during times of warfare. Morgenthau, the father of post–World War II political realism, argued that individuals actualize their will to power through membership in a larger social unit (the nation-state) that pursues an aggressive international strategem (1985: chap. 9). Likewise, Thurow points out that: "When workers join a business firm they are looking for some of the same factors that they seek when joining an army. . . . Together individuals can build something bigger than they could ever dream of building by themselves. Men and women can conquer markets much as they used to conquer neighboring clans" (Thurow 1992: 119–21).

An analysis of the changing nature of power in the post–Cold War world by Joseph Nye (1990) also directs our attention to the expanding global role played by MNCs. Nye's most useful insight is his claim that nation-states are moving from "hard" power methods to "soft" power in order to protect their national interests. Hard power consists of military force and other sanctions that can compel compliance by another state. These were the tools of classical realpolitik. Soft power, by contrast, consists of culture, ideology, and institutions that can set agendas, set the terms for international debates, and induce other nations to "want what we want." MNCs represent, for Nye, a key element of soft power (1990: 112). The 20 largest MNCs have annual incomes greater than those of 80 LDCs, and 40 percent of the largest MNCs have their headquarters in the United States (1990: 178–92). Therefore, as the nature of international power evolves, MNCs become more important in their own right and as a possible tool for protecting the interests of the most powerful nations.

In Donaldson's philosophical treatment of corporations and morality, postmodern trends toward MNC dominance are highlighted in his claim that "the central issue is that of economic justice. . . . In the confrontation between developed and underdeveloped nations, do multinationals aggravate or help solve social and economic problems?" (1982: 11). The evidence that might answer Donaldson's question is, to date, conflicting and controversial. The conflicting claims regarding MNCs require new research that will refine our theories and add to our empirical understanding of development in the Third World.

Theoretical and Empirical Factors

MNCs as a determinant of human rights have been overlooked by prior theoretical and quantitative analyses of the relationship between rights and development.[1] Most empirical studies to date have focused on economic development and governmental policy as causal factors for human rights in the Third World. Variables analyzed in these prior studies include: civil and political rights ranked on an ordinal scale; the physical quality of life index (PQLI) as an indicator of socioeconomic rights; levels of government spending for education, the military, and welfare; urbanization; and ethnic or cultural diversity (a review of these studies appears later). Introducing a measure or measures of MNC activity in the Third World would bring an important new actor into the ambit of these studies.

Theories that posit broad generalizations pertaining to human rights and development would similarly benefit from new attention to MNCs. Multinationals, as external actors that locate in LDCs, represent an important transnational dimension that is missing from existing theory. I propose to expand our understanding by extending questions raised in the past about development and human rights to the relatively new area of MNCs.

Reasons for looking more closely at MNCs and human rights come from a combination of the considerations listed above. New research on MNCs and rights in the Third World will improve our theoretical understanding of political and economic trends in the Third World; bring systemic transformations of international relations, especially those toward the increasing power of nonstate actors, to bear on human rights research; provide new evidence as to the pernicious or beneficial effects of MNCs on rights in LDCs; and bring human rights research up to date with recent developments regarding philosophies of corporate responsibilities and corporate morality.

The remainder of this chapter will summarize the conflicting theoretical views and policy prescriptions regarding MNCs in the Third World, propose a way to operationalize these arguments for empirical study, test the operational models with data drawn from more than 50 LDCs during the period 1983–90, and draw implications from the empirical tests for the theories that served as our point of departure.

TWO THEORIES OF HUMAN RIGHTS AND DEVELOPMENT

Two schools of thought are readily identifiable when it comes to theories of MNCs, development, and rights in the Third World. One view is generally pro-MNC and prefers to highlight the advantages provided for LDCs by multinationals. This I refer to as the "engines of development" school. The more critical or anti-MNC view stresses the negative impact of multinationals on developing nations. I will refer to the critical viewpoint as the "Hymer thesis," because it was heavily influenced during its early development by the work of economist Stephen Hymer. Central elements of the Hymer thesis are congruent with, at times almost indistinguishable from, those of dependency theorists (Amin, 1979; Cardoso and Faletto, 1971; Sunkel, 1979). Although both views, pro-MNC and anti-MNC, were developed to identify the economic impact of multinationals, and although theorists on both sides rarely refer to human rights as such, their implications for human rights in the Third World are easily derived. As we shall see, each view is also supported by competing policy proposals from the supporters of the two camps.

Engines of Development

The pro-MNC view holds that multinationals directly promote second generation economic and social rights. MNCs also indirectly support first generation civil and political rights according to this view. Kathleen Pritchard cites as a "tenet of faith among politicians, financiers, and academicians" the belief that "economic development enhances human rights conditions" (1989: 329). To the extent that MNCs promote development, therefore, they must also enhance human rights. Socioeconomic rights are singled out by Pritchard as those rights most likely to be promoted by development. Rights like those to unemployment protection and social security "depend on the level of economic development" (1989: 329). MNCs that promote development by creating jobs, by bringing new capital and new technology, and by providing such employee benefits as health care would therefore necessarily be promoting economic and social rights.

The possible connection between MNCs and civil or political rights is much less direct. Early theories of development supported infusions of foreign investment and foreign business into LDCs as a way to create expansion of a politically stable middle class (Lerner, 1964). Growth via MNCs would create an urban middle class. The new middle class would, in turn, enhance stability and political tolerance (the political side of Lerner's "cognitive flexibility" created by modernization). Hence, civil and political freedoms (for example, democracy) would expand as Third World nations modernized.

The United States' post–World War II foreign policies on aid and investment were based in part on this logic that MNCs are engines for Third World development. The Alliance for Progress of the 1960s, the Reagan-Bush Carribean Basin Initiative, the Baker Plan, the Brady Plan, and Reagan's bilateral investment treaties all included provisions to open the Third World to greater U.S. investment and a larger MNC presence. An open environment for direct foreign investment (DFI) by MNCs has often been proposed by Washington as a tool to expand development, increase welfare, and promote democracy in the Third World, all at the same time (Department of State, 1990).

The Hymer Thesis

A second view holds that MNCs directly contribute to violations of human rights. The most carefully elaborated theoretical support for this position can be found in the work of Hymer. Hymer's thesis posits development in the Third World via MNCs as a force that creates violations of rights (although Hymer himself does not use the language of human rights). Hymer supports his claims by analysis of the organizational structures of MNCs.

Hymer begins with two laws of economic development: the law of increasing size and the law of uneven development. In an often-quoted passage, Hymer describes the first law. "Since the beginning of the Industrial Revolution, there has been a tendency for the representative firm to increase in size from the *workshop* to the *factory* to the *national corporation* to the *multi-divisional corporation* to the *multinational corporation*" (1979: 386).

Hymer predicted that multinationalization would increase greatly in the 1980s. He was correct. He also argued that the first law leads directly to the second law, entailing "the tendency of the system to produce poverty as well as wealth, underdevelopment as well as development" (1979: 387). This is because of the very structure of the MNC itself. Drawing on the work of Alfred Chandler and Fritz Redlich (1961), Hymer identifies three levels of MNC organization.

Level III, the lowest level of the MNC, is concerned with day-to-day operations. Level II coordinates managers at Level III. Level I, top management, sets goals and planning for the entire firm, "strategy rather than tactics." This is the level at which we would find French's corporate internal decision structures. Furthermore, location theory "suggests that Level III activities would spread themselves over the globe according to the pull of manpower, markets and raw materials. . . . Level II activities . . . tend to concentrate in large cities [near Level III]. . . . Level I activities, the general offices, tend to be even more concentrated than Level II . . . located close to the capital market, the media, and the government" (Hymer, 1979: 393–94). The United States, specifically New York City, is given as an example of a Level I location. The organizational structure of MNCs necessarily creates uneven or dual development: "It is not technology which creates inequality; rather it is *organization*" (1979: 395). At the global level, this is "a division of labor based on nationality" and "specialization by nationality can be expected within the multinational corporation hierarchy" (1979: 396). James Caporaso's work (1987) is a more recent example of research that reveals the international structures of corporate or capitalist divisions of labor.

Hymer's work on MNCs is consistent with dependency theory as a description of dual development. Using the dependency theory categories of center and periphery, one would say that Level III is in the rural periphery of Third World nations; Level II is to be found in the urban center of these peripheral, Third World nations; and Level I is located in the industrialized centers of the West. Hymer's unique contribution to theories of dual development is his explanation that the ultimate source of this pattern is to be found within the very structure of the MNC itself.

This system of international domination allegedly leads to a deterioration of human rights in both the civil-political and the socioeconomic spheres. Hymer sees the masses of the Third World as the group paying the greatest cost to maintain the system, while reaping the fewest benefits. These "excluded groups" amount to roughly two-thirds of the Third World's population. In order to perpetuate itself, the system of MNC control "must keep the excluded two-thirds of the population under control." Control is exerted via "family planning or counterinsurgency" (1979: 400). U.S. foreign policy at times has been built around such counterinsurgency programs in the Third World. The Office of Public Safety and the International Police Academy are only two of the many relevant examples. These programs provided the means of repression used by many Latin American and Asian clients of the United States to violate the human rights of oppressed populations (see Schoultz, 1981: chap. 5).

Therefore, if Hymer is correct, the organization of MNCs creates dual development. Dual development creates the need to control the masses. Instruments of control entail repression and denials of civil and political rights for Third World masses.

Those theorists and policymakers sympathetic to Hymer's view are also skeptical of the alleged socioeconomic benefits for LDCs from MNC investment. Relevant studies have contested claims from the engines of development school that MNCs promote economic and social rights by creating jobs, providing capital, and importing technology. Empirical studies of many LDCs, especially those in Latin America, have shown that attracting MNCs has on many occasions eliminated more jobs than it created (Muller, 1979); absorbed local capital without bringing in external funds, thus harming local entrepeneurs (Spero, 1990); and provided technology inappropriate to Third World needs, hence, once again doing more harm than good (Walters and Blake, 1992). If MNCs do more harm than good, then they do not expand second generation socioeconomic rights, they diminish welfare in these areas instead. Noam Chomsky, Edward Herman, and others have further argued that U.S. foreign aid produces essentially the same results (Chomsky, 1988; Chomsky and Herman, 1979). By contributing to repressive elements in both the public and the private sectors, foreign aid and foreign corporations allegedly create a business climate and a political order that are more conducive to their interests. They are allegedly investing in repression.

Hymer's alternative strategy for Third World development is based on policies that move away from MNCs toward a system of regional economic integration. These policy preferences are echoed by the South Commission, chaired by Julius Nyerere, in its final report. The South Commission favors regional integration and new controls over MNCs through regulation of foreign investment (South Commission, 1990: 208, 233; see also Walters and Blake, 1992: 193–94). Theorists and policymakers who advocate "dependency reversal" also tend to caution LDCs against reliance on MNCs in their pursuit of economic development (Doran, Modelski, and Clark, 1983).

Testable Hypotheses

These two theoretical views on MNCs and human rights in developing nations lead us to a set of empirically testable hypotheses. The engines of development school suggests that MNCs promote human rights, especially second generation socioeconomic rights. The Hymer thesis implies that MNCs in the Third World create situations that lead to lower levels of human rights, especially violations of first generation civil-political rights. The null hypotheses must also be kept in mind. It is possible that *both* schools of thought are wrong. MNCs may have *no* discernible relation to human rights in LDCs.

Tests presented in the remainder of this chapter will subject these theories to quantitative evaluations. A series of tests seems to be called for, given the numerous ways in which one might operationalize variables like human rights or MNCs. This study seeks a best-case test of the two theories on human rights and development.[2] I now turn to various types of quantitative human rights indicators and alternative methods for measuring MNC activities. A prior question is begged, however. Is quantitative study of human rights (in any form) a legitimate scientific enterprise?

QUANTITATIVE STUDIES OF HUMAN RIGHTS

Is Quantification Justifiable?

Quantitative study of human rights is especially problematic. Given the nature and importance of this area, quantification has often been criticized as inappropriate. To quantify is necessarily to depersonalize, and even dehumanize, a topic's content. The supreme value of human rights requires that we always keep in mind the specific human costs in terms of lives, pain, and suffering that violations of rights entail. Richard Claude and Thomas Jabine (1986), editors of a special issue of *Human Rights Quarterly* devoted to quantitative studies, stressed this point when they said that the "essential nature of human rights is qualitative, not quantitative." They hasten to add, however, that "it now seems clear that although measurement might not represent the central feature, it *must* play a role in studying, assessing and planning for human rights" (1986: 553, emphasis added; see also the follow-up edition by the same authors, 1992).

Available quantitative data on human rights, although necessary for theoretical and policy reasons, must be viewed with skepticism given the special problems of reliability and validity for these measures. The data are incomplete and soft. Numbers of violations of security of the person (for example, torture) are usually not released by the governments that are the most egregious violators. There are also questions about political bias raised when nations are ranked according to their human rights records by Freedom House and others. Problems unique to particular variables will be addressed as those variables are introduced into the tests. At this point, one would do well to keep in mind the strengths and weaknesses of all quantitative data on human rights.

According to Soble and Weisberg, no single adequate measure or scale of human rights has yet been developed. They believe that academic research, therefore, has a "vital role" to play in establishing new measures (cited by Claude and Jabine, 1986: 558). Robert Goldstein, writing in the same issue of *Human Rights Quarterly*, argues that because there is no single, universally accepted concept of human rights, it is important to develop many different indicators for the many different types of rights (1986: 610). The tests presented here were developed with these considerations in mind.

Claude and Jabine, Goldstein, and Pritchard have also made the case that quantitative studies advance our theoretical understanding while supporting the policies needed to protect human rights. They lament the fact that: "The search has barely begun for theory supported by data" (Claude and Jabine, 1986: 554–55). Goldstein believes that quantification has the potential to reduce subjectivity; enhance testing, replication, and comparative methodologies; and disprove commonly held assumptions about human rights (1986: 607–8). Pritchard argues that "quantification is advisable" because human rights is such an "emotional" term (1989: 331). The science of human rights research, however, must remain closely tied to relevant policy issues. Claude and Jabine go on to argue that good quantitative data enhance the likelihood that human rights will be supported through condemnation of violators and through changes in policy to guarantee rights more strongly (1986: 556).

According to these authors, "every technique that can better inform judgement is now needed. . . . In short, there is an important place for measurement and refined statistical approaches to the subject of internationally defined human rights" (Claude and Jabine, 1986: 554). Goldstein closes by adding a cautionary note: "What must be avoided is a dependence on statistics *alone* in an area such as human rights. . . . What is needed is a combination: statistical information where it is meaningful and reliable, nonstatistical information where it is meaningful and reliable, and judgement too" (1986: 626–27). With these important points in mind, let us turn to a summary of prior quantitative studies.

Prior Tests

Prior quantitative studies begin with the impact of nation-states on human rights. Nation-states and national governments are the primary actors affecting rights in developing nations, according to these approaches.

Pritchard (1989) begins a review of quantitative methods (Moon and Dixon, 1985; Morris, 1979; Sieghart, 1983; Strouse and Claude, 1976) by stating several testable hypotheses (see also Cingranelli, 1988). Relationships between types of rights and the interactions between development and rights are the subjects of these hypotheses. Perhaps the oldest view is that of Lucian Pye (1965). Civil and political rights are "prerequisites for economic development" according to this view (1989: 329). I like to refer to this position as the Butler thesis because it has been most forcefully defended by William Butler, former president of the International Commission of Jurists. During the Salzburg Seminar on Human Rights, Butler consistently maintained that civil-political rights are necessary and sufficient conditions for socioeconomic rights. Butler believes that a nation with civil and political rights can and must use those rights to pressure its government into providing socioeconomic rights.[3]

A later view noted by Pritchard is that most commonly associated with Samuel Huntington, who claimed that development required repression in the Third World. As traditional societies moved through a transitional stage on their way to becoming modern, a curtailment of rights became necessary for providing order (Huntington and Nelson, 1976). Another view, not mentioned by Pritchard, is a reverse of the Butler thesis. The "full-belly thesis" (Howard, 1983) posits socioeconomic rights as more important to LDCs, at least initially, than civil and political rights. The full-belly thesis argues that a trade-off in favor of food, housing, and medical care is necessary and may mean a short-term inability to provide for civil rights (free speech) and political rights (participation).

The Butler thesis and the full-belly thesis set conflicting priorities in a trade-off between civil-political and socioeconomic rights. Pritchard notes two other views in passing. "Today's view" is the belief that economic and political development are interdependent, implying that rights in the two areas are inseparable. Finally, there is also the "most common" view that first generation civil-political rights are (or should be) independent of economic development, but second generation socioeconomic rights depend on achieving a certain basic level of development (Pritchard, 1989: 329). This final view is a somewhat intuitive compromise between the Butler thesis and the full-belly thesis.

Pritchard reviews a series of studies that test these hypotheses. The primary, almost exclusive, statistical technique employed in these studies is the use of simple, bivariate correlations. A more recent study by Han Park (1987) employs the same methodology. Variables employed in the earlier studies include: development measured as per capita GNP; socioeconomic rights measured via the physical quality of life index; civil and political rankings from Freedom House; and government spending per capita. Park's study is slightly more sophisticated. He disaggregates government spending into three categories (each as a percentage of GNP): educational spending, military spending, and welfare expenditures. Park also adds ascriptive and social dimensions by including variables for ethnic diversity, percentages of population that are Christian or Islamic, percentage of population living in urban areas, and income inequality.

Results from these various studies are generally consistent. Pritchard's sample of studies finds positive correlations between the rankings for civil-political (C/P) rights and the socioeconomic rights reflected in the PQLI (ranging from 0.49 to 0.55). Park finds a similar correlation of C/P rights to the PQLI (0.61). There are also weaker positive correlations between GNP per capita and the C/P rankings (0.33), and between GNP and the PQLI (0.39). Government spending per capita is positively correlated to the PQLI (0.59) and to the C/P rankings (0.33). Pritchard's conclusion that these correlations are "moderate at best" is accurate, if not understated (1989: 335). If we think of these results not in terms of simple correlations but in terms of variance explained, the results are even less satisfying in regard to their explanatory power.[4] Correlations in the range of 0.3 to 0.6 translate into variance explained (R^2) of only 0.09 to 0.36. In other words, only 9 percent to 36 percent of the variance in human rights is associated with variance in GNP or government spending. This is not only an incomplete explanation, it is also statistically weak.

When Park turns to other variables not considered in Pritchard's group of studies, he argues that the PQLI is a better predictor of human rights than are the C/P rankings. The PQLI is positively correlated with welfare spending (0.73), with urbanization (0.71), with percentage of population Christian (0.64), and with ethnic diversity (0.52). The PQLI is negatively correlated with educational expenditures (–0.69), military spending (–0.62), and percentage of population Islamic (–0.51). Park makes a contentious assumption based on these data: Christian values are more consistent with the PQLI than are Islamic values (1987: 410).

Park finds that civil-political rankings, like the PQLI, are correlated in a similar (positive) manner to welfare spending (0.34), to urbanization (0.44), to percentage Christian (0.48), and to ethnic diversity (0.26). He finds negative correlations, once again, between C/P rankings and educational expenditures (–0.54), military spending (–0.38), and percentage Islamic (–0.38). The PQLI and C/P rankings are, therefore, consistent in the directions of their correlations to Park's independent variables. Park notes that this tends to discredit the trade-off theories like the Butler thesis and the full-belly thesis. If socioeconomic and civil-political rights stand in similar relationships to the determinants of human rights, then no trade-offs may be necessary.

Park's conclusion that we do not have to think in terms of trade-offs between different types of rights is encouraging. Perhaps all rights are interdependent and inseparable. Other conclusions are more troubling, however. What are we to make of the relationship between education and rights? Spending on education is negatively correlated to rights in both areas, based on Park's results. This seems counterintuitive. Surely one would not argue that rights would be promoted by cuts in educational funding. Park does not speak to this anomaly in his work. Park's claim regarding the superiority of Christian over Islamic values is even more troubling and smacks of cultural imperialism. Finally, Park's work, like that of his predecessors, relies on correlations alone. Variance explained by his determinants is still relatively limited.

More recent quantitative studies of human rights employ multivariate analyses. Steven Poe and Neal Tate (1994: 854) critique the above studies by lamenting their small sample sizes, their lack of data from different time periods, and their bivariate methodologies. Poe, Tate, and Conway Henderson have all turned to multiple regression as a means for advancing quantitative studies of human rights. Henderson's work has found that expansion of democracy and increased equality are associated with enhanced human rights (1991). Henderson also finds rising rates of economic growth and population growth to be associated with decreases in human rights (1991, 1993). Variance in human rights (for example, integrity of the person) explained by Henderson's variables ranges from 41 percent to 55 percent. Henderson's models of rights are parsimonious (1991: 120); the model used by Poe and Tate is more ambitious.

Like Henderson, Poe and Tate find that increases in democracy go along with enhancement of rights. Conversely, Poe and Tate find that increasing population size and involvement in internal or external wars are associated with increased government repression and deteriorating human rights (1994: 861). Poe and Tate also report the highest level of variance explained of any of these studies ($R^2 = 0.75$ to 0.77). Variance explained by that study must be viewed with caution, however. The sheer number of independent variables included in the Poe-Tate model (11 in all) tends to inflate artificially the R^2 values, especially because almost half of those variables do not show up as statistically significant in relation to measures of human rights (1994: 861) (see Pindyke and Rubinfeld [1981: 79] for a discussion of variance explained in relation to nonsignificant independent variables).

Given the results of all of these prior studies, further quantitative analysis with other determinants and additional study employing multivariate techniques would seem warranted.

Empirical Models

The bulk of prior quantitative studies posited rights as a function of development. Rights were operationalized via the Freedom House rankings on civil liberties and political rights and via the PQLI. Development was operationalized as GNP per capita. Simple specifications of these models can be found in Figure 3.1.

FIGURE 3.1
Specification of Prior Models

H1:	HR	= f (development)
H2a:	C/P	= f (GNP)
H2b:	PQLI	= f (GNP)

HR	= human rights
C/P	= rankings of civil liberties and political rights by Freedom House
GNP	= gross national product per capita
PQLI	= physical quality of life index from the Overseas Development Council

Hypotheses H1 states that human rights are a function of development. Hypotheses H2a and H2b operationalize development as GNP; and operationalize first and second generation human rights as civil-political rankings, or as the PQLI, respectively.[5]

As noted earlier, additional variables, such as government spending and cultural characteristics, were factored into some of the prior models, but these have been omitted from Figure 3.1. This study is interested in the MNC as a possible determinant of human rights in developing nations. Initial specification of the MNC model can be found in Figure 3.2.

Hypothesis H3 in Figure 3.2 specifies human rights as a function of development and multinationals. In Hypothesis H4, MNCs are operationalized in terms of DFI. DFI is the most valid and reliable measure of MNC operations in LDCs. To know where MNCs locate, we must follow a trail of money. MNCs find their entrée into LDCs via investment. DFI is used to establish new plants and operational facilities, to buy into

FIGURE 3.2
Specification of the Multinational Corporation Model

H3:   HR   = f (development + multinationals)
H4:   HR   = f (GNP + DFI)
H5a: C/P   = f (GNP + DFI)
H5b: PQLI = f (GNP + DFI)

DFI = direct foreign investment

---

existing plants and operations, or to form joint ventures with local corporations and local governments. For Hymer, MNCs and DFI are virtually synonomous. When listing terms used to describe "the beast," Hymer lists "multinational corporations" and "foreign investment" (among others) as equivalent terms (1979: 388). DFI as operationalized in this study refers only to foreign investment by U.S. firms.[6] U.S. investment is by far the most important individual measure of DFI. U.S. MNCs account for as much as 50 percent of total foreign investment in the Third World (Page, 1987: 28).

Hypotheses H5a and H5b operationalize human rights by means of the civil-political indices from Freedom House, and by means of the PQLI of socioeconomic rights. Recall that these same indices were used in the prior quantitative studies, allowing us to replicate and verify those prior works. In this way, cumulation in quantitative human rights research is advanced.

Freedom House's annual surveys include rankings for each nation on seven-point scales of civil liberties and political freedoms. The original scales have been inverted in this analysis, so that a higher score from Freedom House will indicate a higher level of human rights. Critiques of Freedom House's methodology have focused on the alleged "definitional weaknesses . . . vagueness and ambiguity" said to be inherent in any such "impressionistic" approach to rating human rights within nations (McCamant, 1981: 130–32). Critics also argue that the Freedom House data are "too narrow to provide a framework for general human rights assessment" (Dominquez, 1979: 32). However, "even [these same] critics view the [Freedom House] data as providing useful quantitative information regarding civil and political rights conditions over a relatively large sample" (Pritchard, 1989: 331). John McCamant, despite some criticism, notes that the work by Freedom House is "the only attempt so far to produce an overall measure of a country's performance on civil and political rights" (1981: 130). Dominquez, despite reservations, terms the Freedom House rankings as "useful judgements" that "are needed for particular kinds of political assessment" (1979: 31–32). McCamant endorses the Freedom House data to the extent that the "scoring does not have any obvious geographical or ideological bias" (1981: 132). Poe and Tate (1994: 857) also provide a detailed defense for use of Freedom House data.[7]

Of course, factors other than MNCs and development could help to determine levels of human rights in LDCs. Final specifications of the MNC model factor in U.S. economic aid and total foreign public debt as independent variables (see Figure 3.3). There is a large body of critical literature (written by Chomsky and others) that argues U.S. aid often leads to violations of human rights in the Third World (see Chapter 4 for more detail). A more recent school of thought holds that the Third World debt crisis is a source of rights violations. Debt burdens force LDCs to accept austerity measures and structural adjustments if they want to qualify for loans from the International Monetary Fund or the World Bank. The concomitant reductions in spending on welfare programs are seen by critics as the essential equivalent of curtailing economic and social rights. Furthermore, as popular opposition to austerity erupts, Third World governments turn to repression and violations of civil-political rights to restore order (Sachs, 1989: 91; see also Skogly, 1993, 1994; and Chapter 2 of this book).

Figure 3.3 separates the Freedom House rankings into political rights and civil liberties. The PQLI is also disaggregated into its constituent parts: infant mortality, illiteracy rates, and life expectancy at age one. Proliferating these numerous specifications of both dependent and independent variables will allow for a series of tests that can evaluate Hypothesis H4 most fairly and most accurately.[8] Controlling for other possible determining variables also helps to ensure that we do not arrive at spurious relationships between rights, development, and investment.

DFI itself can be divided into alternative indicators: net income and number of employees. These alternative indicators of DFI will be used in the tests below, but have been left out of Figure 3.3 for the sake of simplicity and brevity. One last reminder is in order before we turn to the data analysis. Keep in mind the null hypothesis (H0); it is a logical possibility that DFI is unrelated to human rights in LDCs.

I will be testing the MNC model over time. Cross-national data on more than 50 LDCs were drawn from two time periods.[9] The first tests look at the MNC model for the years from 1983 (for the independent variables) to 1985 (dependent variables). A second set of tests looks at the

FIGURE 3.3
Final Specification of the Multinational Corporation Model

H6:	CL	= GNP + DFI + Aid + Debt
H7:	PR	= GNP + DFI + Aid + Debt
H8:	ILLIT	= GNP + DFI + Aid + Debt
H9:	INFMOR	= GNP + DFI + Aid + Debt
H10:	LIFEXP	= GNP + DFI + Aid + Debt

Aid	= U.S. developmental aid
Debt	= total foreign debt
CL	= civil liberties ranked by Freedom House
PR	= political rights ranked by Freedom House
ILLIT	= illiteracy rate of adult population
INFMOR	= infant mortality per 1,000 live births
LIFEXP	= life expectancy at age one

same model for the years from 1987 (independent variables) to 1990 (dependent variables).[10] I am assuming a time lag of roughly two to three years between the determinants and the levels of human rights. There is no discussion in the prior literature regarding how long it takes for aid, debt, GNP, or investment to impact upon rights in LDCs.[11]

Prior quantitative study of human rights has been limited primarily to correlation analysis. Although useful, correlations alone tell us relatively little about the interactions between variables. Bivariate correlations are unable to control for additional factors, and therefore can lead to spurious conclusions. David Banks (1986) and Poe and Tate (1994) argue that empirical research on rights must move to ordinary least squares methods. The technique employed here is a form of ordinary least squares: multivariate regression. Multiple regression has the advantage of separating the influence of one determining factor from that of other determinants. Correlation coefficients alone tend to "inflate the importance" of any single independent variable (Lewis-Beck, 1980: 25). Mutiple regression, on the other hand, allows us to separate the impact of one independent variable while holding other determinants constant.

Hypotheses H6 through H10, the models to be tested, have been further elaborated in terms of Equations 1 through 5 (see Figure 3.4). These equations then provide us with the parameters necessary for multiple regression.

FIGURE 3.4
Equations

H6/E1:	CL	$= a + \beta_1 GNP + \beta_2 DFI + \beta_3 Aid + \beta_4 Debt$
H7/E2:	PR	$= a + \beta_1 GNP + \beta_2 DFI + \beta_3 Aid + \beta_4 Debt$
H8/E3:	ILLIT	$= a + \beta_1 GNP + \beta_2 DFI + \beta_3 Aid + \beta_4 Debt$
H9/E4:	INFMOR	$= a + \beta_1 GNP + \beta_2 DFI + \beta_3 Aid + \beta_4 Debt$
H10/E5:	LIFEXP	$= a + \beta_1 GNP + \beta_2 DFI + \beta_3 Aid + \beta_4 Debt$

a = intercept
β_n = standardized coefficients

CONCLUSIONS FROM THE EMPIRICAL DATA

Table 3.1 contains the parameter estimates for Equations 1 and 2 (for 1985 and 1990). Rankings of civil liberties and political rights are compared to levels of GNP per capita, direct foreign investment, U.S. economic aid, and foreign debt.[12] All tables report the standardized coefficients (β weights) for the slope estimates.[13] The tables do not contain correlation coefficients. DFI has been measured via either total employees or net income. T-ratios that are used to gauge statistical significance are in parentheses beneath each β, and variance explained is reported as both R^2 and adjusted R^2 (adjusted R^2 in parentheses).[14] Reading across each line in Tables 3.1 to 3.3 gives us the β values for each equation, with changing indicators for DFI (employment vs. income) from one line to the next. Changing indicators for DFI leads to slight changes in the parameter estimates for the other independent variables (GNP, aid, debt), as well as slight changes in the values for R^2. The results are striking, especially if one pays close attention to the directions of the relationships, statistical significance of the estimates (or lack thereof), and the relative importance of the explanatory variables.

The conclusion from Table 3.1 with the greatest relevance to theories of human rights and development is the positive relationship between the presence of MNCs and levels of C/P rights in the Third World. Foreign investment is positively associated with both civil liberties and political freedoms. This positive association is consistent over time (from 1985 to 1990). It is also consistent across different indicators of DFI. Increased presence of U.S. MNCs goes along with rising levels of civil and political rights across these samples of LDCs, regardless of whether we operationalize DFI as MNC income or as MNC employment. Furthermore, the

TABLE 3.1
Civil and Political Rights

Indicator	GNP	DFI [measure]	Aid	Debt	R^2 (adjusted)
CL 1985	0.27	0.37* [employment]	0.08	0.41	0.22 (0.14)
(N = 52)	(1.89)	(2.08)	(0.48)	(0.69)	
	0.29*	0.15 [income]	0.08	0.27	0.14 (0.06)
	1.97	(0.86)	(0.55)	(1.56)	
PR 1985	0.26	0.41* [employment]	0.07	0.12	0.22 (0.14)
(N = 52)	(1.76)	(2.29)	(0.44)	(0.33)	
	0.27	0.09 [income]	0.06	0.25	0.13 (0.04)
	(1.72)	(0.52)	(0.38)	(1.44)	
CL 1990	0.31*	0.26 [employment]	0.29*	0.17	0.24 (0.16)
(N = 39)	(1.99)	(1.22)	(1.98)	(0.60)	
	0.36*	0.34 [income]	0.28*	0.47*	0.29 (0.20)
	(2.27)	(1.47)	(1.97)	(2.00)	
PR 1990	0.38†	0.22 [employment]	0.26	0.19	0.26 (0.18)
(N = 39)	(2.47)	(1.06)	(1.80)	(0.69)	
	0.41†	0.41 [income]	0.23	0.49*	0.32 (0.23)
	(2.67)	(1.77)	(1.61)	(2.13)	

* = $p < .05$
† = $p < .01$

positive relationship is statistically significant in the 1985 data when measuring DFI via the numbers of employees working for U.S. MNCs. Lack of significance in the 1990 data cautions against generalizing too far beyond the 50+ LDCs in these samples. Still, the beneficial impact of foreign investment on civil-political rights is clear, consistent, and carries theoretical importance.

When we turn to the other determining variables from the MNC model, we find that GNP, U.S. economic aid, and foreign debt also stand in positive association to first generation rights in the Third World. LDCs with higher levels of development, more economic aid, and heavier debt burdens tend to score better in regard to the C/P rankings. The positive relationship between GNP and C/P rights in Table 3.1 is consistent with prior quantitative studies of human rights and development. Even when controlling for DFI, increased development is positively correlated to better human rights, thereby increasing our confidence in the reliability of the prior research. Furthermore, the positive associations between development, aid, and debt, on the one hand, and civil-political rights, on the other hand, are statistically significant in the more recent (1990) data. Hence, we can safely say that these relationships characterize all LDCs, including those not contained in these samples.

One nice advantage of discussing ß weights rather than correlation coefficients is the ability to compare the relative importance of explanatory variables. Betas calculate the changes in a standard deviation of the dependent variables associated with an increase of one standard deviation in an independent variable (while holding the other independent variables constant). Therefore, standardized coefficients can be compared to one another. Table 3.1 shows that GNP is the determinant with the greatest overall effect on changes in civil and political rights. The absolute values for GNP exceed other parameter estimates in almost every case (a notable exception is the 1985 DFI employee data). Although direct investment by MNCs adds less to the explanatory power of the model than does GNP, it is worth restating and stressing the nature of the association between DFI (both measures) and C/P rights. A positive relationship between investment and civil-political rights is consistent across different indicators of DFI (employees, income) and over time.

The fit of the MNC models to the empirical data is also relatively good, especially when compared to the variance explained by prior studies. R^2 values in Table 3.1 reveal that as much as one-quarter to one-third of the variance in the C/P indices is associated with the combined variance of the independent variables in the MNC model. The strength of the MNC model is roughly the same or slightly better than that of other quantitative studies when it comes to accounting for C/P rights. However, the MNC model exceeds the explanatory power of prior models when we turn to the areas of economic and social rights (see Tables 3.2 and 3.3).

Tables 3.2 and 3.3 contain ß values for Equations 3, 4, and 5 (from Figure 3.4). GNP, DFI, aid, and debt are compared to three different indicators of social and economic rights (the three elements of the PQLI).[15] Increasing GNP per capita, once again the single most important determinant, is associated with increased life expectancy, lower infant mortality, and reduced illiteracy. Hence, rising GNP is clearly associated with better standards of public welfare. The positive relationships between development and longer lives, fewer infant deaths, and enhanced literacy are statistically significant over time (from 1985 to 1990).

Increased U.S. investment follows the same general pattern in its associations to the elements of the PQLI as does GNP. DFI tracks the same course as does GNP when it comes to socioeconomic rights. Rising investment is positively associated with increased life expectancy,

TABLE 3.2
Economic and Social Rights (1985)

Indicator	GNP	DFI [measure]	Aid	Debt	R^2 (adjusted)
ILLIT	−0.45**	−0.19 [employment]	0.06	−0.03	0.27 (0.20)
(N = 52)	(3.39)	(1.10)	(0.38)	(0.09)	
	−0.42**	−0.12 [income]	0.11	−0.09	0.26 (0.19)
	(2.94)	(0.72)	(0.80)	(0.55)	
INFMOR	−0.65**	−0.32* [employment]	−0.10	0.31	0.48 (0.45)
(N = 52)	(5.62)	(2.15)	(0.78)	(1.03)	
	−0.62**	−0.10 [income]	−0.01	0.02	0.43 (0.38)
	(5.05)	(0.70)	(0.06)	(0.16)	
LIFEXP	0.64**	0.24 [employment]	0.10	0.07	0.46 (0.41)
(N = 52)	(5.51)	(1.62)	(0.80)	(0.25)	
	0.64**	0.04 [income]	0.09	0.16	0.45 (0.39)
	(5.19)	(0.25)	(0.75)	(1.16)	

*   = $p < .05$
** = $p < .001$

TABLE 3.3
Economic and Social Rights (1990)

Indicator	GNP	DFI [measure]	Aid	Debt	R^2 (adjusted)
ILLIT	−0.55**	−0.36 [employment]	0.10	0.13	0.33 (0.25)
(N = 39)	(3.76)	(1.59)	(0.71)	(0.47)	
	−0.54**	−0.18 [income]	0.15	0.23	0.34 (0.26)
	(3.54)	(0.81)	(1.03)	(1.02)	
INFMOR	−0.64**	−0.38* [employment]	0.09	0.26	0.40 (0.34)
(N = 39)	(4.66)	(2.19)	(0.70)	(1.05)	
	−0.63**	−0.23 [income]	0.12	0.37	0.42 (0.35)
	(4.46)	(1.07)	(0.88)	(1.75)	
LIFEXP	0.79••	0.30 [employment	0.08	−0.15	0.57 (0.53)
(N = 39)	(6.76)	(1.56)	(0.75)	(0.68)	
	0.80**	0.10 [income]	0.05	−0.22	0.59 (0.54)
	(6.70)	(0.56)	(0.46)	(1.22)	

*   = $p < .05$
** = $p < .001$

reduced infant mortality, and reductions in illiteracy. These relations are again consistent over time. Furthermore, the MNC to human rights relationship is statistically significant when we measure DFI as total employment and compare it to infant mortality rates.[16] The facts that these relationships hold across different indicators of DFI, and also hold consistent over time, increase confidence that MNCs are positively associated with improved socioeconomic rights in general. This is certainly true of the nations contained in these samples. A finding of statistical significance would further imply that such relationships hold true for all LDCs.

The connections between the PQLI (on the one hand), and aid or debt (on the other hand) are more problematic. These relationships are not always consistent over time. Economic aid is positively associated with enhanced life expectancy in both 1985 and 1990. A rising debt, however, is correlated to longer life expectancy in the 1980s but negatively correlated to longer lives in the 1990s. One can only speculate on the possible reasons for such a changing trend. Early borrowing would have led to rising levels of welfare if it were used to increase government spending on things like health care. Prolonged debts into the 1990s, however, could be leading to an erosion in the same health services if decade-long debt burdens force limited revenues to be shifted away from welfare programs toward servicing that debt.[17] This speculation also suggests another avenue for future studies. There are probably several ways in which one might research this possible connection between life expectancy and indebtedness. Case studies are one possibility. Another approach could be to compare aggregate data on health care expenditures to total foreign debt across developing nations. A combination of these two methods would probably be necessary to pinpoint the exact nature of this relationship.

Finally, a quick glance at the R^2 values shows the strong explanatory power of the MNC model in accounting for variance in second generation rights within the Third World. Almost 60 percent of the variation in individual PQLI indicators can be associated with the combined variance in the MNC model's independent variables (compare life expectancy, 1990). Hence, preference for the MNC model over all prior quantitative models of human rights is clearest when seeking to explain the causes of socioeconomic rights in developing nations.

THEORIES OF MULTINATIONAL CORPORATIONS AND HUMAN RIGHTS REVISITED

This chapter sought to establish the possible causal nature of mutinational corporations in regard to human rights in LDCs. Two theories of

MNCs and human rights, the engines of development thesis and the Hymer thesis, were used as a point of departure. MNCs were operationalized as direct foreign investment, and DFI was measured by means of two different indicators. MNC investment was found to be positively associated with first generation political rights and civil liberties in the Third World. Like foreign investment, enhanced GNP per capita also has a positive impact upon first generation rights. These relationships were consistent over time and consistent as we moved from one measure of DFI to another.

MNCs, as reflected in direct foreign investment, were also positively associated with the second generation economic and social rights reflected in the PQLI. Life expectancy, literacy, and infant survival rates all tend to go up as MNC investment increases across LDCs within these samples. Again, the trends remain consistent over time and are consistent across alternative measures of DFI. Once again, as with C/P rights, increased GNP has a positive impact on socioeconomic rights.

The implications from the combined studies suggest that the engines of development school is correct in its assertions that MNCs promote both civil-political rights and socioeconomic welfare at the international level. The Hymer thesis is incorrect in its claims that MNC investment tends to go along with violations of civil-political rights and lower standards of welfare in Third World nations as a whole. The best available aggregate data provide no support for Hymer's view.[18]

NOTES

1. Notable exceptions to the general lack of attention to MNCs and human rights can be found in David Kowalewski's studies of MNCs and inequality in the Caribbean (1982), and his research on MNCs and repression in Asia (1989). See also the discussion of David Carleton's research (1989) on human rights and the international division of labor in Chapter 5 of this book.

2. A best-case test is one that would most fairly and accurately evaluate the validity of a given claim on the basis of its own arguments. I want to conduct a series of tests that will produce results directly relevant to the empirical claims imbedded in the theories outlined in this chapter.

3. William Butler, "Human Rights and Foreign Policy," public lecture presented to the Salzburg Seminar, Session 273: Human Rights Across Cultures and Political Systems, Salzburg, May 30, 1989.

4. For a bivariate relationship, variance explained (R^2) is equal to the correlation coefficient squared (Lewis-Beck, 1980: 25).

5. I treat the following terms as synonyms: first generation rights, civil-political rights, and C/P rights. In a second category, and also synonymous with

each other are the terms: second generation rights, economic and social rights, and socioeconomic rights (see Chapter 1).

6. Data for total foreign investment in Third World nations (U.S. DFI plus non-U.S. DFI) are not generally available. U.S. foreign investment by country serves as the most accurate available indicator of total DFI. U.S. DFI is the largest single source of total DFI.

7. Although there is an almost endless debate in the prior literature over the validity and reliability of indices of rights, such as that published by Freedom House and others, I choose not to involve myself in that debate for the purposes of this study. Beyond the reasons listed above, use of indicators such as the PQLI and Freedom House rankings allow for replication and cumulation of quantitative research on human rights.

8. See note 2 above.

9. Nations in the samples: 1985 sample (N = 52); Algeria, Argentina, Bangladesh, Bolivia, Brazil, Burundi, Chad, Chile, Colombia, Costa Rica, Dominican Republic, Ecuador, El Salvador, Egypt, Ghana, Guatamala, Haiti, Honduras, India, Indonesia, Jamaica, Jordan, Kenya, Liberia, Malawi, Malaysia, Mauritania, Mexico, Morocco, Nicaragua, Niger, Nigeria, Pakistan, Panama, Paraguay, Peru, Rwanda, Senegal, Sierra Leone, Singapore, Somalia, Sudan, Syria, Thailand, Tunisia, Turkey, Uganda, Uruguay, Venezuela, Zaire, Zambia, and Zimbabwe. 1990 sample (N = 39): Argentina, Bangladesh, Bolivia, Brazil, Chile, Colombia, Costa Rica, Dominican Republic, Ecuador, El Salvador, Egypt, Ghana, Guatamala, Honduras, India, Indonesia, Jamaica, Kenya, Malaysia, Mexico, Morocco, Nicaragua, Nigeria, Pakistan, Panama, Paraguay, Peru, Singapore, Somalia, Sudan, Syria, Thailand, Tunisia, Turkey, Uruguay, Venezuela, Zaire, Zambia, and Zimbabwe. These samples contain LDCs from all regions of the Third World. They also represent slightly less than half of all LDCs. Problems with availability of data preclude taking a random sample that has sufficient size. Data collection began by gathering information on all 88 LDCs for which Freedom House, the Commerce Department, the World Bank, and the Agency for International Development publish data (see sources in note 12 in this chapter). I sought to make the study as inclusive as possible. Listwise deletion then eliminated cases with missing data for any of the variables. There are sound statistical reasons for preferring listwise deletion. Furthermore, I chose not to substitute alternative indicators for missing data as has been commonly done in prior studies using multiple regression (see, for example, Poe and Tate, 1994). This process left 52 nations for the 1985 data and 39 nations for the 1990 data. Although not a random sample, this group of LDCs is large enough and diverse enough to allow for robust testing. Conclusions drawn from these samples therefore apply to the Third World as a whole.

10. The sampling for this study was done during 1992–93, at which time the most recent available data for the combined indicators (dependent variables) was the year 1990. I also went back five years to 1985 data (dependent variables) for a second sample. Comparing results from the 1985 and 1990 data allows us to see

if the trends in the data hold up over time. An obvious step to follow up on this study would be to analyze data for 1995. Such a follow-up study would also indicate whether the prior relationships between DFI, rights, GNP, aid, and debt identified here have changed during the post–Cold War era.

11.   A lag of at least two years would seem necessary to allow the effects of DFI to find their way into a nation's political economy. A lag of more than three years runs the risk of compounding the effects of DFI with too many other extraneous factors (changes in governmment, and so forth).

12.   Data on civil liberties and political rights are from Gastil at Freedom House, *Freedom in the World* (1985 and 1990); data on GNP are measured per capita and are also from Freedom House; all data on foreign investment are in U.S. dollars (or total employees) and are from the Bureau of Economic Analysis, U.S. Department of Commerce, *U.S. Direct Investment Abroad* (1983 and 1987); data on total public debt, illiteracy, infant mortality, and life expectancy are from the *World Development Report* published by the World Bank (1983, 1985, 1987, 1990); and data on total economic assistance in U.S. dollars are from the Agency for International Development, *Development and the National Interest* (1989).

13.   Values for the intercept (constant) in each equation are not reported because there is no intuitive interpretation for those numbers. A given intercept would equal the estimated value for the human rights indicator(s) of a nation with no GNP, no DFI, no aid, and no debt. Obviously, there could not be such a country (hence the nonintuitive nature of intercepts in these data).

14.   Adjusted for sample size and for the number of independent variables in the model.

15.   See note 12 above.

16.   This would indicate that employment is a better gauge than net income when measuring the impact of foreign investment on socioeconomic welfare in the Third World. Employment is also a more satisfactory operationalization of DFI than is income when comparing foreign investment to civil and political rights (see Table 3.1).

17.   Recent case studies from Africa tend to support this interpretation. The government of Zimbabwe increased public expenditures for health and education and significantly decreased military budgets after independence in 1980. Spending for health and education combined was equal to 84 percent of the military budget in 1984. Health plus education as a percentage of military spending jumped to 188 percent by 1989 (United Nations Development Programme/ World Bank, 1992: 189–93). During this same period, infant mortality decreased and life expectancy rates increased in Zimbabwe (Meisenhelder, 1994: 87). In 1990, Zimbabwe implemented a structural adjustment program because of its heavy foreign debts. The government was forced to reduce expenditures on schools and medical care. Subsequently, many of the advances made in the 1980s were reversed (1994: 87–88). For example, maternal mortality rates had declined to 101 deaths per 100,000 births by 1989. This rate more than tripled to 359

maternal deaths per 100,000 births in 1991 (Van Hook, 1994: 298). Hence, the imposition of structural adjustment was followed by a drop in social welfare.

18.   Research from this chapter shows no support for the Hymer thesis at the international level. For evidence that Hymer's claims might be more valid at a lower level of analysis, see the case studies of Chile, India, and Mexico in Chapter 5.

4

Human Rights and Foreign Aid

FOREIGN AID AND FOREIGN INVESTMENT

Third World nations are heavily dependent on the advanced, industrialized world for a number of important economic inputs. Hard currency, manufactured goods, expertise, and technology all flow from the North to the South. Chapter 3 analyzed the impact of direct foreign investment by U.S. multinational corporations (MNCs) on human rights in the Third World. Equally important, and in some cases even more important than private investment, is the form of public investment that comes through foreign aid. The relationship between foreign aid and human rights in less developed countries (LDCs) has attracted more scholarly attention than has the connection between MNCs and human rights. However, quantitative studies rarely conceptualize foreign aid as a possible determinant of human rights in the Third World. Although there is much to be learned from these prior quantitative analyses, there is also much work yet to be done to establish the exact nature of the foreign aid-to-human rights connection. A comparison of foreign aid to foreign investment raises a series of interesting and potentially fruitful questions regarding external determinants of human rights within the Third World.

The origins of U.S. foreign aid as we know it date back to January 1949. President Truman in his inaugural address laid out four points of emphasis for his new administration. Point Four called for a "bold new program" of economic aid and technical assistance from the United States to the poorest countries (Lumsdaine, 1993: 34). Since that time, U.S. aid to the Third World has totaled more than $233 billion (Zimmerman, 1993: 234). Total aid from all donors (United States plus others) during the period of 1950–94 was $500 billion (Hook, 1995: 3). By comparison, total private investment in LDCs from the North during roughly the same period amounted to $521 billion (Lumsdaine, 1993: 35). This latter figure includes direct foreign investment (DFI) plus portfolio investment and private bank loans. Private investment in the form of DFI alone was $226 billion (1993: 35). During the period 1950–70 total aid was greater than total foreign investment. During the years 1971–85 total foreign investment exceeded total foreign aid; and from 1986 to 1989 aid once again was greater than total foreign investment (see Lumsdaine, 1993: table 2.1). On average, annual aid levels were double that of DFI per year (1993: 34).

The sheer size of foreign aid as compared to foreign investment highlights the importance of aid for developing nations. There are also economically significant and politically necessary connections between these two forms of largess. Most U.S. foreign aid is tied aid. Aid is tied when it is extended based on the condition that aid dollars must be used to make purchases in the United States from U.S. corporations. Hence, aid monies that are tied will effectively circulate back into the U.S. economy. Tied aid indirectly subsidizes purchases by LDC governments from U.S. businesses.[1] Although Lumsdaine's excellent analysis of foreign aid includes the often repeated claim that tied aid is a minority of total aid (1993: 40), his own figures show that tied aid constitutes the majority of U.S. aid. The percentage of U.S. aid that was untied (for selected years) was only 9 percent in 1968, 39 percent in 1980, and 37 percent in 1988 (1993: 236). In 1988, 48 percent of U.S. aid was fully tied and 15 percent was partially tied, for a grand total of 63 percent of all aid that was tied to some extent (1993: 236). According to Robert Zimmerman, more than 70 percent of all U.S. aid dollars are spent here in the United States on goods and services provided by U.S. corporations (1993: 11).

Tying aid creates a close relationship between foreign aid in a given year and DFI by MNCs in subsequent years. This is, at least in part, the rationale for tying aid in the first place. In the words of one former president of the World Bank, "The function of foreign aid is to promote and marginally support the flow of private loans and direct investment capital to the developing countries" (cited in Hook, 1995: 30). Tied aid turns into new sales and new markets for U.S. MNCs. New sales and new markets, in turn, open the doors to new DFI opportunities. America's business clients are more likely to want and need U.S.-owned corporations in their country after they have been softened up by tied aid. Tied aid can be used to establish consumer loyalties, market shares, and a demand for service and parts from U.S. corporations. All of these factors tend to increase the likelihood of expanded investment opportunities in the Third World as an indirect result of tied aid.

The relationship between DFI and aid was touched on in Chapter 3. In the data analysis that specified the connections between DFI and human rights, U.S. economic aid was factored into the tests as a way to control for an exogenous variable (see Tables 3.1 to 3.3). Those tests showed DFI to be positively associated with first and second generation rights in LDCs. The same tests, however, were inconclusive regarding the possible impact of aid on rights. Economic aid showed up as a nonsignificant variable in most of the tests. The notable exception was when aid was regressed on civil liberty rankings for 1990 (see Table 3.1). In that case, increased economic aid across the sample of 39 LDCs was associated with an increase in civil liberties. Although this result is somewhat intriguing in its own right, it tells us little about the systemic interaction between levels of aid and levels of human rights. More study is needed to specify the exact nature of such interaction.

How does U.S. foreign aid affect human rights in Third World nations? What forms does such aid take, and what is its impact? Do economic and military aid have similar effects, or is there a differential impact on rights from differing types of aid? How does such aid influence first and second generation rights? How have aid flows changed over time, and is the impact of aid consistent over time? This chapter seeks to answer these questions through a quantitative analysis of aid and human rights in the Third World. The remainder of this chapter will describe the nature of aid flows from the United States to developing nations, review prior quantitative studies of the relationship between aid and rights with a view toward extending and improving upon those studies, summarize the conflicting theoretical literatures that see different causal connections between aid and rights, test the theoretical claims through analysis of aid and rights data drawn from 1983 to 1990, and draw conclusions from the data analysis that address the impact of aid on rights in LDCs. The conclusion of this chapter will also draw some tentative generalizations regarding the combined impact of DFI and aid and then point us toward the final step in this book, that of case studies.

THE STRUCTURE OF U.S. FOREIGN AID

Foreign aid has become one of the most contoversial aspects of U.S. foreign policy in the 1990s. Foreign assistance in fiscal year 1995 was $14.8 billion (Doherty, 1994: 3566). Total aid to the Third World from all donors is currently more than $50 billion per year, distributed to more than 100 nations (Hook, 1995: 15). The primary recipients of U.S. aid are Israel ($3 billion per year) and Egypt ($2 billion per year). A second tier of the top aid clients for the United States includes the nations of Bolivia, Costa Rica, El Salvador, Guatemala, Honduras, India, Liberia, Pakistan, Panama, the Philippines, Peru, and Zaire. Figure 4.1 shows the international distribution pattern of U.S. foreign aid.

U.S. aid as a percentage of total Organization for Economic Cooperation and Development (OECD) aid dropped from 57 percent in 1955 to only 16 percent in 1989 (Lumsdaine, 1993: 257).[2] Although most OECD members have been increasing their aid as a percentage of national GNP, the trend for the United States is in the opposite direction. The OECD standard (or goal) is for aid to equal at least 0.7 percent of GNP. The figures for the United States are: 0.3 percent in 1970, 0.23 percent in 1980, and 0.18 percent in 1990 (Hook, 1995: 178). Although U.S. aid has increased in absolute dollar amounts over this time, it has decreased significantly as a percentage of national economic output.

Most OECD nations have increased that portion of their aid that is distributed through multilateral institutions. The United States, once again, is a notable exception to the overall trend. U.S. assistance in the form of multilateral aid was 31 percent of all aid for the years 1980–84, but multilteral aid was only 20 percent of U.S. foreign aid in 1989 (Lumsdaine, 1993: 261).

Total U.S. military aid for the years 1962–89 was $104 billion (Hook, 1995: 126). Fully 90 percent of this aid was tied to purchases from U.S. suppliers (1995: 133). Military aid accounted for 25 percent of total U.S. aid in 1978 and 37 percent of all aid in 1988 (Zimmerman, 1993: 4). The military aid budget for 1993 equaled about 23 percent of total U.S. aid (Doherty, 1993: 93). However, military aid accounts for half of all U.S. bilateral aid (Lumsdaine, 1993: 93).

Military aid is given as: Foreign Military Financing (FMF) for purchases of U.S. military equipment and services; International Military Education and Training (IMET) to train both military officers and civilian police forces from other countries; and funds for United Nations (UN) peacekeeping forces (a $1.2 billion expenditure for FY 1995) (Doherty, 1994: 3566). FMF is by far the largest single element of military aid.

FIGURE 4.1
Distribution of U.S. Foreign Assistance Obligations by Country (Fiscal Year 1991)

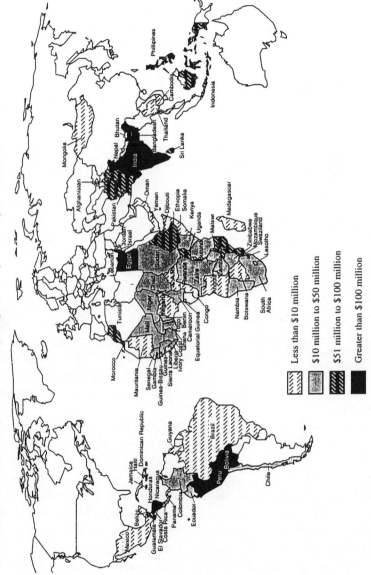

Source: **Adapted from General Accounting Office (1993). Countries not listed did not receive U.S. bilateral foreign aid.**

Some 27 countries received FMF aid in 1989; the smaller programs for IMET clients included 86 nations in the same year (Hook, 1995: 126). FMF funding can run into billions of dollars for countries like Israel and Egypt. IMET expenditures, by contrast, are normally less than $1 million per year for each nation selected (1995: 126).

Most aid to the Third World is in the form of economic assistance. Total U.S. economic aid during the period 1962–89 was $175 billion. Economic aid covers a wide range of programs. The Agency for International Development (AID) disburses the vast majority of these funds. Developmental Assistance (DA) projects target areas such as the acquired immune deficiency syndrome epidemic, children's programs, conservation, education, and nutrition. Economic Support Funds are usually given directly in cash payments or as financing for LDC imports of U.S. commodities (Doherty, 1993: 79). AID also funds programs for population assistance (family planning), disaster assistance, and Food for Peace. Non-AID economic assistance through the State Department and other agencies provides funding for refugees, the war on drugs, the Peace Corps, and the Overseas Private Investment Corporation loans and loan guarantees (for a detailed summary, see Doherty, 1993: 75–81).

Over time, the United States has softened the terms of more and more of its aid. This trend entails increasing the concessional nature of aid. More aid is given in the form of grants (which are not repaid). Concessional aid also includes soft loans, which carry below-commercial rates of interest. Aid has also tended to go increasingly to the poorest of the poor, and away from the newly industrialized countries of the Third World. For example, South Korea, once an aid recipient, has graduated in the 1990s to become the newest member of the OECD and an aid donor itself (Hook, 1995: 28).

The end of the Cold War has also brought about significant changes in aid policies, although not always in the directions one might expect. Total aid levels have not declined, despite the lack of a global communist threat as ready justification for aid. According to Steven Hook, the "scope and complexity of aid relations have only increased in the 1990s" (1995: 3). Hook cites the emergence of Eastern Europe as a new aid recipient and the addition of structural adjustment requirements from the International Monetary Fund and World Bank as examples of such new complexities. DA funding from both the United States in particular, and the OECD in general, continues to rise since the end of the Cold War. Certain consistencies remain, however, in the distribution of aid. Africa and Asia combined continue to absorb two-thirds of all DA aid (1995: 31). Aid also remains equivalent to as much as 10–50 percent of the GNP of many recipients (1995: 31). These factors have not changed as compared to aid flows during the Cold War era.

What has changed in the post–Cold War era is the rationale for defending aid. J. Brian Atwood, director of AID in the Clinton administration, has argued that aid in the post–Cold War era must meet the "new strategic threats" facing the United States. Atwood lists these threats as population growth, environmental degradation, repression in the Third World, and obstacles to global economic growth (Hook, 1995: 179). This view was shared by former Secretary of State Warren Christopher. This approach is also reflected in Clinton's advocacy of sustainable development as a guiding principle for post–Cold War aid to LDCs. Sustainable development is defined as that which allows for economic growth, environmental protection, promotion of democracy, improvement in the quality of life, and preservation of these same benefits for future generations (see Doran, 1994: 2).

A final significant political factor for aid in the 1990s is the movement by Congress to cut aid expenditures and to eliminate aid programs. Republican leaders in Congress have proposed doing away with AID altogether (Doherty 1994: 3566). Although the agency has survived such threats, it still finds its budgets and field offices politically threatened. More than 20 AID overseas missions were closed between 1989 and 1995 (Hook, 1995: 180). In 1996, Clinton announced plans that would drop the number of foreign missions from its Cold War peak of 120 to only 75 by the year 2000.[3] A 1993 report to Congress from the General Accounting Office (GAO) is also highly critical of AID's management structure. The GAO report faults AID for a lack of clearly defined objectives, sloppy evaluations of program results, a lack of accountability, and improper training of staff (General Accounting Office, 1993).

Thus, U.S. foreign aid has become one of the most controversial aspects of foreign policy in the post–Cold War period. Overlooked in most of the political debate over aid, however, are the economic, political, and social impacts that aid has on developing nations. The purpose of this chapter is to establish the nature of aid's impact, especially the effect of aid on human rights in LDCs. A brief review of prior quantitative studies of rights and aid will serve as background for the research design used here.

QUANTITATIVE STUDIES OF
AID AND HUMAN RIGHTS

The connection between U.S. foreign aid and human rights has been a concern for Congress since at least 1974. Section 502b of the Arms Export Control Act and the Harkin Amendment established linkages between aid and rights (see Chapter 2). Under such laws, Congress decreed that aid to the Third World would be based in part on respect for human rights. Section 502b and the Harkin Amendment threatened to reduce or to cut off aid to regimes that are guilty of human rights abuses. This legislation has also stimulated scholarly interest in the connections between rights and aid. Researchers have sought to answer the question of whether these laws have had a measurable impact on the distribution of foreign aid.

Almost all of the quantitative work done on human rights and aid seeks to establish whether violations of rights in the Third World lead to subsequent curtailment of U.S. aid to the abusive regimes. A series of articles by numerous scholars addresses these issues: Carleton and Stohl (1987); Cingranelli and Pasquarello (1985); Hofrenning (1990); Poe (1990); Poe et al. (1994); Poe and Sirirangsi (1994); Schoultz (1980); Stohl, Carleton, and Johnson (1984). These studies conceptualize human rights as a determinant of U.S. aid. They want to know if changes in human rights lead to related changes in aid flows. Quantitative studies rarely consider a reversed causal chain. That is, rarely do these prior studies ask about the causal impact that aid may have on human rights. Doran's work (1978) is a notable exception. Doran has sought to determine the effect of aid on levels of stability in the Third World. This chapter is more akin to Doran's approach, asking what causal impact U.S. aid has on levels of human rights in LDCs.

Although prior quantitative studies, on the whole, see aid as a function of human rights, the methodology of these studies is useful when we ask whether human rights are a function of foreign aid. The research designs of these prior studies, especially those employed by Carleton and Stohl, Cingranelli and Pasquarello, and Poe, inform the approach taken in this chapter.[4]

An interesting debate over aid and rights can be found in an article by Cingranelli and Pasquarello, versus a follow-up study by Carleton and Stohl. Cingranelli and Pasquarello (1985) postulate aid as the dependent variable and human rights as the independent (determining) variable. Drawing on Schoultz (1980), these authors also postulate a "two-stage allocation process." The first stage in aid allocation is gatekeeping. At this stage, the decision is made whether or not to distribute any assistance to a given nation. Once the gatekeeping decisions are made, a second stage of allocation decides on the level of economic and military aid for each aid recipient. Cingranelli and Pasquarello, who drew their sample from Latin America, also argue that El Salvador must be excluded from aid analysis as an outlier. El Salvador alone accounts for 27 percent of all bilateral aid within their sample. Recipients of unusually large amounts of aid were nonidicative of the overall patterns between aid and rights, and "would have distorted the findings" (1985: 545).

The conclusions of their study indicate that, at the gatekeeping stage, economic aid is determined according to levels of economic development, not according to human rights. They argue that economic aid goes to nations most in need of developmental assistance, and that human rights records have little or nothing to do with the decision on whether to extend economic aid. Gatekeeping decisions for military aid, however, are based primarily on respect for human rights (Cingranelli and Pasquarello, 1985: 554). Countries with higher levels of economic development tend not to get economic aid. Countries that were more serious abusers of rights tended to be excluded from military aid. At the second stage of decisionmaking, nations with better human rights records tended to get more economic aid, but human rights violations had no relationship to deciding levels of military aid (once the gatekeeping stage was passed) (1985: 560).

In a subsequent issue of the same journal, Carleton and Stohl do a reanalysis of the Cingranelli-Pasquarello data. Carleton and Stohl (1987) begin by noting that in most prior works there is either no significant relationship between aid and rights or the relationship between aid and rights was found to be negative (aid went primarily to violators of human rights). Thus, they note that the Cingranelli-Pasquarello study differs from similar research in its claim that human rights are connected to military aid at stage one (gatekeeping) and in that economic aid is found to be positively associated with human rights at stage two (when setting levels of aid) (1987: 1003–4). Carleton and Stohl take Cingranelli and Pasquarello to task for their conclusions, but both studies share the same analytic approach and the same basic research design.

Both studies measure rights by means of the annual State Department country reports on human rights. Both studies find strong positive correlations between human rights reports from the State Department, from Freedom House, and from Amnesty International. Carleton and Stohl then go a step beyond Cingranelli-Pasquarello to employ "multiple sources of information" through the use of several scales that measure human rights (1987: 1008). Carleton and Stohl also argue that El Salvador is not the only outlier; they list Honduras, Jamaica, and Nicaragua as others that must be excluded from their sample (1987: 1009).

The results of the Carleton-Stohl study find that the relationships between aid and rights established by Cingranelli-Pasquarello hold only when using State Department data. These connections are not statistically significant when constructing human rights scales based on data from Amnesty International or Freedom House (Carleton and Stohl, 1987: 1013). From these results, the latter study concludes that there is "prima facie evidence" that "human rights have little effect on the distibution of U.S. economic aid" (1987: 1015).

A third study in this body of literature sticks with the two-stage methodology and also focuses on the region of Latin America. Poe and his co-researchers (1994) extend and improve upon the methodology of the above studies and apply their methods to a larger period. Noting that the prior studies were "hindered because they were limited to conducting analyses on single year samples" (1994: 545), the team led by Poe draws their data from the period 1983–91. They postulate a two-year time lag between their independent variable (human rights) and their dependent variables (economic and military aid). The results of this study are generally consistent with those of Cingranelli-Pasquarello in regard to economic aid. Poe's group finds that "human rights abuses do have an impact on economic aid allocation in 'routine' cases, once the effects of countries like El Salvador, that receive a disproportionate amount of aid due to their strategic importance, are controlled" (1994: 552). They also find that, after controlling for outliers, there is a significant inverse relationship between human rights abuses and U.S. military aid. In the "final model" used by Poe's team (excluding outliers), increases in human rights abuses are associated with decreases in U.S. security assistance (1994: 555). This finding contests Cingranelli-Pasquarello's claim that there is no relationship between military aid and human rights once the analysis is beyond the gatekeeping stage. Poe and his co-researchers find a connection between security assistance and rights even at the second stage of determining levels of aid to chosen recipients.

This spate of articles employing quantitative techniques to study aid and human rights leaves us with a combined set of results that are at times consistent, at other times not. It is especially interesting to note, however, that all three studies are generally congruent in their approaches and methodology. All three acknowledge the importance of the two-stage design. All three also note the importance of using proper safeguards to omit outliers and nonindicative cases. Finally, all three assume rights to be the independent variables and economic and military aid to be the dependent variables. The quantitative methodology employed in this chapter follows the research model established by this prior literature. The significant difference between this study and the prior research is in the causal chain of events.

The empirical work of this chapter postulates aid as the independent (determining) variable, and assumes that levels of human rights are the dependent (determined) variables. Before turning to the empirical analysis itself, a useful prelude would be to consider those prior works that, like this study, consider foreign aid to be a possible determinant of human rights in the Third World. Prior studies that postulate aid as a cause of human rights in LDCs tend to be nonquantitative in nature. These studies are more theoretical and anecdotal. It is to a review of these prior theoretical works that I now turn.

THEORIES OF AID AND HUMAN RIGHTS

Aid as a Negative Causal Factor

Prior literature that postulates aid as a causal factor for human rights in the Third World tends to focus on the negative impacts of economic and military aid. This large body of literature presents three types of arguments regarding the pernicious effects of aid for rights. First, it is asserted that security aid is used to enhance torture and political repression within LDCs. Second, aid is said to harm key economic structures in recipient nations. Finally, aid is argued to have certain antidemocratic results, including the reinforcement and enhancement of existing inequalities. I shall discuss a representative sampling of the research that alleges aid is a negative factor for rights by reviewing these three arguments.

Claims that security aid is used to increase repression are the most common arguments within the literature that focuses on the negative impact of aid. For example, a 1976 report from Amnesty International (AI) identifies half of the security officers guilty of using torture in the Philippines as former students of the U.S. IMET programs (cited in Schoultz, 1981: 236). A more recent AI report details similar examples from the 1990s. The 1995 AI report says that the "link between human rights abuses and security assistance [is] most disturbing" (1995: 3). AI argues that "US weapons and training should not be used . . . to strengthen regimes that are brutal and repressive" (1995: 1). This document then goes on to detail the alleged link between aid and repression in 19 countries.[5] The general thrust of AI's 1995 security analysis is to argue that: "Without careful monitoring of security aid, without a realistic set of measurements in the human rights arena, and without the will to cut assistance where necessary, the United States may find that it will be complicit in human rights violations" (1995: 2). To argue that the United States is complicit in human rights violations is to argue that U.S. security assistance is a (partial) cause of those violations.

AI's theme is echoed by a plethora of authors. Kevin Danaher, Phillip Berryman, and Medea Benjamin argue that military aid strengthens Third World elites and "makes rebellion inevitable" (1987: 13). Noam Chomsky and Edward Herman point to IMET training that is used to enhance the power of military dictators and indirectly increases the use of torture (1979: 47–49). Loretta Rose cites military aid as something that adds to "the coercive resources of abusive governments" (1988: 24). At least two quantitative studies have also supplied empirical data to support claims of a link between military aid and repression. Deborah Gerner notes that "state terror" (for example, coercion by military or police) of the local population is possible without U.S. arms because alternative suppliers exist. However, according to Gerner, U.S. arms transfers to the Third World "ha[ve] made such terror easier to accomplish" (1988: 260). Gerner also finds a weak positive relationship between U.S. arms transfers and repression within LDCs. This relationship is statistically significant, but only for recipients of substantial military aid (defined by Gerner as military aid in excess of $65 million per year [1988: 268]). A final study by Charles Doran (1978) locates a strong positive relationship between military and economic aid (combined) and subsequent social unrest. Doran postulates a possible explanation for this trend: such aid must be used by foreign governments to repress their people (1978: 445).

A second set of arguments about the damage to human rights done by U.S. aid focuses on the economic dislocations allegedly caused by such aid. Economic structures within the Third World are said to suffer due to aid. Zimmerman claims that, because aid is used mainly to promote U.S. security interests, achievement of developmental goals becomes virtually impossible for Third World nations (1993: 1). Aid combined with U.S. diplomacy produces dependency in the Third World, with "perverse consequences" for recipients (1993: 1). Among the "perverse consequences" identified in related literature are the increased unemployment and declining real wages that have coincided with massive economic and military aid to Central America (Danaher, Berryman, and Benjamin, 1987: 1). U.S. aid policies that promote agriculture for export have allegedly caused increased hunger within client states (1987: 3; see also Lappe, Collins, and Kinley, 1980: 121–22). Food for Peace also has a downside. This aid comes in the form of credits. The actual commodities themselves are often sold on the world market at a profit by the recipient governments. However, this common practice effectively prevents the low-cost grains from reaching hungry people in target nations (Danaher, Berryman, and Benjamin, 1987: 3–4). Export-oriented growth promoted by U.S. aid also increases income inequalities and enhances the concentration of land ownership in the hands of a relative few (1987: 14-15).

Desmond McNeill's research lists numerous failures of foreign assistance. These failures include aid that tends to go primarily to capital intensive projects that cannot be sustained over the long term. For example, new schools are built, but no moneys are left over to hire adequate teaching staffs (1981: 72). McNeill also points to a brain drain stimulated by aid programs. Aid funds are often used to educate students from the Third World in the West, students who then decide not to return to their native lands. Other programs serve to siphon the best and brightest in LDCs away from local employment for the benefit of foreign interests (1981: 76–77). Furthermore, a values gap develops to divide the masses from indigenous middlemen who serve foreign interests and who come to identify with the values and goals of these foreign interests. Chomsky and Herman point to the tax breaks, rights to repatriate profits, and anti-union activities of foreign MNCs that are allegedly part and parcel of the requirements for receiving U.S. aid (1979: 247–49).

A third set of arguments about the negative impact of aid on rights has to do with the antidemocratic results of aid programs. Chomsky and Herman's ideologically tinged attack on aid is based on the claim that "U.S. controlled aid has been positively related to investment climate and inversely related to the maintainance of a democratic order and human rights" (1979: 44). Aid is used, according to these authors, to promote a "favorable climate for investment" which means, in effect, hindering democracy. Echoing the Hymer thesis reviewed in the previous chapter of this book, Chomsky and Herman charge that aid is used to marginalize 80 percent of the Third World's population, excluding them from the political process and denying them their legal and human rights (1979: 54). Aid allegedly enhances stability at the expense of "the well-being of the bulk of the population" (1979: 250). Other authors provide numerous examples that seek to illustrate such assertions.

In a case study of aid to Egypt, Zimmerman cites evidence that aid increases the power of the ruling party, the National Democratic Party. This aid serves to hinder the development of a "genuine democracy." Elites within the National Democratic Party benefit from U.S. aid, but the Egyptian masses do not (1993: 101). Hook also points to aid as something that serves elite interests in both the North and the South and as a force that reinforces inequalities within LDCs (1995: 38–40). McNeill agrees that aid benefits only a relative few, mainly the high income earners in developing nations (1981: 69).

Frances Lappe's study of aid as an obstacle to be overcome by LDCs arrives at similar conclusions. Aid strengthens repressive governments and decreases the chance for egalitarian reforms (1980: 23–26). Aid programs funded under the heading of "Food and Nutrition" were in fact used to electrify rural areas controlled by wealthy landowers and prosperous shopkeepers. The resulting mechanization led to reduced employment for the local labor force (1980: 35). Lappe could find only 6 percent of AID's total budget for agriculture and rural development devoted to promoting land reform for the benefit of the poor (1980: 79).

A slightly more sophisticated and more troubling version of this argument links increased inequality from aid programs back to the violent forms of repression that were summarized under the first set of arguments about aid and human rights abuses. Danaher, Berryman, and Benjamin argue that the austerity measures imposed on LDCs by AID (and the various international financial institutions that distribute aid) lead to lower standards of living for the masses, which in turn lead to strikes and protests. The political unrest then produces enhanced repression by the local government. Therefore, austerity-based aid is indirectly a cause of subsequent state terror (1987: 7). Doran's more recent work cites studies that find no improvement in democracy after the receipt of aid. Doran also reminds us of his own earlier findings that show increased aid leads not to democracy but rather to rising instability and unrest in the Third World, most likely due to a ratcheting up of repression facilitated by the increased aid (1994: 8–9). To sum up, according to the critical view, "U.S. foreign aid programmes have not promoted or restored human rights, nor have they strengthened democracy" (Conteh-Morgan, 1990: 25).

However, the critical view is not the only view expressed in the literature regarding aid and human rights. A smaller body of works seeks to establish the positive impact of foreign aid on human rights in Third World nations.

Aid as a Positive Causal Factor

A less voluminous but no less important body of literature stresses the positive impact of U.S. foreign aid on human rights in LDCs. The 1993 GAO report on AID contains a listing of the stated objectives for the 1961 Foreign Assistance Act (FAA), as amended.[6] Many of these objectives are directly related to promotion and protection of first generation civil-political rights, second generation socioeconomic rights, and even third generation solidarity rights.

FAA objectives include: alleviating poverty, promoting self-sustaining economic growth with equitable distribution of benefits, increasing opportunities for participation by the poor, encouraging democratic institutions, reducing infant mortality, improvements in health, reducing illiteracy, enhancing the status of women and integrating them into national economies, addressing needs for shelter, and "food security" (General Accounting Office, 1993: 66–67). Pursuit of these objectives would tend to promote equality and democracy (first generation rights) and to provide for enhanced standards of welfare (second generation rights). Third generation rights to a clean environment and humanitarian assistance are also addressed under the additional objectives of "reducing environmental degradation" and "providing international disaster assistance." Foreign aid is also charged with the task of "strengthening the development and use of cooperatives" (1993: 66). Lappe's research has found evidence of AID funding and U.S. officials successfully helping peasants in Ecuador to form agricultural cooperatives (1980: 81–82).

The federal government is also keenly aware of the connection between aid and private investment discussed earlier. FAA goals go on to specify "encouraging U.S. private investment" as an objective of foreign assistance (General Accounting Office, 1993: 67). Finally, the GAO singles out "supporting human rights by not providing assistance to countries that engage in a consistent pattern of gross violations of these rights" as a distinct goal of foreign aid (1993: 66).

A discussion of aid and human rights by Rose assumes that economic aid has a beneficial impact on rights in the Third World. Aid has the potential to alleviate poverty, hunger, inequality, and environmental distress (Rose, 1988: 23). With a play on words, Rose refers to aid as "a 'good' which [donors] control" (1988: 24). Here the word good is used in two ways. Aid is a good in the sense of being a good thing. Aid is also a good in the sense of being like other goods and services that donors have the power to deny to abusive regimes (this is Rose's policy preference). Rose argues in favor of an enhanced "aid-rights link," and advocates continuing aid to nations with repressive regimes only if the aid is channeled through nongovernmental organizations, such as the Red Cross (1988: 25). The GAO report concurs, advocating the use of, "whenever feasible, private and voluntary organizations" (1993: 66). AID distributes 20 percent of its annual budgets for Africa through nongovernmental organizations (Beinart, 1996: 158).

Additional research that touches on the potential positive effects of aid can be found in the work of Earl Conteh-Morgan and David Cingranelli. Conteh-Morgan finds anecdotal evidence of aid reducing instability in some Third World nations. He argues that economic support funding has "helped to promote economic and political stability" in El Salvador, Pakistan, and Turkey (1990: 31). Cingranelli's history of U.S. foreign policy on human rights praises the benefits provided by policies and programs dating back to the Kennedy administration. Cingranelli (1993) cites three goals for Kennedy's aid to Latin America under the Alliance for Progress. These are economic development, more progressive taxation and land reform, and support for democratic movements. The goals of such aid (if not the outcomes) were, at least in part, to enhance equality and to foster democracy (1993: 153). Kennedy created the Peace Corps, AID, and expanded Food for Peace for these very reasons.

A number of book-length studies on foreign aid have been published in the 1990s. Of these, Zimmerman's text is the only one that devotes a specific discussion to the relationship between aid and the promotion of human rights in client states. Despite his criticisms of aid policies (noted earlier), Zimmerman does find some worthwhile elements of foreign assistance. He begins by identifying three categories of human rights: economic rights, social rights, and political rights. He believes that "U.S. economic aid has helped developing countries' governments meet social rights in basic education and health for millions of people" (1993: 163). He then lists some of the many ways in which U.S. aid provides the necessary means for promoting rights: building schools and clinics, training teachers and medical professionals, increasing access to food and nutrition, creating employment, providing infrastructure, promoting small businesses, forming farmer cooperatives, vocational training, and organizing labor (1993: 163).

Zimmerman also gives a breakdown by region of the beneficial impact of aid on human rights. AID programs in Asia and the Middle East include human rights projects that train lawyers and judges, help establish democratic elections, promote nongovernmental human rights organizations, and fund research into human rights (1993: 165). In the Caribbean and Latin America, aid has funded civic education and leadership training (1993: 166). AID's Human Rights Fund for Africa sends assistance to 30 countries for seminars and conferences on human rights, educational programs and scholarships, and promotion of local human rights organizations (1993: 166). Aid also finances "participant training" in the areas of law and public administration, often within the United States. Finally, according to Zimmerman: "Local government and decentralization projects [funded by AID] affect human rights and the political process by creating and strengthening local government administration and providing opportunities for local participation in the planning and implementation of development projects" (1993: 167).

Thus, we find strong evidence on both sides of the debate regarding the impact of aid on human rights. In the more balanced treatments of aid, such as that provided by Zimmerman, we find indications of both positive and negative influence. Zimmerman sums up the conflicting data on aid and rights by posing a question, and then pointing to the only viable answer to his question given the current state of research. "Beyond anecdotal indications of impact, have U.S. human rights [aid] activities resulted in measurable improvements? The simple answer is either 'no' or 'we don't know'" (1993: 167). Zimmerman's observation could not be more to the point. We simply do not know if aid has an overall favorable impact, or an overall pernicious impact (or a mixed impact) on rights. This is because nearly all evidence on both sides of the debate is anecdotal evidence. To answer Zimmerman's question requires that we look beyond the anectodal evidence to a more systemic level of analysis. The evidence presented below is based on aggregate cross-national data drawn from the best available data for all Third World nations combined.

DATA ANALYSIS

The research design used here to test theories of the impact of aid on human rights will follow the standards set in Chapter 3. The arguments to be tested are first modeled, the models are then expressed in terms amenable to quantitative methods (for example, multivariate regression), and the subsequent equations are estimated based on the best available data from the largest possible sample. However, one twist on the research design from Chapter 3 will be introduced, a change suggested by the prior quantitative studies on aid and rights reviewed in this chapter. At the proper stage in the tests, outliers will be excluded from the sample in order to give us a more accurate picture of the norm in the relationship between aid and rights in the Third World.

These tests assume that levels of aid are the independent variables and levels of human rights are the dependent variables. That is to say, human rights are conceptualized as something that changes as a result of changes in aid. Human rights as a function of foreign aid is the relationship expressed by hypothesis H1 in Figure 4.2. More detailed variations of this same basic relationship are presented in hypotheses H2 through H8 (see Figure 4.2). Hypothesis H2 conceptualizes human rights in the Third

World as a function of aid plus level of economic development. Controlling for economic development helps to prevent spurious conclusions based on the aid and human rights data. Hypothesis H3a reflects this model in the area of first generation civil-political rights, while H3b models the variables in the area of second generation socioeconomic rights (as measured by the Physical Quality of Life Index, or PQLI). Hypotheses H4 through H8 are the final models to be tested. In each of the last five hypotheses, economic development is operationalized as GNP per capita, and aid is disaggregated into economic aid and military assistance. H4 through H8 also disaggregate human rights into either Freedom House rankings for civil liberties and political rights or into the constituent parts of the PQLI (adult illiteracy rates, infant mortality rates per 1,000 live births, and life expectancy at age one). Readers will recall that these are the same variables introduced in Chapter 3. They proved useful when testing theories of investment and human rights. The same variables from the same sources will also serve to test arguments linking aid to human rights in LDCs. The new data employed here are the numbers for

FIGURE 4.2
Modeling the Relationship between Aid and Human Rights

H1:	HR	= f (aid)
H2:	HR	= f (development + aid)
H3a:	C/P	= f (development + aid)
H3b:	PQLI	= f (development + aid)
H4:	CL	= GNP + ECONAID + MILTAID
H5:	PR	= GNP + ECONAID + MILTAID
H6:	ILLIT	= GNP + ECONAID + MILTAID
H7:	INFMOR	= GNP + ECONAID + MILTAID
H8:	LIFEXP	= GNP + ECONAID + MILTAID

HR	= human rights
C/P	= rankings of civil liberties and political rights by Freedom House
PQLI	= physical quality of life index from the Overseas Development Council
GNP	= gross national product per capita
ILLIT	= illiteracy rate of adult population
INFMOR	= infant mortlity per 1,000 live births
LIFEXP	= life expectancy at age one
ECONAID	= total U.S. economic aid
MILTAID	= total U.S. military aid

economic and military aid.[7] Chapter 3 data on aid were for economic aid alone. Here the tests will compare the distinct impact on rights that comes from each type of aid.

The samples of Third World nations used here and the basic techniques for drawing those samples are also carried over from Chapter 3. The data are drawn from the period 1983 to 1990. This is almost identical to the period discussed by Poe and others (their timeframe was 1983–91; see Poe et al., [1994]). As was the case for the MNC model, the aid model will also be tested over time. The first tests look at the aid model for the years from 1983 (for the independent variables) to 1985 (for the dependent variables). A second set of tests looks at the aid model for the years from 1987 (independent variables) to 1990 (dependent variables). The two year or three year time lags between variables are important, and reflect the methodology employed by Poe (1994) and by Doran (1978). Doran has offered the most fully developed articulation for use of such time lags (see 1978: 445), a defense that I shall not try to recreate here.[8]

The samples contain LDCs from all regions of the Third World. The larger sample (Table 4.1) represents slightly less than half of all LDCs. Problems with availability of data preclude taking a random sample that has sufficient size for testing. Data collection began by gathering information on all 88 LDCs for which Freedom House, the World Bank (PQLI variables) and AID (economic and military aid) publish data. I sought to make the study as inclusive as possible. Listwise deletion was used to eliminate cases with missing data for any single variable. There are sound statistical reasons for using listwise deletion. I chose not to substitute alternative indicators for missing data as has been commonly done in many prior studies using multiple regression (see Poe and Tate, 1994 as an example). The sampling for this study was done in 1992–93, at which time the most recent available data were from the year 1990 (for the dependent variables). I also went back five years to 1985 data (dependent variables) for a second sample. Comparing results from the 1985 and the 1990 data will allow for conclusions as to whether the trends in the data hold up over time. Also, although not a simple random sample, this group of LDCs is large enough and diverse enough to allow for robust testing. Conclusions drawn from these samples, therefore, will be discussed in regard to the Third World as a whole.

Parameter estimates for the equations that test hypotheses H4 and H5 are contained in Table 4.1.[9] Table 4.1 represents that stage referred to in the prior literature as gatekeeping. This is the first stage at which one inquires into the relationship between human rights and U.S. aid for all

Third World nations, whether they receive U.S. aid or not, and regardless of the levels of economic or military aid that they might receive. The sample of LDCs in Table 4.1 contains 42 or 46 nations, depending on the year.[10]

Results from the first test contained in Table 4.1 show a positive relationship between economic aid from the U.S. and civil-political rights in Third World nations. As economic aid increases across these samples of 40-plus LDCs, political rights and civil liberties also increase. This is true for both periods, 1985 and 1990. Furthermore, these relationships are statistically significant at less than a .05 level (two-tailed test), allowing us to reject the null hypothesis of no relationship between aid and rights. The tie from economic aid to civil and political rights in the Third World is significant and consistent over time (from 1985 to 1990). Therefore, the positive relationship between economic assistance and civil-political rights is a generalization that most likely applies to all LDCs as a group. Throughout the Third World, an increase in U.S. economic aid is likely to be associated with improvements in first generation rights during subsequent years.

TABLE 4.1
Aid and Civil-Political Rights

	PR85	CL85	PR90	CL90
GNP	0.39†	0.40†	0.42†	0.43†
Standardized	0.0005†	0.0004†	0.001†	0.0007†
(t-ratio)	(2.72)	(2.89)	(3.16)	(3.20)
ECONAID	0.77*	0.90*	0.62*	0.50*
standardized	0.009*	0.008*	0.008*	0.004*
(t-ratio)	(2.05)	(2.47)	(2.50)	(1.98)
MILTAID	−0.63	−0.74*	−0.46	−0.29
standarized	−0.005	−0.005*	−0.005	−0.002
(t-ratio)	(1.70)	(2.05)	(1.85)	(1.15)
N	42	42	46	46
R^2	.18	.22	.23	.22

$* = p < .05$
$† = p < .01$

The data also show that development stands in the same relationship to human rights as does economic aid. Increased GNP per capita is associated with improving civil-political rights for Third World nations in both the 1980s and 1990s. Here the data also reveal statistical significance in the parameter estimates for development measured as GNP per capita.

Military aid is quite a different story. Military aid is inversely related to levels of rights in Table 4.1. The negative impact of military assistance on civil and political freedoms is consistent over time. It is also statistically significant when compared to civil liberties in 1985. Because the trends are consistent over time, it would appear that military aid is clearly a negative factor for first generation rights in the Third World as a whole.

What about aid and second generation rights? Measures for the PQLI were left out of Table 4.1 because, in these larger samples, almost none of them showed up as statistically significant in relation to U.S. economic or military aid.[11] Because of this nonfinding between both types of aid and socioeconomic rights at the gatekeeping stage, one might simply assume that the null hypothesis holds in this case. Perhaps there is simply no connection between U.S. aid and welfare rights in LDCs. On the other hand, it may be that we have yet to look hard enough to specify this relationship properly. In an effort to leave no stone unturned, and seeking a best-case test,[12] the tests must proceed beyond the gatekeeping stage. Stage two of these tests examines smaller samples that exclude those states that received no U.S. aid and also excludes a notable outlier.

Table 4.2 presents the data for U.S. economic and military aid in relation to second generation rights for the smaller samples. Table 4.2 goes beyond the gatekeeping stage. These samples eliminate all LDCs that received no aid. Also omitted is the most significant outlier, Egypt. Aid to Egypt (approximately $2 billion per year) is so much larger than aid to any other developing nation that inclusion of Egypt can tend to skew the distribution in any quantitative study of foreign aid. Hence, to omit Egypt is consistent with the precedent set in prior quantitative studies of aid and rights that argue against inclusion of outliers. Finally, and following Gerner (1988), I eliminated from this final model all nations that did not obtain substantial amounts of U.S. aid. I have defined substantial aid as assitance in excess of $1 million per year.[13]

When looking at the data from the final model in this series of tests, one finds that there is a significant relationship between both types of aid and the PQLI in Third World nations that receive substantial aid. Putting the floor for aid in this final test at $1 million per year eliminates from the discussion those LDCs that are granted only nominal economic assistance, and those LDCs that are included in International Military Education and

TABLE 4.2
Aid and Socioeconomic Rights

	INFMOR85	ILLIT85	LIFEXP85	INFMOR90	ILLIT90	LIFEXP90
GNP	−0.75*	−0.83*	0.88†	−0.67*	−0.49	0.71*
standardized	−0.06*	−0.05*	0.01†	−0.05*	−0.03	0.02*
(t-ratio)	(3.33)	(3.45)	(3.56)	(2.45)	(1.54)	(2.70)
ECONAID	−1.04*	−0.97*	0.43	−0.33	−0.24	0.32
standardized	−0.33*	−0.24*	0.03	−0.07	−0.04	0.02
(t-ratio)	(3.41)	(2.90)	(1.25)	(1.22)	(0.77)	(1.25)
MILTAID	1.22†	0.77*	−0.27	0.34	0.04	−0.15
standardized	0.31†	0.15*	−0.01	0.07	0.04	−0.01
(t-ratio)	(3.95)	(2.26)	(0.78)	(1.23)	(0.15)	(0.58)
N	10	10	10	11	11	11
R^2	0.73	0.68	0.66	0.46	0.27	0.51

* = $p < .05$
† = $p < .01$

Training aid only.[14] Nations in the more generous Foreign Military Financing program, or nations in both the FMF and IMET aid pools remain as part of the smaller samples. Table 4.2 shows that, in the sample of nations receiving substantial aid, both increased GNP and increased economic aid across the samples are associated with better social and economic rights. As GNP or economic assistance increases, illiteracy and infant mortality both decline and life expectancy improves. The tie between development (GNP) and rights is generally significant and consistent over time. The tie between economic aid and socioeconomic rights is also consistent over time. Furthermore, the tests show that statistically significant declines in both mortality rates and illiteracy are associated with increased economic aid during the 1980s. This strengthens the case for rejecting the null hypothesis and tends to indicate that economic aid helps to improve welfare rights in all nations that are lucky enough to receive substantial levels of assistance.

The results from Table 4.2 are also very revealing in regard to the connection between substantial military aid and socioeconomic rights. The impact of military aid runs in exactly the opposite direction. Increased military aid across these samples is associated with declining levels of second generation rights. As military aid goes up, infant mortality and illiteracy also increase and life expectancy declines. Once again, these relationships are consistent over time (from 1985 to 1990). Once again, the variables load significantly for mortality and illiteracy rates in the 1980s.

The combined results presented in Tables 4.1 and 4.2 allow for some generalizations about aid and rights. Development as measured via GNP per capita tends to produce increases in both first and second generation rights in the Third World (a finding consistent with the results of Chapter 3). Increases in U.S. economic aid are likewise associated with enhanced civil-political rights in all LDCs, and economic aid has a similar positive impact on socioeconomic rights in those developing nations that are granted substantial assistance. Conversely, military aid is negatively associated with first generation rights at the gatekeeping stage (that is, in all LDCs), and military aid is also inversely related to welfare rights in those Third World nations that are showered with substantial security assistance.

AID, INVESTMENT, AND HUMAN RIGHTS

Here I will seek to summarize and restate the combined results from the tests in Chapters 3 and 4. This is done with an eye toward the final steps in the arguments laid out in this text.

Total foreign aid plus total foreign investment flowing into the Third World since 1950 (from all donors combined) adds up to more than $1 trillion. This number is staggering. On the face of it, such external economic inputs would be expected to produce some kind of domestic political and social outputs within the Third World. It would be naive to assume that moneys in these quantities would not have some sort of impact on mechanisms of repression and social welfare. The political economy of first and second generation rights in LDCs is necessarily linked to these external inputs. The domestic outputs are best summarized by discussing them in relation to the individual determinants of rights considered by this study: economic development, direct foreign investment, economic aid, and military aid.

All tests from both chapters show that with increased economic development comes improvement in human rights. These results are consistent with classical democratic theory and conform to the predictions of early post–World War II theories of development. It has long been argued that enhanced economic production in any nation will eventually lead to a larger middle class, if development can be sustained over the long run. Democratic theory and developmental theory both argue that a rising middle class will tend to enhance political stability and social tolerance. Results presented here could be interpreted as lending credence to those views.

Futhermore, direct foreign investment and economic aid both follow this same general pattern. As DFI increases across Third World nations, first and second generation rights tend to get better (see Chapter 3). Similarly, with increased economic aid comes better first generation rights, and with substantial amounts of foreign economic aid (more than $1 million per year) comes better second generation rights.

Military aid stands as the lone villain in this scenario. Increased levels of military aid across LDCs are associated with declining levels of civil and political rights. Military aid has an intimate relationship with repression in the Third World. This, perhaps, is not surprising. Even more notable in some ways is the connection between substantial military aid (greater than $1 million per year) and declining levels of socioeconomic rights within the United States' major security assistance clients. Here one can find evidence that the militarization of an LDC political economy via foreign security aid serves to endanger social welfare. Militarization draws resources away from programs for education, health, and social welfare. Militarization steers more of the limited internal and external funding available for LDCs into the military industrial complex of developing nations. The long-term results of these trends are becoming all too evident in post–Cold War failed states, such as Liberia, Somalia, and Zaire.

Tentative conclusions suggest themselves at this point. DFI and substantial economic aid are elements of the international political economy that, if available, bode well for better human rights in LDCs.[15] Furthermore, military aid, especially in large amounts, should be avoided by Third World governments as a threat to their liberties, rights, and national well-being.

Such generalizations are revealing, but they still do not tell us enough about the internal machinations of Third World rights as a function of foreign economic inputs. To specify the differences between Third World nations and to detail the relevant policy alternatives open to LDC governments, one must turn to a different level of analysis. This book will now move to a series of case studies that seeks to flesh out the details of the international political economy of human rights in Third World nations. Three states are especially indicative of the global trends. Three newly industrialized countries of the developing world have, in the decades of the 1970s, 1980s, and 1990s, experimented with almost the entire range of policy options. Chile, India, and Mexico have (as a group) run the entire gamut in the post–World War II era from strident economic nationalism to more recent policies of wide open environments for foreign corporations. These three nations have used, at different times, policies that range from nationalization of foreign investment to virtually no restrictions on foreign corporations. The research of this text has reached the stage at which studies of U.S. MNCs in particular LDCs have become necessary.

The case studies themselves will then lead in turn to a concluding chapter that will pull together what has been learned from the various conceptual, philosophical, foreign policy, quantitative, and case study analyses of this book. Included in the final chapter are some ruminations about the nature of modern social sciences and the ability of social science to test adequately or to explain sufficiently the causes and effects of human rights in developing nations.

NOTES

1. This is a fact that is normally lost on those politicians and voters who see aid as merely a handout for LDCs.

2. The OECD includes the advanced industrialized nations of North America, Western Europe, and Asia.

3. "U.S. to Reduce Foreign Aid," *Los Angeles Times*, March 12, 1996.

4. I have not sought to present a comprehensive review of quantitative studies of aid. Rather, I will summarize certain seminal and representative articles, especially those studies that are most relevant to the analyses that follow.

5. The nations studied in AI's 1995 report are Bolivia, Brazil, Chad, Colombia, Egypt, Ghana, Indonesia, Israel, Kenya, Pakistan, Peru, Philippines, Saudi Arabia, South Africa, South Korea, Thailand, Tunisia, Turkey, and Venezuela.

6. The 1961 FAA is the governing legislation for foreign aid.

7. Data on civil liberties and political rights are from Gastil at Freedom House, *Freedom in the World* (1985, 1990); data on GNP are measured per capita and are also from Freedom House; data on illiteracy, infant mortality, and life expectancy are from the *World Development Report* published by the World Bank (1985, 1990); and data on economic and military aid for all years are from AID, *U.S. Overseas Loans and Grants* (1993).

8. See also Chapter 3, note 11 for a discussion of testing with lagged variables.

9. For the sake of simplicity and brevity, translation of hypotheses H4 through H8 into differential equations has not been presented in this chapter. Instead, I proceed directly from the hypotheses themselves to the presentation of the parameter estimates. See Figure 3.4 for an example of the step omitted here. Also, tabular presentation of the statistics for foreign aid and human rights in this chapter does not use the same format as that used in Chapter 3. Instead, here I present the data in a manner akin to the tables found in the prior quantitative studies of aid and rights that were reviewed in this chapter (Poe et al., and so forth).

10. Nations in the sample for 1985 (N = 42): Bangladesh, Burundi, Cameroon, Central African Republic, Chad, Colombia, Costa Rica, Dominican Republic, Ecuador, El Salvador, Gabon, Ghana, Haiti, Honduras, India, Indonesia, Jordan, Kenya, Liberia, Malaysia, Morocco, Nepal, Niger, Pakistan, Panama, Paraguay, Peru, Philippines, Rwanda, Senegal, Sierra Leone, Somalia, Sudan, Thailand, Togo, Tunisia, Turkey, Uganda, Uruguay, Venezuela, Zaire, and Zimbabwe. The 1990 sample (N = 46) includes all of the above nations and the additional states: Guatamala, Malawi, Mexico, and Singapore.

11. In the samples of 42 and 46 nations, from 1985 and 1990 (respectively), only life expectancy data for 1990 loaded as significant, and only in relation to economic aid. In other words, when testing for a tie between aid and the PQLI in the larger samples, LIFEXP 1990 alone was significant (and positive) in relation to economic (but not military) aid. Complete data are available from the author upon request.

12. See Chapter 3, note 2 for a definition of best-case testing.

13. Nations remaining in the smaller samples are: (1985, N = 10) Colombia, Costa Rica, El Salvador, Guatemala, Honduras, Liberia, Pakistan, Panama, Philippines, and Zaire; the 1990 sample in Table 4.2 (N = 11) includes the above ten nations plus Jordan. These are the nations of the Third World (along with

Egypt) listed as "primary aid recipients" by Hook (1995: 191). A sequence of regressions was run that winnowed down the samples until this final model of 10 or 11 nations was reached. First, the nations that received no aid were eliminated. Then Egypt was cut as being the most obvious outlier. In each successive iteration, parameters were checked for statistical significance and found wanting. In other words, elimination of LDCs without aid and elimination of Egypt resulted in no grounds on which to reject the null hypothesis of no relationship between aid and second generation rights. However, once nations with aid levels below $1 million were cut from the sample, the results were dramatically different. For the sake of simplicity, the tests that resulted in nonfindings have not been presented here. Again, complete data are available from the author on request.

14.   According to Hook, IMET funding is usually less than $1 million per year (1995: 126).

15.   The standard rejoinder to arguments about the beneficial impact of aid and investment is to point to the same external inputs as causes of increased dependency for Third World nations. I admit not having refuted these arguments about aid and investment as forms of neoimperialism. To test such arguments, however, would require the ability to measure levels of dependency in LDCs, and a subsequent comparison of levels of dependency to levels of aid and investment. Measuring dependency is a task that many have attempted but none, to my mind, has accomplished successfully. It may even be an impossible task (see, for example, Cardoso and Faletto, 1971: Preface). In any event, if aid and investment do lead to dependency, that possibility remains unchallenged by my research. However, given the post–Cold War global trends that exhibit a headlong rush by nearly all LDCs toward the liberal economic model of the West (see Chapter 5), I tend to agree with Hook that the alternatives to aid and investment preferred by neo-Marxist "structural critiques" have largely become moot in terms of their political relevance (1995: 38–40).

5

Case Studies of Multinational Corporations and Human Rights

THE AGGREGATION PROBLEM

An interesting critique of the research on multinational corporations (MNCs) and rights presented in Chapter 3 has been offered by Morton E. Winston, professor of philosophy at The College of New Jersey and chair of the board of directors for Amnesty International USA. Winston presented this critique within the context of an address to Mobil Corporation's World Affairs meeting in 1996.[1] After a precis of the analyses and results from Chapter 3, Winston presented a critical review that advanced several arguments. First, he pointed out that the results from Chapter 3 show only correlations between MNCs and human rights but not causation. Results from Chapter 3 show that as direct foreign investment (DFI) by MNCs increases, first and second generation rights also tend to go up. However, these same results cannot be used to claim that increases in human rights are caused by increases in DFI. The nature of the statistical procedures used in Chapter 3 is such that one cannot necessarily infer causation from the covariance in the indicators for MNCs and rights. Winston then offered plausible but competing explanations for the positive relationship between human rights and DFI.

It could be that human rights are good for business. Perhaps a positive relationship exists between rights and DFI because Third World countries with greater political freedom and higher standards of welfare attract more corporate investment. If this were the case, then better human rights are the cause of increased business investment. Or it could be that business is good for human rights. This is what I referred to in Chapter 3 as the engines of development thesis. Perhaps increased investment leads to subsequent improvements in first and second generation rights. A third possibility is that these factors interact with each other; it may be that human rights are good for business, and business is good for human rights. Winston's first critique was simply to point out that the statistical information presented thus far cannot tell us with certainty which way the causal chain runs. In that respect, Winston is correct.

Winston's second critique is even more telling. Chapter 3 reveals the overall international trends between rights and investment. However, one cannot conclude, based on the evidence from Chapter 3, that any particular MNC will have a positive (or negative) effect on human rights in a given less developed country (LDC). According to Winston, the "fundamental problem with Meyer's approach . . . [is that] Meyer's model cannot distinguish between the MNCs that do, in fact, promote human rights and those which in fact do not."[2] Winston referred to this as the "aggregation problem."

Once again, Winston is right on the money in his critique of my work. He is also correct in his third and final point that corporations, like individuals, must be judged on the merits of their individual behavior. However, the deficiencies inherent in the cross-national study presented in Chapter 3, deficiencies that are highlighted by Winston's critique, are weaknesses that typify any study of that sort. Any quantitative study using multivariate regression to explain the variance in a given indicator (for example, levels of human rights) by means of fluctuations in another set of variables (for example, DFI or development) produces results that are properly understood only in terms of statistical correlation. Correlations, no matter how strong, are not the same thing as causal explanations. Because political scientists often slip from speaking of correlations into speaking about causality, we sometimes need to be alerted against committing this fallacy. Results from Chapter 3 were carefully stated with these considerations in mind.

More relevant to the subject of this chapter is Winston's second point. Chapter 3 was designed to show the overall trends between rights and MNCs across the samples of Third World nations. Knowledge of the overall trends is crucial to an adequate understanding of how MNCs affect human rights. Chapter 3 provides information along these lines that cannot be found in any other study of MNCs. Nor was such information to be found in any prior study of human rights and development in the Third World. However, Winston's point about the aggregation problem is still well taken. A cross-national study employing aggregate data is unable to speak to the impact of particular MNCs in particular nations. To understand the effect that a given corporation has on rights in a given nation requires that we go to a different level of analysis. The overall trends are important, because case studies alone could not tell us much about the relationship between rights and DFI at the global level. Hence the statistical analysis of Chapter 3 was a necessary but incomplete first step toward an adequate understanding of the ties between human rights and MNCs in Third World nations. One must move to the level of case studies to address Winston's useful critique regarding the positive or negative effects of individual MNCs.[3]

CASE STUDY SELECTION AND METHODOLOGY

The utility of case studies for political and economic research is necessarily connected to selecting the proper cases and analyzing those cases in a valid and appropriate manner. The cases studied here (India, Mexico, and Chile) are uniquely important for understanding the impact of MNCs on human rights in the Third World. They are important individually because of the lessons that can be learned from the particulars of each case. These three countries are also important as a group because of their similar positions within the Third World as a whole. All three are examples of newly industrialized countries (NICs). NICs are the "handful of less developed countries in Latin America and Asia experiencing rapid industrial growth and great success in exporting manufactured goods to advanced industrialized states" (Walters and Blake, 1992: 43). Examples of other NICs include Brazil, Singapore, South Korea, Taiwan, and the People's Republic of China province of Hong Kong.

Case studies of MNCs in the Third World must necessarily focus on NICs. These are the nations in the Third World that attract the lion's share of total DFI. These are also the nations that have had the longest history of dealing with and trying to control the pernicious effects of foreign MNCs. Little would be gained from studying nations that attract insubstantial amounts of DFI. Furthermore, NICs are those Third World nations that have had the opportunity to advance furthest along the learning curve that governments must travel in their dealings with international corporations. Hence, NICs as a group must be the primary focus of any study involving the political economy of MNCs and human rights. Beyond their collective identities as NICs, India, Mexico, and Chile are especially instructive for other reasons as well.

India is the Third World nation with the unfortunate distinction of having suffered the world's worst industrial accident, an accident that was caused by an MNC whose (majority) ownership was foreign. The disaster in Bhopal was an extreme case of human rights violations by an MNC. As such, the manner in which India's government sought to hold Union Carbide accountable for Bhopal, as well as subsequent Indian policy to regulate DFI and MNCs in general, stand as a key study of one NIC's attempt to mitigate the worst effects of MNC activities. MNCs in India are especially important if we are to understand the impact of multinationals on first generation rights (the right to life) and MNC impact on third generation rights (the right to a clean environment).

Mexico is that country of all the NICs that is being most rapidly integrated into the regional economic blocs that typify international trade in the post–Cold War era. As the newest member of the North American Free Trade Agreement (NAFTA), Mexico is experiencing an influx of DFI and new MNCs at an unprecedented rate. Successes and failures associated with Mexico's opening up to foreign MNCs as part of NAFTA (and NAFTA's precursors) stand as harbingers for the future of other LDCs seeking membership in a regional trade pact with the Organization for Economic Cooperation and Development (OECD) nations. The case of Mexico is especially informative in regard to problems caused by MNCs in the areas of second generation rights (workers' rights) and third generation environmental rights.

A final case study on Chile will aquaint us with the long history of MNC presence in a country with a turbulant political history. Allegations of antidemocratic activities by U.S. MNCs in Chile date back to the International Telephone and Telegraph (ITT) scandal of the early 1970s. The possible linkage between foreign corporations and internal sociopolitical repression in Chile warrants an investigation into MNC impact on first generation democratic rights and on second generation workers' rights.

For each case, I will summarize the foreign MNC presence, focusing mainly on U.S. MNCs. Government policy to regulate MNCs by each of the host nations will also be presented. The most obvious weakness of case studies in general is that they do not always lead to "reliable and valid statements of regularity about sets of cases" (Eckstein, 1975: 97). Therefore, I will be looking for patterns of human rights abuses by MNCs that exist across these individual case studies. I will also be looking for similarities and differences in how the respective governments have sought to deal with MNCs through public policy or through the courts.

One final point regarding selection of cases and case study methodology is in order. No doubt many readers have already noticed that the cases selected, even at a cursory glance, are nations whose experiences with MNCs tend to run counter to the findings of Chapter 3. The overall tendency found in Chapter 3 is for increases in DFI by MNCs to be associated with improvement in both first and second generation rights in the Third World. Data analysis from Chapter 3 confirms as much when it comes to the political economy of MNCs and rights in the Third World. However, the cases that have been selected for detailed study (India, Mexico, Chile) are ones in which violations of rights by U.S. MNCs have either been patently obvious or long suspected by critics of U.S. businesses. This is not by accident. I have intentionally selected case studies that will focus on allegations of harm done by U.S. MNCs.

I have three reasons for concentrating the case studies on nations where there is the most prima facie evidence of human rights abuses. First, I wanted to subject the conclusions drawn in Chapter 3, conclusions that are based on broad statistical measures, to the toughest possible test. I have sought out case histories with the potential to present counterevidence to the results of Chapter 3. I do so not in order to refute my own findings. I stand by the analysis presented in Chapter 3, including the conclusions I have inferred from my data. The overall trends linking MNC investment to human rights are beneficial for the Third World as a whole. This does not mean, however, that MNC presence in LDCs is always and uniformly beneficial. To be as unbiased as possible, my case study evidence will consider the most notable exceptions to the rule.

A second reason for focusing on the particular cases discussed here is to overcome Winston's aggregation problem. The broad positive impact of MNC investment on rights in LDCs is an observation valid only when discussing MNCs as a group. To disaggregate requires that I address particular MNCs in particular Third World nations. However, the lower level studies will not be designed as a way to merely confirm the conclusions of Chapter 3. I will not be looking primarily for examples of beneficial behavior by MNCs. Rather, as a way to present a more balanced picture in this book as a whole, the disaggregated analyses will seek to emphasize what the conclusion of Chapter 3 tends to downplay: likely violations of human rights due to MNC activities.

Finally, and in a more theoretical vein, I will be conducting what Lijphart (1971) has termed "theory infirming" case studies. In a seminal article, Lijphart developed a useful typology for case studies. A theory infirming study is one that uses case studies to raise doubts about a theory's validity, although theory infirming studies alone cannot refute any theory in its entirety (Collier, 1993: 106). The theory in question is the engines of development thesis. Aggregate data from a set of more than 50

LDCs provided evidence that tended to confirm the engines of development view. Having presented that confirmation of the theory at the broad international level, I now propose to undermine the same theory by presenting case study evidence to the contrary. I seek to infirm at the national level the very theory I confirmed earlier at the international level.

No doubt it may strike many readers as counterintuitive to claim that a theory can be confirmed at one level while being discomfirmed to some extent at another level of analysis. How can this be? Is Meyer contradicting himself? The short answer to this question is simply no. I am not contradicting myself, nor am I especially concerned if the case study evidence runs contrary to the aggregate, cross-national data. In fact, I would be more concerned about the validity of my own work if all the evidence I produced at all levels of analysis was consistent in every respect and always mutually reinforcing. However, a longer and more detailed discussion of the inconsistencies separating Chapter 3 from the case studies is also in order. I choose to present this longer defense of my work after presenting the case studies themselves. Chapter 6 will include an explanation of how and why the infirming results of the case studies do not necessarily refute the confirming results of Chapter 3. The coexistence of both confirming and infirming evidence is the most likely outcome from comprehensive testing of any theory as broad as the engines of development thesis.

INDIA: BHOPAL AND BEYOND

Government Regulation of Multinational Corporations Prior to Bhopal

In 1984, Bhopal, India was subjected to the worst industrial accident in history. Any consideration of human rights and MNCs in India must focus on the many dimensions of the Bhopal disaster. The plant in Bhopal is a majority-owned subsidiary of Union Carbide (UC). UC is headquartered in Danbury, Connecticut. UC owns 51 percent of Union Carbide of India (UCI), the subsidiary with responsibility for day-to-day operation of the plant. Estimates of those killed in Bhopal as a direct result of the 1984 disaster run between 2,000 and 10,000 (Bogard, 1989: viii). Personal injuries from the accident may have exceeded 300,000 (1989: viii). Toxic substances released during the disaster continued to do damage to the local environment well into the 1990s.[4]

The massive death toll, the injuries to hundreds of thousands of victims, and the environmental destruction wrought in Bhopal are, when stated in the terminology used in this study, egregious violations of fundamental rights. The right to life and the right to a clean environment are basic human rights that were contravened by the persons and corporate agents responsible for the disaster. The horrors of Bhopal, however, must also be understood within the larger context of MNCs and government policy in India. Prior to a discussion of the disaster itself, I will summarize government-MNC relations in India in the years leading up to the disaster.

India achieved its independence from Britain in 1947. In the years that immediately followed independence, the Indian government pursued a developmental strategy based on government control, government intervention, prohibitions on direct foreign investment, and government domination of planning and investment (Das, 1997: 104). The goal of this strategy was to promote import substitution industry (ISI). ISI was a developmental alternative championed by the United Nations Conference on Trade and Development (UNCTAD) and by its first secretary-general, Raul Prebisch (Walters and Blake, 1992: 45). UNCTAD was the voice of the Third World during the early post-colonial era when it came to the international politics of trade and investment. UNCTAD and India were among the strongest supporters of ISI. ISI strategies sought to create indigenous industries within Third World nations that could produce locally manufactured substitutes for those items that the Third World had imported during colonial rule. Although there was a large private industrial sector in India, the government also relied heavily on five-year plans and "considerable regulatory control," including creation of state-owned enterprises (SOEs), and tight regulation of DFI from foreign companies (Marton, 1986: 225). Government permission and industrial licenses were required before foreign corporations could start production in India. The government even went so far as to set production capacity for individual enterprises (1986: 225).

In 1956 India adopted the Industrial Policy Resolution. This act of parliament closed off many economic sectors to foreign MNCs altogether. SOEs were given exclusive access to key economic sectors. The goal of this policy was self-sufficiency for India's core industrial base. Some 17 core industries were reserved for SOEs. After 1956 these areas included steel, oil, drugs and pharmaceuticals, heavy electrical or mechanical equipment, and machine tools (Marton, 1986: 226–28). In 1969 India's banks were nationalized, enabling the government to control credit power according to its perceptions of national priorities. In 1970 government control of the economy was expanded into the consumer goods sector as well (1986: 226–28).

Regulation of foreign investment displayed a "high degree of selectivity" regarding those MNCs allowed into India (Marton, 1986: 228). Policy focused on acquisition of certain advanced technologies. Industrial licensing was used to regulate production levels and expansion of MNCs (1986: 228–29). This early period of India's development strategies culminated in the Foreign Exchange Regulation Act (FERA) of 1973, which gave sweeping new powers to the Indian government in its campaign to control foreign MNCs.

Marton provides an excellent summary of the provisions of the 1973 FERA (1986: 229 ff.). FERA required that all MNCs obtain permission from the Reserve Bank of India for their operations in India. Three levels of entry were allowed: 40 percent, 51 percent, and 74 percent. MNCs already in India in 1973 could retain a majority share in their enterprise only by bringing in sophisticated technology or by exporting more than 40 percent of production. Most MNCs in India could not (or would not) meet these requirements, and therefore were forced to reduce their ownership to less than 40 percent of total equity. Many MNCs disinvested in order to meet the requirement of a 40 percent maximum share. Others, such as IBM and Coca-Cola, pulled out of India altogether rather than diluting their equity shares to less than 40 percent (MacDonald, 1992: 40). The overall effect of FERA was to create a net outflow of capital from India and to drive MNCs out of low-tech production (Encarnation, 1989). After FERA, foreign-owned MNC subsidiaries in India dropped from a high of 188 in 1974 to only 111 in 1981 (Marton, 1986: 229).

MNCs that wanted to retain more than 50 percent equity in their operations after 1973 (for example, UC's plant in Bhopal) were required to make "major new investments and expansions in core or priority industries" (Marton, 1986: 230). This requirement was most often met by diversification of production. For example, "Union Carbide expanded its production activities to new chemical products" (1986: 230). The pesticide plant in Bhopal, which started operations in 1969, diversified production to allow UC to retain majority ownership under FERA guidelines.

Such was Indian policy on MNCs and foreign investment prior to the 1984 disaster at Bhopal. It was a strategy based on ISI, FERA restrictions on DFI, and "Indianization" of the economy (Encarnation, 1989: 81). Marton concludes her review of this policy phase with the following observations: "Thus largely as a result of the government's selective policy toward direct foreign investment inflow, and the rather rigorous regulatory measures applied to such companies, the role of foreign subsidiaries has remained far more limited in India than in other developing countries with similar growth . . . in Mexico, with a much smaller economy, they [DFI flows] are about five times higher" (Marton, 1986: 230–31).

A comparative perspective on India's developmental strategy prior to 1984, such as Marton provides in the above quote, is important. During this period, DFI into Mexico was five times greater than DFI into India. DFI flowing into Brazil during the same period was ten times greater than in India (Marton, 1986: 230–31). India was unique in that, of the Third World NICs, it adopted policies that kept the tightest reins on Western MNCs. India used a highly restrictive approach to MNCs and DFI as a means to promote its self-sufficiency and as a way to protect the best interests of its people. India used controls on foreign investment and foreign technology in order to prevent MNCs from exploiting its citizens. "India was the first among developing countries to control the inflow of foreign technology [and DFI], and has the most experience with such measures" (1986: 231).

It is ironic, therefore, that India, which had the most experience in dealing with MNCs as well as the most restrictive approach to DFI after independence, should also be the Third World country to suffer from the worst industrial disaster, a disaster involving a Western MNC. Even given its wealth of knowledge in regulating foreign MNCs, and in spite of its tight control over MNC operations, India's government was unable to prevent the tragedy in Bhopal.

The Bhopal Disaster

On December 2, 1984, employees discovered a methyl isocyanate (MIC) leak at 11:30 p.m. in the UCI plant in Bhopal. MIC was used to create pesticides at the Bhopal plant. Intensive use of pesticides was part of the agricultural policies of the green revolution, policies designed to produce significant and rapid increases in crop yields for Third World nations. The plant supervisor on duty at the time, believing it was most likely a water leak, postponed investigation of the problem until after his work break was over. By the time action was taken, it was too late to prevent a catastrophe.

Bogard lists a series of factors that interacted to turn the MIC leak into a major disaster. These factors have to do with the interrelated failures of several distinct procedures and safety systems:

1. A refrigeration unit designed to inhibit dangerous chemical reactions in the storage tanks had been shut down months before the accident for cost-cutting reasons.

2. A vent scrubber designed to detoxify escaping gases was inoperative.

3. Water spouts intended to neutralize MIC vapor by transforming it into relatively safe organic compounds failed.

4. A 30 meter high flare tower designed to burn toxic gases high in the air, rendering them harmless, was ineffective.

5. A spare tank built to hold an accidental release of MIC was full at the time of the leak and could not be used.

6. Instruments at the plant for detecting pressure and temperature levels were unreliable.

7. There was a lack of redundancy measures (automatic shutoffs, alarm systems, etc.) that might have detected the gas leak before it spread beyond the plant.

8. Pipes at the MIC production unit had been cleaned by an improperly trained technician, possibly introducing a small amount of water into the MIC storage tank, and then causing an unstable chemical reaction.

9. Finally, shortly after the disaster, UC claimed that they believed the leak may have been caused by the deliberate sabotage of a disgruntled employee (Bogard, 1989: 3–4).

Bogard's investigation of the Bhopal disaster considers this case within the larger context of hazards created in the Third World by modern industry. Bogard defines a hazard as an accident waiting to happen (1989: 52). He is concerned with the larger problem of hazards in general because "at a global level, hazardousness and vulnerability to hazards appear to be increasing" (1989: 65). This is especially true in Third World nations as an indirect result of attracting Western MNCs. Bhopal is Bogard's key case for study because it is the worst example of what is a growing international trend.[5]

During initial construction and licensing of the Bhopal plant, the hazards of pesticide production were "redefined" by UC to focus on the plant's "mitigative potential" (Bogard, 1989: 50). UC's corporate attitude was one of calculated risks. UC convinced the Indian government that the economic and agricultural benefits from pesticide production would far outweigh the dangers of the productive process itself. They stressed to Indian officials the benefits that chemical manufacture would create in regard to increased food supplies, economic growth, and modernization.

Little information was given to residents near the plant about the possible dangers. Alarms were installed in the plant but, prior to December 1984, they went off so frequently that residents came to ignore them. Residents did not know how to protect themselves in the event of a real disaster. Few of them knew that a simple damp cloth placed over the face could have saved them from lethal exposure at the time of the 1984 leak (Bogard, 1989: 21).

UC chose not to distribute such information to residents of Bhopal and preferred instead to consistently downplay the hazards of chemical production. Bogard charges that the executives of Union Carbide were guilty of "technocratic arrogance." He claims that UC officials simply assumed the Indian public to be ignorant and politically apathetic. UC seemed to assume that if the public were told of the risks at all, then the masses would tend to overreact and overestimate the dangers (Bogard, 1989: 121). Therefore, the public was not informed of the hazards necessarily associated with the UCI plant, nor were the people included in "decisions which fundamentally affected their well-being" (1989: 121). The participatory rights of India's people were largely ignored in order to reduce possible opposition to the plant.

There were a few attempts by India's media to alert the residents of Bhopal to the dangers of the plant. In 1982 a local journalist warned the townspeople that UCI had not experienced one accident-free year since its opening (Manning, 1985: 54). He stressed the fact that, in 1981, a leak of phosgene gas had caused 1 death and 24 injuries. In 1983 yet another gas leak warning went unheeded (Ram, 1984). By the time the major disaster hit in December 1984, the people of Bhopal were almost powerless to cope with its effects.

The effects of the disaster were horrific. Approximately 1,500 people died within three days of the MIC leak.[6] By 1994 the death toll had climbed to 7,000, including those who perished due to the effects of long-term exposure to MIC.[7] Survivors of the disaster suffered injuries akin to those inflicted upon soldiers exposed to chemical warfare. The most common injuries were to the eyes and the lungs. Burning, inflammation, and watering of eyes, partial blindness, cataracts, and respiratory failure were prevalent. Neuromuscular symptoms included weakness of muscles and loss of coordination. Vomiting, diarrhea, and abdominal pain were common.[8] Doctors also found injuries to kidneys, livers, and immune systems.[9]

Women and children were especially hard hit. Fully 93 percent of the children affected by the gas had damage to their lungs. Spontaneous abortions and infant death rates were ten times greater in Bhopal than in other parts of India for almost a decade following the disaster.[10] Gynecological problems included excessive vaginal discharge and irregularities in menstrual cycles, with some women having four to five periods per month. Lactating women experienced a decrease in milk output, a change in the taste of their milk, and infants with a loss of appetite. Women who were pregnant at the time of the MIC leak suffered from retarded uterine growth, indicating that fetuses were not growing normally.[11]

Environmental destruction from the toxic gases has also been a direct result of the Bhopal disaster. Studies have found higher than normal levels of thiocyanates in the residents of Bhopal. High thiocyanate levels are indicative of chronic cyanide ingestion. These findings suggest that MIC may have been partially converted to cyanide and then to thiocyanate. High thiocyanate levels are also persistent in Bhopal's water. Chronic ingestion of high levels of thiocyanate may reduce thyroid gland function, because these chemicals are known to block the thyroid gland. Of 250,000 Bhopal residents believed to have been directly exposed to MIC, 44,000 suffered from moderate medical disabilities, and 63,000 suffered severe medical disabilities.[12]

Altogether, 65,000 people filed lawsuits in Indian and U.S. courts against UC as a result of the Bhopal disaster. Some 14,000 of these suits sought compensation for the loss of a family member.[13] UC's lawyers tried unsuccessfully to get all lawsuits in both countries dismissed. The government of India sought $3.3 billion in total damages. In June 1985, UC offered $100 million in compensation to families of the deceased. Certificates of death were required to receive compensation. Inaccurate medical records excluded many names from the death toll. There were no post-mortem records for hundreds of casualties who had been cremated immediately after the disaster. Furthermore, many families complained that medical authorities demanded bribes before they would write gas-related causes into the death certificates (Singh, 1985).

As the court cases progressed, UC tried to deny all responsibility for the disaster. Warren Anderson, UC's chief executive officer at the time of the leak, claimed that UCI was responsible because: "Compliance with safety procedures is a local issue."[14] UC's lawyers also argued that India's government (which owns 26 percent of the plant) was guilty of contributory negligence because its licensing, inspection, zoning, and land use policies added to the severity of the accident (the plant is located in a heavily populated area within the municipal limits of Bhopal). UC had collaborated with UCI in the design and operation of the plant, but UC argued, in its own defense, that UCI had not used the design package recommended by UC, and that UCI had direct control over management of plant operations at all times.

By the end of 1985 a compromise was reached regarding legal jurisdiction in the case. All lawsuits would be heard in India's courts first, but all cases would also be subject to appeal in the United States. In 1989,

India's Supreme Court set total compensation from UC at $470 million. The Court dropped murder charges that had been filed against Anderson after the accident. The court also refused to grant Anderson immunity from prosecution, one of the terms that UC demanded as part of any settlement.

In 1992 India's Supreme Court approved the transfer of $470 million from UC to welfare offices in the Indian government for subsequent distribution. Also in 1992 a court in Bhopal filed manslaughter charges against Anderson and began extradiction proceedings. Although the United States and India do have a mutual extradition treaty, the United States has never agreed to extradiction in Anderson's case. In 1993, the court in Bhopal filed manslaughter charges against eight local Indian officials employed by UCI, but none of these individuals has ever been brought to trial. The compensation process has also been bogged down with what seems to be an endless series of legal delays and bureaucratic red tape. More than a decade has passed since the tragedy in Bhopal, and most victims still have not received compensation.

Multinational Corporations in India after Bhopal

Given the massive destruction caused by the disaster in Bhopal, and given that the human and environmental traumas from the MIC leak are still evident to this day, one might expect the government of India to be even less open to MNCs coming into its country in the post-Bhopal era. In fact, just the opposite is the case. In the 1990s, India adopted an open door approach to DFI and foreign MNCs. Among the many U.S. MNCs now operating in India are: Amoco, B.F. Goodrich, Colgate, Dow Chemicals, DuPont, Ford, General Electric (GE), General Motors (GM), IBM, Kaiser, Kelloggs, Merck, Pepsi, Phillips Petroleum, Proctor & Gamble, Siemens, and Unilever. This is just a sampling, not a comprehensive listing. In all, more than 2 dozen U.S. MNCs are in India today. Foreign MNCs are opening new operations at the rate of about 300 new projects per year in India (MacDonald, 1992: 40).

Why would India open up to MNCs in a big way, in spite of all that its people have suffered since 1984? The explanation for India's newfound attraction to DFI and MNCs involves both push and pull factors. Some reasons push MNCs to expand beyond their homes in OECD nations and into the Third World. Other reasons pull MNCs into India (and other NICs) because of new policies geared toward attracting DFI.

Bogard accounts for the rapid expansion of chemical MNCs into the Third World by invoking the analyses of dependency theory and Wallerstein's world systems theory (1979). The central argument of these theories is that the world is divided into a developed core of advanced industrialized nations (the OECD members of North America, Western Europe, and Japan), versus an economically depressed and politically weak periphery (the Third World). The world system has a single, integrated division of labor and capital that divides rich and poor states. In the relation between core and periphery, economic exchange becomes increasingly unequal (to the advantage of the core) and leads to underdevelopment and poverty in the periphery. Furthermore, production technologies within core countries, especially those that are hazardous and those that do harm to the environment, have come under increasing state regulation by core governments. These regulations drive up both the political and economic costs of production, creating falling rates of profit for production within the core. The result is to put mounting pressure on the MNCs who control such technologies to relocate production to states in the periphery. In the periphery, costs of production are lower because environmental regulation is less strict and labor rates are cheaper (Bogard, 1989: 91–93). MNCs are pushed out of the core and into the periphery, especially in regard to hazardous production, because of the rising costs of production in the core and because of the relative economic and political advantages gained by relocating to the periphery.

Bogard also points to the pull factors that promote MNC expansion into the Third World: "The states making up the periphery, in their desire to modernize, often see in these technologies the promise of economic benefits and the reduction of political pressures stemming from poverty and population problems" (Bogard, 1989: 93). India's policies on MNCs and DFI in the 1990s are an important example that tends to confirm the additional pull on MNCs promoted by NIC policies to attract investment and technology.

The first halting steps toward liberalization of DFI policy were taken by Prime Minister Rajiv Ghandi's administration in the 1980s. Ghandi's focus was primarily on advanced technologies and computerization (Das, 1997: 104). High-tech production was promoted by easing regulation of DFI in export processing zones (EPZs). Six new EPZs were created, and electronics industries were allowed to own up to 100 percent equity of new firms established inside the EPZs (Encarnation, 1989: 159). However, outside of the EPZs, strict control over DFI was still the rule. Government control over MNCs not in the EPZs remained so tight in the immediate post-Bhopal era (mid- to late-1980s) that India was hit with trade sanctions by the United States because of its restrictions on DFI. Consistent with the terms of the Trade Act of 1988, India was named as an unfair trader under section 301 of the U.S. trade bill (so-called Super

301). In May 1989, India was cited under Super 301 for restricting foreign investment (Subhash, 1993: 37). Super 301 then required mandatory trade sanctions, including tariffs of up to 100 percent on India's exports to the United States.

As a trade war between India and the United States heated up in the early 1990s, India also came up against a monetary crisis. Weakness of the Indian currency in international markets during 1991 brought India's economic problems to a head. The fall of the rupee on the international currency exchange was a problem that India's government lacked the resources to avoid. India did not have the hard currency to support the rupee, due at least in part to the nation's age-old policy of restricting foreign investment.

The economic crisis of 1991 was a watershed event in India's history. It forced a "major break with the past" (Das, 1997: 104). From 1991 to 1996, Prime Minister P. V. Narasimha Rao instituted a systematic process of liberalization and deregulation. He dismantled "the cobweb of controls" and created "space for investment and international trade" in India's economy (1997: 104). MNCs in the EPZs were given five-year exemptions from corporate income taxes. Other foreign corporations were granted tax cuts in the hope that this would enhance DFI and economic growth. Rao eliminated the shackles on MNCs contained in the notorious FERA of 1973: he removed the Reserve Bank of India's power to micromanage foreign MNCs; he gave MNCs the freedom to open branch offices without having to create independent subsidiaries; he opened virtually all industrial, commercial, and trading sectors to foreign investment; and he gave MNCs the right to use foreign brand names (for example, Pepsi) without requiring that they develop hybrid names especially for the Indian market (for example, Lehar-Pepsi), as they had been forced to do in years past (MacDonald, 1992: 40). Joint ventures between foreign MNCs and Indian partners were also liberalized under the new policies. The 40 percent equities were given automatic governmental approval to become 51 percent equities, and 51 percent equities became 74 percent or more (Das, 1997: 110).

These economic reforms stimulated rapid increases in U.S. direct investment into India. The rate of return on investments in India came to exceed returns on U.S. investments into similar industries in Canada (UNCTC, 1992). DFI from the United States into India rose from $350 million in 1990 to $2 billion in 1996 (Subhash, 1993; Haniffa, 1996). Estimates are that U.S. DFI in India by the year 2000 will be $10 billion or more.[15]

Economic reforms in India have revolutionized its policy on MNCs and DFI. The same policies, however, have also stimulated much debate and even some political backlash. Indian politics in the 1990s, and the policy debates over foreign corporations, have been conducted within a three-way split in the nation's body politic. The three major players in the dispute are the Congress Party, the Bharatiya Janata Party (BJP), and the socialists in the Janata Dal (or "people's party"). The Congress Party has ruled India for all but a few years since independence. It is the party of prime ministers Nehru, Ghandi, and Rao. The Congress Party created the anti-MNC policies of the 1973 FERA, but it is also the party that put India on the path toward liberalization by adopting MNC-friendly reforms under Rao.

Today Congress is the pro-DFI party in India. Its leaders believe that attracting DFI and MNCs will not compromise India's sovereignty.[16] However, Congress' move to a pro-DFI position has also cost it popular support. Congress lost control of India's parliament in the elections of 1996.

The BJP is Congress' principal opposition. BJP, a party of Hindu nationalists, prefers a go-slow approach to foreign investment. When the Congress Party adopted its pro-DFI reforms in the early 1990s, the BJP organized a "buy India first" campaign in response. The BJP also killed a major infrastructure deal negotiated by a U.S. MNC. Enron Corporation of Houston, Texas had its contract to build a power plant voided because of political opposition to the deal led by the BJP. A renegotiated contract forced Enron to cut the cost to India for the plant by $300 million.[17]

The BJP calls its philosophy on MNCs *Swadeshi*, which means self-reliance or the "India-can-do-it-spirit." *Swadeshi* was the "buzzword of the party during the Enron controversy."[18] According to the leader of the BJP, "We were opposed to Enron's earlier agreement . . . and got it cancelled, but worked with equal dedication to get a world class competitive deal from the same Enron."[19] The BJP's skepticism about foreign investment was evident from further remarks that: "we wish to be on guard to ensure that we are not exploited or taken for a ride. Some such exploitation almost occurred in the Enron case."[20]

The BJP approves of DFI only in high-tech industries and wants to preserve the consumer goods sector exclusively for indigenous industries. Its political slogan for the DFI debate is "computer chips, not potato chips." The socialist Janata Dal tends to side with the BJP in this dispute, arguing that India must "insulate" its economy from foreign MNCs.[21]

India's foreign policy in the 1990s has been consumed with the debate over economic liberalization versus continued control of MNCs.

However, none of the major parties is advocating a return to the highly restrictive days of the FERA. Even strident nationalists in the BJP agree that "globalization is now here to stay" (Das, 1997: 104). Although the BJP has maintained the largest bloc of votes in parliament, no party has been able to achieve an outright majority since 1996. This has produced an unstable political environment with a series of short-lived coalition governments. The rapid turnover in governments is caused by political scandals in the two major parties (Congress and the BJP), combined with the polarizing effects of the debate over MNCs.

What can we learn from the case of MNCs in India that will illuminate our understanding of MNCs in other parts of the Third World? The most striking facts of the Indian case involve the catastrophe of Bhopal, as contrasted with recent Indian policy on foreign MNCs. India is a leader of the Third World. It was a founding member of the nonaligned movement during the Cold War. Many developing nations are sure to follow India's lead regarding MNCs in the twenty-first century. Despite the disaster in Bhopal, India has scrapped its decades-old policies of restricting foreign investment. This is further evidence that, in the post–Cold War era, the liberal model of economic growth is the only model relevant to Third World modernization. The old global debate that once pitted free markets against command economies is now dead. The collapse of the Soviet Union has brought with it a rejection of centrally-planned and government-controlled economic sectors. Privatization and multinationalization are sweeping the Third World. No developing nation can hope to avoid this global change in the international political economy. Even India which, given its history, has good reason to fear the dangers that can follow from MNCs, is rushing headlong into liberalization. The lesson of India is that almost nothing will deter Third World nations from full integration into the capitalist world economy, not even disasters on the scale of Bhopal.

Now that nations that once championed self-sufficiency and ISI have turned to globalization instead, there is a concomitant desire to reap as many benefits as possible from the liberal model of development. That means, ultimately, seeking the fullest possible paticipation in the global and regional free trade associations organized by the Western powers. The country that has progressed furthest along this path is the subject of my second case study: Mexico.

MEXICO, THE NORTH AMERICAN FREE TRADE AGREEMENT, AND MULTINATIONAL CORPORATIONS

Multinational Corporation Regulation: The Early Years

Like India, Mexico embarked upon an ambitious program of modernization after World War II. Unlike India, however, Mexico's developmental strategy was heavily reliant upon attracting foreign MNCs. Both nations sought to create import substitution industries. India did so by keeping out most MNCs and promoting self-sufficiency in the early postwar period. Mexico, by contrast, developed ISI by bringing in foreign (especially U.S.) MNCs.

Mexico's policy on MNCs and DFI in the 1950s and 1960s was designed to create ISI production by means of U.S. MNCs. A relatively "unrestricted inflow of foreign capital and technology" was promoted through tax concessions for MNCs (Marton, 1986: 257–58). MNCs were allowed to establish majority-owned subsidiaries that manufactured consumer goods for the domestic market. Automobiles were assembled in Mexico with little or no local content. GE and Westinghouse were among the first to produce consumer electronics (1986: 257–58).

Other sectors of the economy were reserved for Mexican industrial groups or SOEs that controlled petroleum (foreign oil corporations had been nationalized in 1938), production of electricity, steel, mining, paper, and transportation. Indigenous industrial groups were given exclusive rights in the areas of cement, breweries, and agro-processing (Marton, 1986: 257–58). Mexican-owned companies were unable to compete with MNCs, however, when it came to high-tech assembly. Compared to India during the same period (which had kept out high-tech MNCs in favor of SOEs), Mexico had almost no local technological capabilities for production of machinery and heavy equipment. Manufacture of spare parts and other engineering goods by Mexican-owned enterprises was also limited (1986: 259).

Mexico tried to develop ISI by attracting MNCs that would bring their own technology with them. High dependency on foreign technology prevailed. MNCs did little or no research and development in Mexico. MNC production perpetuated Mexican dependence on imported technology and foreign technological services (Marton, 1986: 259). By the late 1960s and early 1970s, Mexico suffered from large balance of trade deficits because of imports of industrial equipment and capital goods (1986: 258). Fears that MNCs had too much control over technology, combined with the slow but significant growth in local industrial groups, led Mexican leaders to adopt a big change in policies in the 1970s.

The change of course for Mexico in the 1970s was spurred by desires for a more self-sufficient form of growth. New policies were contained in the Echeverria laws, named after President Luis Echeverria (1970–76). The Echeverria laws directed Mexico's ISI strategy away from MNC production of consumer goods and toward local development of intermediate and capital goods. Echeverria also created policies that involved closer scrutiny of MNC operations and procedures to review the impact of MNCs on national development. The new policies increased Mexico's control over vital economic sectors and imposed new regulations on foreign MNCs (Marton, 1986: 260).

In 1973, Mexico adopted the Law for Regulation of Foreign Investment (LRFI). The LRFI, combined with other Echeverria laws governing investment and technology, sought to Mexicanize the Mexican economy. The 1973 LRFI had three goals. The first was Mexicanization of ownership. Foreign shares of joint ventures were reduced to less than 50 percent. Mexican ownership grew as a result. A second goal was to steer DFI into new areas according to the government's perceptions of national priorities. A final goal of the new law on regulating foreign investment was to reserve some economic sectors for SOEs and Mexican companies. SOEs were given control over petrochemicals, nuclear energy, and utilities. Transportation, communication, and forestry were reserved for Mexico's industrial groups (Marton, 1986: 260).

The Echeverria laws imposed new limits on foreign equity (Marton, 1986: 260–61). There was a 34 percent maximum for foreign equity in all mining operations, and a 40 percent maximum for auto component enterprises. Other sectors were governed by a 49 percent maximum share for MNCs. As was the case with India's FERA of 1973, foreign corporations with an equity share of more than 49 percent had to reduce their holdings under Mexico's 1973 LRFI. Enforcement and oversight powers regarding the Echeverria laws were given to the National Commission on Foreign Investment. MNCs had to operate through joint ventures with Mexican partners holding the majority share, and not, in most cases, by maintaining foreign-owned subsidiaries.[22] The National Commission on Foreign Investment had to appprove all new DFI proposals, any expansion of MNC operations, new product lines, and any other form of growth or diversification.

Despite these new controls on MNCs and DFI, foreign investment continued to increase in Mexico. According to Marton "introduction of regulatory measures on foreign investment appears to have had little impact on the inflow of foreign capital [after 1973]" (1986: 262). The validity of this statement is hard to assess, because we have no way of knowing how much greater DFI in Mexico might have been if the Echeverria laws had never been adopted. Total foreign investment into Mexico in 1973 was $4 billion. By 1982 annual foreign investment into Mexico had reached almost $11 billion (1986, 262). Increases in foreign investment in the mid-1970s to the early 1980s "can be mainly attributed to the rapid economic expansion that followed the substantial increase in petroleum exports and increases in public expenditures" (1986, 262). Most of this investment came in the form of loans from private banks. Direct foreign investment by MNCs during this period was concentrated in only a few high-tech industries (chemicals, electronics, machinery). The United States accounted for the lion's share of foreign investment. U.S. investment in Mexico was about 70 percent of total investment each year (1986, 262). Technology supplied to Mexico from the United States accounted for roughly the same percentage of all foreign technology (about 70 percent annually, see Marton, 1986: 266). The United States supplies the vast majority of foreign technology and foreign investment going into Mexico, reflecting the "dominant position of U.S. companies in the Mexican market" (1986: 262).

There was a very important exception to the regulation of foreign technology and the tight control of DFI contained in the Echeverria laws. This was the free hand given to U.S. businesses that were located just inside the Mexican-U.S. border in Mexico. Export-oriented assembly plants that are situated within a 12.5-mile-wide EPZ on the Mexican side of the border have long been favored with special treatment by the Mexican government. This special treatment was largely unchanged under the Echeverria laws.[23]

U.S.-owned plants in the border zone are commonly referred to as maquiladora or maquila plants. Maquiladora is a Spanish word that denotes the assembly of parts that have been manufactured elsewhere. Some 2,000 maquiladora factories have been established by the United States along the 2,000-mile border with Mexico. By 1996, these plants were employing 700,000 workers.[24] Maquiladora businesses import capital goods and raw or partly finished materials that are then assembled into finished or semi-finished products in Mexico. MNCs are allowed to have majority ownership of maquiladoras, and the goods they import into Mexico are usually duty-free. U.S. corporations agree, in return, to export 100 percent of their manufactured goods as a precondition to locating in the maquiladora zone (Meeker-Lowry, 1992: 25).

The maquiladoras date back to 1965. In that year, the Mexican government adopted the Border Industrialization Program (BIP). The BIP had its origins in the bracero policies of 1941–64. Braceros were temporary workers from Mexico brought into the United States to help meet a U.S. labor shortage during and after World War II. A total of 5 million migrant laborers were employed by the bracero program. Mexican workers were recruited to replace U.S. agricultural workers who had been drafted during the war. The braceros were also needed after the war to meet the labor demands of the U.S. postwar economic boom. After the harvest season was over, braceros were expected to return to Mexico. Concerns that these workers were staying in the United States illegally, combined with complaints from U.S. labor unions that the program was driving down wages, led the United States to unilaterally cancel the bracero program in 1965. When the bracero program was terminated, Mexico's government turned to the BIP as a way to absorb and employ the returning migrant labor force.

As originally established, the Border Industrialization Program of 1965 allowed for up to 100 percent foreign ownership for MNCs that created maquiladoras within the 12.5-mile zone. Creation of the BIP was done in such a way as to protect existing ISI programs. The BIP requirement of exporting 100 percent of production ensured that maquiladoras would not compete with ISI plants for the Mexican market. ISI production was shielded from the maquiladoras.

In essence, there were two sets of economic policies in Mexico. The Echeverria laws and other regulations on MNCs and DFI applied to businesses outside of the BIP zone. The maquiladoras inside the BIP zone were regulated under a separate set of policies. Charges of human rights abuses caused by U.S. corporations in Mexico have been leveled almost exclusively at the maquiladoras.

Maquiladoras: Labor Rights and Environmental Rights

A great deal of study and considerable political activism have been devoted to unearthing evidence of alleged human rights abuses by U.S. corporations in the maquiladora zone. These abuses are greatest in the areas of second generation labor rights and third generation rights to a clean environment. Although Mexico has not suffered from any single industrial disaster on the scale of Bhopal, the cumulative effects of U.S. maquiladoras in Mexico have had a pernicious impact that may be no less severe. A review of the hazardous conditions of employment and union-busting activites within the maquiladoras will point to systematic denials of workers' rights. Environmental destruction associated with the maquiladora plants indicates serious rights violations in this area as well.

Understanding the maquiladoras is also crucial to understanding MNCs in the subsequent age of NAFTA. The BIP policies were a precursor for things to come under NAFTA. NAFTA has been referred to as little more than the BIP writ large (LaBotz, 1993). For Mexico, membership in NAFTA was a natural progression from the creation of the maquiladora zone.

The earliest maquila plants were small and produced piecework for the apparel industry. By the 1990s, maquiladoras had grown into huge industrial parks operated by such well-known corporations as Ford, GE, GM, and RCA. In the 1970s an average plant employed 150 workers. By 1990 this had doubled to an average of 300 employees per plant (Williams and Passe-Smith, 1992). Electronic components are now the dominant maquila sector, in terms of both total plants and number of workers. Auto parts are ranked second in terms of total plants, and textiles are second in terms of total employment. Other key industries in the zone include chemicals and food processing.

The maquila labor force is unique in many ways. Women between the ages of 16 and 25 make up 70 percent of the maquiladora workforce (Coalition for Justice in the Maquiladoras [hereafter CJM], 1993: 1). By far, most maquila workers are young, single, childless women with some formal education. Most are not recent emigrees to the maquila zone, but rather have lived there for some time prior to gaining employment. Employers prefer these workers, often referred to as "maquila grade" labor (Tiano, 1994: 152). The MNCs and the Mexican government both take the view that these are the best workers for the maquila plants because young women tend to possess greater dexterity and are therefore more skilled at maquila-type assembly. The government has mounted many campaigns to recruit such workers into the maquila zone, with government ads portraying young women as well suited for these jobs.

Critics have argued that maquiladoras prefer to hire young women because they are a more vulnerable workforce. Young women are allegedly viewed by the MNCs as being more docile and more likely to accept low wages and unsafe working conditions. This allegedly facilitates exploitation of a labor force that is largely powerless to resist (Meeker-Lowry, 1992).

Perhaps MNCs prefer maquila grade women because their physical skills are better attuned to the demands of maquiladora assembly lines. Or perhaps they prefer to employ women in hopes of having a more compliant and docile labor force. Perhaps a combination of these factors is at play. Regardless of the true motives of the MNCs, all observers agree that the maquila labor pool is predominantly young and female. Therefore, if violations of workers' rights do exist, then these violations will tend to fall disproportionately on young women.

Wages and benefits serve as useful indicators of maquiladora treatment of their labor force. According to the Coalition for Justice in the Maquiladoras (CJM), a nongovernmental advocacy group based in Texas, maquila workers earn only $4–$7 per day (CJM, 1993: 1). A study by Susan Tiano (1994) found maquila wages to be equal to the Mexican minimum wage (and no higher). She also found that non-maquila workers in the maquiladora zone had higher average wages, in some cases making up to twice as much as maquila employees. Non-maquila workers also had better chances to improve their salaries via merit pay and seniority raises than did maquila workers (Tiano, 1994).

Some of the benefits provided to maquila workers are mandated by Mexican labor laws. These mandates include access provided by employers to the national health care system, Christmas bonuses, and paid vacations. A few maquiladoras go farther and also offer their workers profit-sharing plans and low interest loans. Benefits provided by non-maquila enterprises in the maquila zone are slightly inferior to the benefits packages provided by the maquiladoras. However, total compensation (wages plus benefits) for non-maquila employment more than makes up for the relative lack of benefits (Tiano, 1994).

On balance, workers in the maquiladora zone who find non-maquila employment are better off economically than are the members of the maquila labor force. Furthermore, increases in productivity by maquila workers are not rewarded by the maquiladora MNCs. A study by Harley Shaiken (1993) shows that productivity in the maquiladora plants increased by 41 percent between 1980 and 1992. However, wages plus benefits during the same period actually declined by 32 percent. According to LaBotz (1993: 92), the decline in real wages during this period was even worse than Shaiken estimates. LaBotz estimates that real wages actually fell by almost 50 percent. Shaiken also points out that, although maquila workers regularly achieve up to 80 percent or even 100 percent of U.S. productivity levels, maquila wages are equal to only about 14 percent of the wages paid for comparable jobs in the United States.

Perhaps the most troubling violations of worker rights inside the maquiladora zone involve what appears to be a widespread and persistent pattern of union-busting. The right to organize and the right to strike have been abused by many of the maquiladoras. Mexican labor laws recognize the rights to collective bargaining and union organizing. The government has a Conciliation and Arbitration Board that mediates labor disputes. The arbitration board also has the power to determine the legality or illegality of strikes. A strike is considered legal under Mexican law only when it has been organized by a labor union that has been recognized by both the employer and the board. Unions obtain official recognition when a contract between the employer and the union has been filed with the board. The Mexican government, in its efforts to favor the maquiladoras, often "restricts the rights of workers . . . manipulates union activities and intimidates dissident union leaders."[25] Jerome Levinson (1993) believes that the Mexican government is in collusion with the maquila MNCs in these anti-union activities.

According to Levinson, the arbitration board routinely allows maquiladoras to ignore aggressive worker-established unions, and to negotiate instead with compliant maquila-created "unions" that can consist of as few as one worker. Employers are then legally free to refuse to negotiate with any other union, even one that has the support of the majority of the plant's workers (Levinson, 1993). If the workers go on strike, the board can declare the strike illegal because it was not organized by the official (pro-management) union. Workers who participate in the illegal strike lose all their job-related rights and can be fired (U.S. Department of Labor, 1993). The government can also move forcibly to reopen the plant, impose binding arbitration, and dictate a settlement to the workers. Through these legal and political maneuvers, MNCs in cooperation with the Mexican government can resolve labor disputes in the maquiladora zone at will. The arbitration board and Mexican presidents have a long history of direct intervention into labor disputes.

Agapito Gonzales, head of the Day Laborers and Industrial Workers Union, has attempted to unionize many of the U.S.-owned factories in Mexico. Gonzales has also been prominent in his efforts to demand increased wages at these plants (Levinson, 1993). After the companies complained to the Mexican government, Gonzales was arrested on charges of tax evasion and detained for months before his eventual release. Contract negotiations that were finalized in Gonzales' absence provided wage scales that were substantially lower than he had been demanding.[26]

Additional examples of anti-union activities by the maquiladoras and by their supporters in the Mexican government abound. In 1993, workers at a Volkswagon maquila formed an independent union and went on strike, protesting low wages and long working hours. The government intervened and voided the collective contract for that plant. The corporation was then free to hire strikebreakers and cut salaries.[27] Also in 1993, ten workers at a GE plant in Juarez were fired after they accused the corporation of safety and health violations, exposing workers to hazardous chemicals, and failing to pay overtime. Six of the workers were later reinstated. At about the same time 21 employees were fired by Honeywell in Chihuahua when they tried to organize workers at the plant. None of the Honeywell union activists was ever reinstated (Alexander and Gilmore, 1994).

A Mexican union organizer testified before the U.S. Congress in 1993 regarding blacklisting by MNCs. Alma L. Molina of Ciudad Juarez tried to organize workers at the Clarostat maquila. Clarostat is a U.S.-owned electronics MNC. She was fired because of her union activites. She then found work at the nearby GE plant. After only seven days on the job with GE, she was called into a personnel office and shown her name on a list that was kept on file by GE. According to Molina, "The personnel man told me that he did not know why my name was on the list but that he would have to fire me anyway."[28] This is not an isolated incident. There has been a pattern of behavior involving union intimidation and blacklisting by many MNCs in the maquiladora zone. Eligio Rodrigues once worked as an industrial engineer for a Mexican subsidiary of Vishay Intertechnology. Vishay is an MNC based in Malvern, Pennsylvania. Rodrigues was fired for trying to organize a union and now believes that he has been blacklisted by Vishay and other maquiladoras.[29]

Further violations of workers' rights can be found in those cases where there is a lack of safety and the presence of hazardous working conditions. A study by Sylvia Guendelman and Monica Silberg (1993) compared job-related injuries for maquila and non-maquila industries in Mexico. They found no significant differences between the two groups of factories in regard to physical injuries. However, their samples included only those employees who were recommended for the survey by maquila plant managers, raising questions of possible bias in their results. An earlier study by Maria Fernandez-Kelly (1983) had found that fully 60 percent of maquila electrical workers suffered from job-related optic-nerve weakness. Roughly the same percentage of seamstresses employed by maquiladoras suffered from lumbago. A 1994 study discovered that most managers in maquila plants were unaware of the dangers from ergonomic problems associated with factory work. The same study showed that lack of proper equipment in the maquila plants created a high incidence of muscular-skeletal disorders in long-term maquiladora workers.[30]

Exposure to hazardous substances has also been a prevalent problem in many maquila enterprises. Acute health problems commonly associated with overexposure to toxic chemicals are widespread among maquila workers (LaBotz, 1993). Some 200 workers from Matamoros employed by Mallory Capacitor, a U.S. MNC with headquarters in Indianapolis, have experienced miscarriages and birth defects in their children (for example, missing limbs, mental retardation) allegedly because of their exposure to toxic materials on the job.[31] According to the Mallory workers, the MNC did not warn mothers about the risks of exposure, nor did it supply them with protective equipment. They were exposed to polychorinated biphenyls on the job, leading to headaches, nausea, and fainting (Juffer, 1988: 27). Seventy of these "Mallory children" were born with facial deformities and mental retardation (Selcraig, 1994: 60). Although two lawsuits were filed by parents of the Mallory children, "liability is uncertain since Mallory has been bought and sold many times; at one time being owned by Kraft, then Black and Decker, and today by the North American Capacitor Co." (Meeker-Lowry, 1992: 28).

Legal liability has also been hard to exact in many cases involving Mexicans who suffer from the effects of MNC toxic wastes. Entire communities have been put at risk by the environmental destruction created by maquiladoras. U.S. companies operating in Mexico have "poured chemical wastes down drains, dumped them in irrigation ditches, left them in the desert, burned them in city dumps, and turned them over to Mexican recycling firms not qualified to handle toxic waste" (Juffer, 1988: 24).

The most notrious case is that of Stepan Chemical and other MNCs along Chemical Row in Matamoros, just across the border from Brownsville, Texas. At various times in the 1990s, Stepan has dumped chemical wastes into ponds and then covered over these lagoons, plowed under a canal behind its plant that had been used to discharge toxic wastes, and experienced ammonia leaks and explosions on the grounds of its plant (CJM, 1993: 5; Selcraig, 1994: 62). Stepan, a Chicago-based chemical MNC, used the canal to dispose of xylene, a toxic substance that is known to cause brain hemorrhaging and damage to lungs, livers, and kidneys. Xylene has also been linked to birth defects. Four other MNCs in Matamoros, including a GM plant, have also dumped xylene and methylene chloride (Meeker-Lowry, 1992). In Matamoros, 42 babies were born in 1992 with severe neurological defects. Another 42 afflicted babies were born to families living very close to the border in Brownsville. Babies in the area have been born with "devastating brain and spinal-cord malformations at three times the expected rates."[32] The defects, principally anencephaly and spina bifida, are classified as neural tube defects and are caused soon after conception. A crease in the embryo's tissue fails to close fully into the tube that would normally develop into the brain and spinal cord. Anencephalic babies are born with partial or missing brains. They are stillborn or die soon after birth. Spina bifida is a defect that usually leaves the spinal cord open. The lives of some babies with spina bifida can be saved by surgery, but they still suffer paralysis and other maladies.[33]

In the U.S. as a whole, the rate for these defects is less than 5 per 10,000 births. In the Brownsville-Matamoros area in 1992 (at the height of the dumping along Chemical Row) the rate of defects was 15 per 10,000 births.[34] Many health experts believe these defects to be connected to the maquiladora toxic wastes (Selcraig, 1994: 60).

Stepan Chemical and the other MNCs denied that the rash of birth defects was related to their operations. Stepan officials were adamant at first, insisting that they would not pay damages to the community (Selcraig, 1994: 62). They also refused to fund cleanup efforts that would have removed the toxic substances from water and soil (CJM, 1993: 6). The chief of manufacturing at Stepan's Illinois headquarters even went so far as to claim that his corporation had improved the environmental conditions in Matamoros and "made the place much safer" (Selcraig, 1994: 62).

MNCs involved in the Brownsville-Matamoros birth defect lawsuits put pressure on the Mexican government to assist them in the cases. The president of the Matamoros maquila association allegedly wanted Mexico's Interior Ministry to intimidate Domingo Gonzales (Selcraig, 1994: 601–12). Gonzales is the cofounder of the CJM and a leader among Stepan Chemical's critics. The case was finally settled when the Matamoros maquiladoras agreed to pay $17 million to the families who had suffered. The out-of-court settlement included no admission of guilt or responsibility by the MNCs. General Motors continued to stick to arguments that the birth defects were caused by lack of proper nutrition on the part of the mothers.

The incidence of birth defects in the maquiladora zone has dropped significantly since its peak during the 1992 epidemic. However, environmental problems persist in northern Mexico, some of which have been exacerbated since the implementation of the North American Free Trade Agreement, which went into effect for the United States, Mexico, and Canada on January 1, 1994. The deleterious effects of U.S. MNCs on labor rights and environmental conditions prior to NAFTA have carried over into the NAFTA era.

Multinational Corporations and the
North American Free Trade Agreement:
Labor Rights and Environmental Rights

Maquiladoras operated in Mexico for almost 20 years prior to the enactment of NAFTA's free trade arrangements. There is a detailed historical record of the impact of the maquiladoras. Because MNCs in Mexico under the NAFTA regime are a relatively new phenomenon, there is much less evidence to go on when assessing the positive and negative effects of MNCs under NAFTA. Supporters of NAFTA argue that the trade pact can be a useful tool in forcing MNCs and the Mexican government to improve treatment of workers and environmental protections. Negotiated during the Reagan and Bush administrations, the NAFTA accord was also backed by President Clinton. Clinton went beyond the agreements negotiated by his predecessors to add side agreements to NAFTA that specifically addressed labor and environmental issues. Alas, based on the evidence to date, the facts show that union-busting and toxic wastes are still serious problems in Mexico, but there is also some hope for improvement in the future under NAFTA.

NAFTA requires Mexico and the United States to drop most of their preexisting barriers to free trade across the border. NAFTA provides for a free flow of goods, services, and investment between the two countries. The political debate in the United States over the merits of NAFTA prior to its ratification by Congress focused mainly on the likely effect it would have on jobs in the United States. Opponents of the treaty, led by Ross Perot of Texas, argued that NAFTA would lead to massive layoffs and high unemployment in the United States. NAFTA's critics feared that MNCs would quickly transfer production to Mexico in order to take advantage of cheaper labor rates and weaker environmental laws. Proponents of NAFTA looked to the long-term gain in jobs that could result from increased exports to Mexico, once that country was forced by NAFTA to drop its tariffs and quotas on U.S.-made goods.

Subsequent studies that have tried to quantify net gains and losses in U.S. jobs due to NAFTA have produced conflicting results. Some research points to lost jobs, other studies claim to have found increased employment in the U.S. due to NAFTA. Problems of political bias enter into the equation on both sides of this debate, with research funded by NAFTA's opponents producing the negative results, although research from NAFTA's supporters shows the opposite. A few of the more objective studies claim to prove that the net impact on U.S. jobs has been either neutral (no net gain or loss) or so small as to be economically insignificant. I see no need to review these studies for the purposes of this book. Furthermore, the fixation on jobs in the United States, although understandable, misses the more important larger issues of NAFTA and even tends to distort the true significance of NAFTA for changes in the international political economy. NAFTA is usually described as a treaty on trade, which naturally turns the debate toward issues of goods, services, and jobs. The most important dimension of NAFTA, however, is its provisions liberalizing international investment. NAFTA's provisions for foreign investment take the advantages once reserved for MNCs in the maquila zone and extend these pro-MNC policies to all parts of Mexico. MNCs anywhere in Mexico can now enjoy the open environment for DFI that was first developed for maquiladoras by the BIP of 1965.

Investment policy is the single most important factor determining global location of MNCs. Hence, to talk about NAFTA only in relation to trade can be misleading and could lead one to think only in terms of trade barriers, trade deficits, and employment levels. The heart of NAFTA, in fact the heart of all international free trade zones, is the way that DFI is freed to seek new homes for MNCs. A single-minded focus on jobs is misleading because "the fundamental purpose of NAFTA is to facilitate . . . investment" (Koechlin, 1995: 26). "NAFTA is not primarily about trade; it is about the ability of capital to move without regard to national borders" (Brecher, 1993: 685). During the first year of NAFTA, U.S. DFI into Mexico doubled. Direct U.S. investment by MNCs was $4 billion in 1994, as compared to $2 billion in the previous year (Koechlin, 1995: 26). A sampling of the U.S. corporations in Mexico includes: Chase Manhattan, Chrysler, DuPont, Ford, GE, GM, IBM, ITT, Johnson & Johnson, Kodak, Memorex, Pepsi, Proctor & Gamble, Rockwell, Stepan Chemicals, Sunbeam, Union Carbide, United Technologies, and Zenith. This is only a representative listing, not a comprehensive roll call. Scores of U.S. MNCs have already located in Mexico, with more arriving almost daily since the passage of NAFTA.

The side agreement to NAFTA on labor is the North American Agreement on Labor Cooperation (NAALC). The NAALC created a labor grievance system and national committees to investigate abuses of labor rights. These committees are known as the National Administrative Offices (NAOs). NAOs receive complaints from labor unions and other nongovernmental organizations and then determine if the complaints meet the criteria stated in the NAALC to give an NAO jurisdiction. The NAALC does not set any transnational standards for labor rights above or beyond the existing labor laws of the three nations. A violation of labor rights under the NAALC, therefore, would have to be a contravention of a national law by an MNC within the country in question. For example, an MNC in Mexico could be brought before an NAO for violating Mexican labor laws, but not for violation of a U.S. labor standard that is missing from Mexican law.[35]

Complaints come under the jurisdiction of an NAO if they meet three criteria. The alleged violation must involve a consistent pattern of failure to enforce labor standards, must affect trade between states that are parties to NAFTA, and must relate to labor laws that are mutually recognized by the parties to the agreement (Levinson, 1993: 4). If the complaint meets these criteria, an NAO can investigate the allegations and call for consultations between the labor ministers (or labor secretary) of the countries in question. Petitioners are free to bring their complaints before the NAO of any of the three states. The NAALC holds open the possibility that trade sanctions could be imposed for violations of labor laws, violations of child labor prohibitions, failures to meet health and safety standards, or for violating minimum wage requirements.

The first cases brought before the U.S. NAO came from four separate groups regarding several SONY plants in Nuevo Laredo, Mexico. Workers at the plants charged that they had not been allowed to organize freely or to register their own independent union with Mexico's arbitration board. SONY allegedly fired union organizers and activists, tampered with union elections, and relied on excessive force from police who were called in to break up a strike. The NAO found in favor of the petitioners in regard to the first complaint and agreed that the union had been unjustly denied its right to register with the arbitration board. The NAO failed to reach a decision regarding the other complaints filed in the SONY case. The NAO took the strongest action open to it in regard to the first issue (registration of the union). It called upon the U.S. Secretary of Labor to admonish Mexico's Minister of Labor for not enforcing Mexico's own laws in this case.[36] SONY is, of course, a non-U.S. MNC. When the U.S. NAO heard complaints of similar union-busting activites by GE and Honeywell in Mexico, it chose to make no recommendations for action by the U.S. government. Even in the case of SONY, the U.S. reaction was mild, to say the least. Diplomatic expressions of displeasure alone bring little pressure to bear on government officials or corporate executives.

A strike in 1995 by workers at a Ford plant in Mexico raised some of the same issues that were salient in the SONY case. Rumors circulated that Ford was preparing to call in strikebreakers as had been done at the SONY plants. The CJM stepped in on behalf of the workers and pressured Ford to allow new union elections. The strike had been called when workers objected to the terms of a contract negotiated between the MNC and union bosses that Ford preferred to deal with (who neglected to consult with rank and file union members). That contract had provided pay raises for the union bosses, but not for the bulk of the assembly line workers (CJM, 1995). Fortunately in this case a mutually acceptable resolution to the crisis was adopted by Ford and their workers (with significant mediation by the CJM). This case did not drag on as long as the SONY strikes and did not need to go to the level of the NAO. Perhaps there is some hope from this case that MNCs and workers are finding more amicable ways to settle their disputes in Mexico. During the Ford strike, an MNC gave in to worker demands for control over their own union and for legitimate representation in the collective bargaining process. In this one case at least, labor rights were eventually respected by the corporation.

Hopes raised by the resolution of the Ford strike for better treatment of workers must be balanced, however, by the continuing evidence of violations of labor rights in Mexico. A 1996 report was released by the Women's Rights Project of the New York-based Human Rights Watch. Human Rights Watch is a widely respected human rights nongovernmental organization (NGO). The report details a widespread pattern of discrimination against women in the maquila zone. Researchers interviewed workers from more than 40 plants in five cities. The results show that the Mexican government has failed to protect women from labor rights violations by MNCs. Companies routinely screen out pregnant women when recruiting new hires, and often fire those who become pregnant. Other pregnant women have been pressured into resigning, sexually harassed by their bosses, shifted to harder tasks to encourage them to quit, and in at least one case, suffered a miscarriage on the job when refused permission to leave a shift.[37] Mexico's Labor Department forbids firing or mistreatment of pregnant women and takes the position that discrimination against women in hiring is also illegal. Unfortunately, as with so many Mexican labor laws, the government continues to do little or nothing to enforce these standards.

Violations of workers' rights have carried over from the maquila era into the age of NAFTA. Similarly, denials of the right to a clean environment characterize MNC operations in Mexico both before and after NAFTA went into effect. The side agreement to NAFTA on environmental protection, like the NAALC on labor rights, contains enforcement procedures that are almost nonexistent.

After the parties to NAFTA signed the trade agreement in 1993, they concluded the concomitant North American Agreement on Environmental Cooperation (NAAEC). The NAAEC created a Commission on Environmental Cooperation (CEC). The CEC has its headquarters in Montreal.

The CEC is the institutional framework for promoting environmental protection under the NAFTA regime. When they created the CEC, the U.S. and Mexico also promised a joint effort to clean up the environmental mess along the border caused by the maquiladoras. A program to direct $8 billion in cleanup funds was announced with much fanfair. A North American Developmental Bank (NADB) was founded and assigned $1.5 billion to distribute to initial cleanup projects. The World Bank also promised to chip in $600 million to aid in the cleanup.[38]

The Sierra Club and other environmentalists criticized the border plan for being too small. They estimate the costs of the cleanup to be at least $20 billion (Selcraig, 1994: 64). Even the less ambitious plans of the NAFTA governments have not been carried through as promised. By 1995 Mexico was trying to back out of its commitments to contribute funds for the cleanup.[39] In its first two years of operations, the NADB did not issue a single loan.[40] The lack of an effective cleanup plan for the border region is just one of the many problems with the NAAEC. The environmental review process under the authority of the CEC is another.

The CEC contains the cabinet-level environmental officials from each government. Individuals and NGOs can file complaints before the CEC. If the CEC agrees to hear a given complaint regarding pollution in Mexico, then a long process of review and dispute settlement begins. In all, this process can take up to 18 months (Selcraig, 1994: 64). First, the CEC informs the Mexican government of the nature of the complaint. Next, Mexico's government can ask to have the investigation halted if the case is the subject of a "pending proceeding" inside Mexico (for example, if Mexico is seeking either voluntary or court-imposed compliance from the MNC to stop polluting) (1994: 64). If the Mexican government does not object, the CEC prepares a report based on public records. After the CEC files its report, the governments of both the United States and Canada must agree that the issue should be brought to the next stage, dispute resolution with Mexico. During the dispute resolution stage, Mexico can avoid fines or other economic sanctions "simply by claiming that it doesn't have the money" to implement its own environmental laws (1994: 64). The final step in this process is the (unlikely) possibility that fines would be levied against the Mexican government for failing to enforce its environmental laws. The fines assessed, if any, would be imposed on the Mexican government, not against the MNC that did the polluting.

Besides the obvious problems with the weak CEC enforcement regime, critics decry what they see as the undemocratic nature of the CEC process. The CEC can hold its hearings in secret, because the NAAEC has no provisions to require open meetings.[41] State-to-state submissions before the

CEC (complaints filed, defenses offered) are not to be released to the media or to the public.[42] There are also no provisions in the NAAEC to allow NGOs that are not direct parties to the dispute to file friend-of-the-court briefs.[43]

The first petitions filed before the CEC dealt with the mysterious deaths of 40,000 birds at a Mexican reservoir in December 1994 and January 1995. The Silva reservoir in central Mexico near the city of Leon is used by more than 50 species of birds during their annual migrations. The Silva catastrophe was one of the worst bird kills in North American history.[44] The Leon area is the shoemaking capital of Mexico and home to more than 800 tanneries.[45] The tanneries discharge their chemical wastes directly into rivers and streams that flow into the Silva reservoir. There is also a large chemical plant in the area. The most likely cause of the bird kill is hexavalent chromium used by the many tanneries upstream from the reservoir.[46]

The Mexican tanneries moved into this area from the United States years ago to escape problems they had experienced with unions and environmental regulations in the United States.[47] High levels of chromium were detected in the reservoir after the bird kill and it had to be drained. Unfortunately, the environmental problems that caused the 1995 bird kill are not isolated incidents. According to Public Citizen, a populist NGO founded by Ralph Nader, many environmental problems in Mexico have escalated since the enactment of NAFTA. A 1996 report from this organization reviews NAFTA's record during its first two years. The report points to evidence of increased illegal dumping of toxic wastes, worsened air pollution, and higher incidences of diseases caused by maquiladora pollutants.[48]

Perhaps the most hotly debated dimension of the NAAEC is its requirement that the parties to NAFTA harmonize their environmental regulations. Critics of NAFTA argue that harmonization of environmental standards will be in a downward direction, effectively weakening environmental protections in the United States. The critical view argues that it is in the nature of NAFTA-NAAEC to push environmental standards down toward a lowest common denominator.

The NAAEC sets no environmental standards itself. Rather, the goal is to get the three governments better to enforce their own, preexisting laws. U.S. environmental policies, although not ideal, set high standards for clean air and water. The United States also devotes considerable resources to monitoring emissions, cleanup of toxic sites, and development of newer, cleaner, greener industrial technologies. Mexico, on paper, also has very good environmental laws; even opponents of NAFTA will concede this point. The primary problem in Mexico is getting the Mexican government to enforce its own standards, impose sanctions on polluters, and clean up toxic dumps.

To the extent that environmental laws do differ, the NAAEC requires all three states to work toward uniformity of standards. For example, Mexico allows the production and sale of household batteries that contain mercury; the U.S. does not (Knight, 1995: 30). Canada allows the production and installation of some types of asbestos. U.S. laws require the phase-out of all forms of asbestos, including the less hazardous types manufactured in Canada.[49] Critics fear that the United States will have to lower its environmental standards to accept batteries from Mexico and asbestos from Canada under the free trade provisions of NAFTA. The other governments have the option to charge that U.S. environmental prohibitions of these goods constitute nontariff barriers to trade. NAFTA provisions for free trade forbid unreasonable environmental restrictions against imports; such unreasonable restrictions would be considered a type of nontariff barrier.

Supporters of NAFTA believe that the NAAEC will have the opposite effect, forcing other countries to raise their environmental standards if they want to sell their goods in U.S. markets. The terms of the NAAEC explicitly state that all three governments have the right to maintain their existing environmental standards (Knight, 1995: 30). All three countries also have the right to ban imports that do not meet their higher standards. Finally, the NAAEC allows state and local governments to set their own environmental standards that are tougher and more restrictive than any national or international standard (1995: 30). For example, in California any product with even trace elements of carcinogenic chemicals must carry warning labels clearly stating this fact. The California requirement is much tougher than federal laws in this area. The wording of the NAAEC is such that the California standard would remain intact under the terms of NAFTA. Critics argue that the exact opposite is true. They fear that the federal government will pressure California and other states to weaken their local environmental regulations.[50]

Critics of the NAAEC underestimate the political influence of state and local governments when it comes to setting environmental standards. The critics also seem to underestimate the political power of the U.S. environmental lobby and the environmental concerns of the average voter. It is highly unlikely that popular opinion would allow the importation of products deemed hazardous in this country (mercury batteries, Canadian asbestos) simply because an unfair trade suit might be filed by a foreign government. Furthermore, no sovereign government is going to weaken its environmental protections simply because it enters into an international free trade agreement. If NAFTA and the NAAEC represent threats to the environment, it is not because these treaties will force the United States to accept some lowest common denominator on environmental protection in order to keep our trading partners happy.[51] Rather, the dangers to the environment from NAFTA are the same old problems that have existed at least since 1965 and the creation of the first maquiladoras. The real dangers are that MNCs will flock to Mexico in order to avoid stricter environmental regulations in the United States and Canada. The significant new element brought into the equation by NAFTA is that MNCs are now free to do to the rest of Mexico what they have already done in the maquila zone in northern Mexico. Unless the Mexican government can be induced to strengthen enforcement of its environmental protections that are already on the books, more disasters in central and southern Mexico like the bird kill near Leon are inevitable.

What does a case study of MNCs in Mexico teach us about MNCs and human rights in the Third World? The clearest lesson from the Mexican case is that NAFTA, and more regional free trade agreements like NAFTA, are the wave of the future. NAFTA is a fact that is here to stay. Critics of the treaty and its side agreements on labor and the environment might as well give up any hope of reversing these trends. It is time to accept the inevitability of NAFTA, the free expansion of MNCs to the Third World, and the global flow of DFI. In the twenty-first century, MNCs will increase their globalization of production as NAFTA and other free trade regimes inexorably expand. On this wave of globalization ride the would-be surfers in Third World governments. Third World leaders have little choice but to promote multinationalization of their political economies in a desperate attempt to catch up with the advanced industrialized nations of the OECD. Every NIC wants to experience the rates of growth and modernization that could make them the newest members of the OECD rich man's club (à la South Korea).

India and Mexico are the best examples of these growing international trends. The policy paths carved out by India and Mexico, including abandonment of economic nationalism in favor of unrestrained multinationalization via foreign investment, will be the policy model adopted by most other Third World nations. Self-sufficiency and economic autarky never were viable goals for developing nations. Now that the economic leaders of the Third World have uniformly embraced the liberal model of development, MNCs will become omnipresent. That raises even greater concerns about the likely impact, for good and for ill, of MNCs on human rights.

Some labor and environmental activists in the United States have given NAFTA qualified support in the hope that the new free trade regime can be used to get on the right side of global changes in the international political economy.[52] They would like to see NAFTA channel the inevitable tide of globalization and multinationalization in ways that could protect both the labor force and the environment.

The NAOs and the CEC can be used to increase political awareness on both sides of the border. Clearly MNCs have largely ignored labor rights and environmental laws in Mexico in years past. The massive bird kill in Leon, the charges of abuse from Public Citizen and Human Rights Watch, and the foot-dragging by NAFTA governments in regard to the border cleanup all indicate that conditions are not going to change radically for the better in the near future. However, there have also been some signs of hope.

Environmental protection may be improving in some areas. Mexico has imposed a temporary shutdown of the Stepan chemical plant on at least two occasions. A large PEMEX petroleum refinery has been closed near Mexico City. Mexico's environmental agency has also imposed temporary closures of "numerous noncompliant plants" (Knight, 1995: 31). One of the newest plants constructed by a U.S. MNC boasts that it will incorporate the same green technology in Mexico as it uses in its U.S. plants to meet U.S. environmental standards (1995: 32–33). NAFTA also makes new institutional resources available (the CEC, the NADB) that could address and redress the worst environmental problems if these resources were used effectively. If the international structures of NAFTA have been weak until now, that is all the more reason for political pressure to be exerted by interested parties in the public and by environmental NGOs. Citizens in all NAFTA countries need to take on a "watchdog" role to "hold their governments accountable through the glare of public attention" (Selcraig, 1994: 64).

There are also some encouraging signs regarding NAFTA's impact on labor rights. Women are still being discriminated against and union-busting activities continue in some cases, but there have also been some victories for labor under NAFTA. The NAALC and the NAOs have increased awareness and activism regarding labor rights in North America. "The pressure of U.S. public opinion, significantly heightened in the NAFTA era, is often the only effective defense available to Mexican organizers" when maquiladoras try to deny labor rights.[53] Kirkwood Industries, a U.S.-based MNC, recently tried to fire 100 workers in Mexico for supporting a union drive. The Teamsters union in the U.S. protested, publicized the action by Kirkwood, and pressured pro-labor members of

Congress to condemn Kirkwood's tactics.[54] The political pressure from the U.S. forced Kirkwood to capitulate, allowing a unionization vote in their plant to go forward. This case shows that, slowly but surely, "NAFTA may be altering the terms of labor-capital relations in Mexico" for the better.[55]

The future impact of NAFTA on labor rights and environmental protection is important not only for Mexico but also for potential new members of NAFTA as well. Chile is likely to become the next member of NAFTA in the near future. Chile's experience with MNCs is important to an understanding of human rights in the Third World because Chile's governments have granted free access to MNCs and DFI for a much longer time than either Mexico or India. At about the same time that Mexico and India were imposing new restrictions on MNCs in 1973, Chile's elected government was overthrown by a bloody coup d'état. The military regime that seized power quickly opened Chile to a free inflow of DFI. MNCs flocked to Chile during the rule of the Pinochet regime, making the impact of MNCs on human rights in Chile an important final case study.

MULTINATIONAL CORPORATIONS AND HUMAN RIGHTS IN CHILE

Multinational Corporations in Chile before 1973

The military regime that controlled Chile from 1973 to 1990 was one of the world's most notorious violators of human rights. Of the three nations examined in this chapter, Chile has experienced the worst violations of rights by far. Chile also has the most open environment for foreign investment and MNCs. This combination of factors might lead one to wonder if there is any connection between the two facts. Could there be some identifiable link between the egregious violations of human rights by Chile's military government and the pro-MNC policies created by the same administration?

MNCs in Chile have been highly controversial. However, they have not been accused of murder (as in Bhopal) or even of union-busting (as in the maquila zone). Rarely have MNCs in Chile been accused of direct violations of human rights. MNCs might be responsible for human rights abuses in Chile only in an indirect way if at all. MNCs have often been accused of supporting, aiding, and abetting repressive governments in Chile. Therefore, to study human rights and MNCs in Chile requires a different approach than the one used in my other case studies. Here I will review the human rights atrocities committed by Chile's former government. Then I will consider the extent to which MNCs may be culpable, either as accomplices to the regime or as beneficiaries of the economic changes that accompanied the repression.

There are good reasons to suspect that MNCs may have dirty hands in regard to violations of rights in Chile. A first reason to be suspicious is because of the actions of one notable MNC. ITT was involved in a "bizarre plot" during 1970 to subvert democratic elections in Chile (United States Senate [hereafter, U.S. Senate], 1979: 226). The ITT affair will be described in detail later.

Another reason to suspect that MNCs might have played a role in Chile's repression comes from prior empirical study. Carleton has investigated the relationship between "export-oriented industrialization [by MNCs] and the incidence of state repression in Latin America" (1989: 211). When MNCs shift their production facilities to the Third World, the result is a "new international division of labor" and export-oriented development (1989: 211). Carleton has tested claims that industrialization in Latin America via MNCs is closely tied to repression of labor rights. Drawing on D. Nayyer (1978) and others, Carleton postulates two relationships that could link MNCs to repression.

The first hypothesis tested by Carleton is that MNCs "desire and seek out those nations that are most repressive" (1989: 218). This is the repression as cause argument. Repression is the alleged cause for MNCs locating in Latin America. According to this view, increased repression of labor rights by Latin American regimes induces MNCs to locate in Latin America, attracted by the existence of a docile and powerless labor force. The second hypothesis tested by Carleton states that increased MNC presence in Latin America leads to enhanced repression. This is the repression as effect argument, a variation on the Hymer thesis reviewed in Chapter 3. According to this view, MNC industrialization in Latin America causes superexploitation of the labor force, which in turn creates political opposition, followed by authoritarianism, and then political repression of the opposition.

Carleton uses data from Freedom House to measure human rights. He measures MNC production for export by means of the percentage of total exports made up of manufactured goods. Statistical analysis of manufactured exports as compared to human rights leads Carleton to the conclusion that "as the Latin American countries become integrated into the new division of labor [based on MNC production], the regimes in power increase repression" (1989: 226). Carleton's study tends to support his second hypothesis, indicating that repression is an effect caused by increased MNC production. In the case of Chile, Carleton's research would lead us to expect that, as more MNCs move into the country, repression would escalate as a result.

Carleton's study, like my analysis from Chapter 3, uses aggregate data to test theoretical claims linking MNCs to human rights. As such, it is open to Winston's critique regarding the aggregation problem. As a rule, Carleton finds that increased integration of states into the international division of labor (and increased reliance on MNCs) will tend to go along with increased repression in Latin America. However, this is not necessarily true in all cases. Some countries could be exceptions to this rule. To see if Carleton's generalization applies to Chile requires a review of the particulars of the Chilean case. Before reviewing human rights abuses in Chile's recent past, I will summarize Chile's prior policies on MNCs and DFI.

Foreign investment has played an important role in Chile's economic development since the nineteenth century, especially in regard to tapping Chile's natural resources. Chile has some of the richest deposits of copper in the world. Two U.S. MNCs came to dominate Chile's copper production in the early twentieth century. Kennecott bought its first interests in Chile in 1914. Anaconda began mining copper in Chile in 1923. These two U.S. MNCs were part of a seven-firm oligopoly that controlled up to 70 percent of the noncommunist world's copper production during the Cold War (Kline, 1992: 3). Foreign control of the mining industry has often stimulated resentment in Chile. Because sales of copper were contolled by U.S. MNCs, Washington was able unilaterally to set the price the United States paid for imports from Chile. Citing wartime economic necessity, the U.S. government established its price for copper from Chile during the Korean War at only one-half of the world market price. This action "seemed to confirm [in Chile] classic [dependency theory] notions that perceive collusion between foreign MNCs and home governments to exploit the resources and maintain the subserviance of developing countries" (1992: 4).

Control of copper by foreign MNCs led to reactions by both the intelligentsia and the government in Chile. Raul Prebisch, who advocated development via import substitution industry as an alternative to reliance on MNCs, first developed his ISI theories as an economist at the Economic Commission for Latin America (ECLA) in Santiago, Chile. Prebisch developed his theories in favor of ISI from a model based on Chile's experience. The ECLA structural approach called for state intervention into Third World economies to foster local control of industrialization (O'Brien and Roddick, 1983: 57).

Chile's political system became hostile to foreign investment in the 1960s, when large landowners expressed opposition to the land reform requirements of President Kennedy's Alliance for Progress and when it became fashionable to blame economic problems in Chile on foreign MNCs (Kline, 1992: 6). In 1964, President Frei instituted a policy of Chileanization of the economy and forced MNCs to reduce their ownership in the mines to 49 percent or less. Frei's policies resulted in local majority ownership of mining operations, but the mines remained such a lucrative enterprise that DFI by mining MNCs continued to increase. New DFI into the copper industry totaled more than $500 million in 1968 alone (1992: 8).

By 1970, massive U.S. DFI into Chile was on a collision course with leftist political parties that were rising to prominence. Chile helped to create the Andean Common Market (ANCOM) in 1969, which also included Bolivia, Columbia, Ecuador, and Peru. ANCOM established common tariffs on imports among its members and instituted unified regulations on DFI that limited foreign MNCs to a 49 percent equity share in all enterprises. During the early 1970s, Chile was the "most aggressive" member of ANCOM when it came to enforcing these restrictions on foreign investment (Kline, 1992: 9–10). This policy was instituted during the administration of President Salvador Allende.

Salvador Allende, founder of Chile's Socialist Party, was elected to the presidency in 1970. Allende campaigned on a platform that promised extensive land reform and nationalization of key industries, most of which were controlled by foreign capital (U.S. Senate, 1979: 227). He garnered only 36 percent of the popular vote in a national election, but, because no candidate in the three-way race received an absolute majority of votes, the presidency had to be decided by a vote of Chile's Congress. Allende's Popular Unity coalition of Socialists, Communists, and Social Democrats carried the vote in Congress by a wide margin.

Once in office, Allende embarked on ECLA-inspired structural reforms of Chile's economy. Wages were raised and strict price controls were imposed to redistribute national income downward, toward the poor and the lower middle class (O'Brien and Roddick, 1983: 23–24). Banks and industries were slated for takeover by the government. Copper MNCs were the first target of Allende's nationalization program. He proposed a complete takeover of Anaconda and Kennecott. Allende's administration also claimed that, because many MNCs had made excess profits in years past on which they had paid no tax, no compensation needed to be paid for expropriated properties from the copper mines and other industries. Total uncompensated takeovers by Allende amounted to $800 million and involved the assets of Anaconda, Armco Steel, Bank of America, GM, ITT, Kennecott, Ralston Purina, RCA, and others (Kline, 1992: 11–12).

ITT had been in Chile since 1930, and owned a 70 percent share in the Chilean telephone company (Chiltelco). Chiltelco operated as a government-regulated monopoly. In May 1971 Allende announced the complete takeover of Chiltelco and offered ITT $24 million in compensation (U.S. Senate, 1979: 238). ITT protested, claiming their share of Chiltelco to be worth $153 million (Kline, 1992: 11). A short time later, columnist Jack Anderson published a series of articles showing that ITT had conspired with the Central Intelligence Agency (CIA) in an attempt to prevent Allende's election. Allende's government was outraged and broke off all talks with ITT regarding compensation for Chiltelco. For Allende's government, the ITT affair "came to symbolize the darkest fears of developing countries that foreign MNCs might conspire with home governments to compromise a host nation's political sovereignty" (1992: 12).

ITT's efforts to deny Allende the presidency in 1970 are the most blatant example on public record of antidemocratic activities by a U.S. MNC in the Third World. In collusion with the CIA, ITT first schemed to prevent Allende from winning the popular election in September 1970. When the lack of a clear-cut victor in the popular election shifted the contest to Chile's Congress, ITT continued in its anti-Allende efforts. Even after the Congress voted to confirm Allende as president, ITT and the CIA persisted, doing their best to unseat Allende from office. If they had succeeded, ITT would have denied the people of Chile their democratic rights to choose their own leaders and to determine their own politicoeconomic structures. As it was, despite the ultimate failure of ITT's plots, their interventions into Chile's political system constituted threats to first generation political rights of all Chileans.

Because the ITT-CIA affair in Chile became a major scandal in U.S. foreign policy, the Senate Foreign Relations Committee established a Subcommittee on Multinational Corporations to investigate. The Subcommittee on MNCs held nine days of hearings; interviewed dozens of executives from ITT, other MNCs, and the CIA; and subpoenaed documents from ITT and the State Department. The final report released by the Senate subcommittee establishes the facts of the case.

Early in 1970 members of ITT's board of directors began to fear an Allende victory in the upcoming September election. Led by board member John McCone (a former Director of the CIA), and supported by ITT's chief executive officer Geneen, ITT brought a number of proposals to Richard Helms, head of the CIA in the Nixon administration. In July 1970 ITT offered to supply funds to Allende's opponents in the election, if the moneys could be controlled and channeled through the CIA (U.S. Senate, 1979: 229). Helms rejected this offer, based on advice from his Chief of Clandestine Services Broe.

After the presidential contest shifted to the arena of Chile's Congress, McCone took an offer authorized by Geneen to Helms and Henry Kissinger. At that time, Kissinger was working as Nixon's National Security Advisor. ITT was prepared to put up as much as $1 million in support of any plan that would deny Allende confirmation by the Chilean Congress (U.S. Senate, 1979: 229–30). Once again, the CIA and the White House declined ITT's offer.

Undeterred by the CIA's initial reluctance to support its suggestions, ITT went ahead on its own with plans to fund an anti-Allende media campaign in Chile and in Europe. ITT's staff also drafted a list of possible ways to defeat Allende, including a proposal to bring about a constitutional crisis that would induce Chile's army to intervene and prevent Allende's election by the Congress. Broe, head of covert operations for the CIA, "approved the recommendations" (U.S. Senate, 1979: 233). Broe went even further and proposed a plan to ITT whereby the CIA and U.S. MNCs would create "economic chaos" in Chile to pressure Congress into voting against Allende. Broe's plan suggested that U.S. banks in Chile either withhold credit or close their operations. MNCs would withhold capital, deny goods on order, and refuse to supply spare parts (1979: 233–34). Geneen and McCone found Broe's plans to be unworkable, however, and did not follow through on them. Broe then suggested that ITT maintain economic pressure on Chile in some way, perhaps by promoting a run on its banks.

After Allende was elected to the presidency by Congress in October 1970, ITT helped to organize an Ad Hoc Committee on Chile that included other MNCs doing business in Chile (for example, Anaconda, Kennecott). The goal of the ad hoc committee was to keep pressure on Kissinger and others in Washington to punish Allende. The ad hoc group wanted Washington to block loans to Chile from the World Bank and the Inter-American Development Bank. They hoped that economic pressure would force Allende to negotiate with the MNCs on favorable terms. Anaconda and ITT were especially strident in pushing this "hard line approach to Dr. Allende" (U.S. Senate, 1979: 237).

ITT's schemes against Allende culminated with an October 1971 memo to Kissinger's staff. In it, ITT proposed a plan of economic sabotage. An 18-point plan of economic pressure was designed to see that Allende would not "make it through the next six months." The plan proposed that: public and private banks should deny loans to Chile; U.S.

markets should be closed to Chile's exports; U.S. stockpiles of copper should be used as an alternative to purchases of Chilean copper; and U.S. currency and U.S. fuel supplies should be denied to Chile (U.S. Senate, 1979: 239). There is no evidence that Kissinger supported or acted upon these ITT proposals.

All of ITT's efforts against Allende came to naught when, in early 1972, Jack Anderson broke the ITT story based on documents he obtained from ITT's files. The ensuing scandal was an embarrassment for ITT, for the CIA, and for the Nixon administration. In its conclusions regarding the ITT affair, the Senate Subcommittee on MNCs stated that:

ITT sought to engage the CIA in a plan covertly to manipulate the outcome of the Chilean presidential election. In so doing the company overstepped the line of acceptable corporate behavior. If ITT's actions in seeking to enlist the CIA for its purposes with respect to Chile were to be sanctioned as normal and acceptable, no country would welcome the presence of multinational corporations. Over every dispute or potential dispute between a company and a host government in connection with a corporation's investment interests, there would hang the spectre of foreign intervention. No sovereign nation would be willing to accept that as the price for permitting foreign corporations to invest in its territory. The pressures which the company sought to bring to bear on the U.S. Government for CIA intervention are thus incompatible with the long-term existence of multinational corporations. (U.S. Senate, 1979: 242)

The Senate subcommittee did not mince any words in its final report. Not only was ITT's behavior inimical to the democratic rights of the Chilean people, it was also a threat to the existence of MNC operations in the Third World. Fortunately, ITT actions in Chile are an exception to the norm for corporate behavior. However, the story of U.S. involvement in Chile does not end here. The ITT scandal was just one chapter in what has become a long tale of possible U.S. involvement in human rights violations in Chile. The next chapter of this story opened in September 1973.

Human Rights in Chile after 1973

Allende had powerful opponents both inside and outside of Chile. Even while it condemned ITT's actions in Chile, the Senate Subcommittee on MNCs also expressed its strong objections to Allende's nationalizations without due compensation. By 1973, Allende's takeovers had spread to domestic corporations in Chile as well. Nationalization of more than 500 domestic firms spurred internal opposition and labor unrest (Kline, 1992:

12). Huge budget deficits combined with hyperinflation destabilized Chile's economic and political spheres. Despite higher wages, lower unemployment, and increased income equity under Allende, labor demonstrations shut down many factories in 1973 to protest economic hardships felt by the middle class. The most virulent opposition to Allende's neo-Marxism was to be found in the right-wing political parties and in the military. Ideological ferver on the right erupted into a military coup in September 1973.

The September coup took Allende's life and led to yet another radical change in Chile's political economy. The early days of the coup were a bloodbath. Estimates of those killed immediately after the military seized power range from a low of 1,000 (Donnelly, 1993: 54) to a high of 30,000 (O'Brien and Roddick, 1983: 110). A study on human rights in Chile by Phil O'Brien and Jackie Roddick cites an unofficial report from the U.S. State Department indicating that "10,800 people had been killed by December 1973" (1983: 110). The military junta that held power for the next 17 years was dominated by General Pinochet.

Pinochet's regime was guilty of massive human rights violations. Tens of thousands of people were tortured. Congress was dissolved and all leftist parties were outlawed. A state of emergency was declared and all civil rights were suspended. Media were tightly censored. There have long been suspicions that U.S. spies and military personnel may have been involved in the plotting or the execution of the coup in 1973. These suspicions are stimulated, at least in part, by memories of the ITT-CIA affair of 1970. Proof of direct U.S. involvement in the 1973 coup, however, has never materialized.

In addition to torturing and murdering its political opponents, the military regime under Pinochet also reversed the economic reforms of the Allende administration and embarked upon a program of free market capitalism. Although there has been no proof of U.S. involvement in the coup and U.S. MNCs have never been accused of contributing directly to Pinochet's grab for power, almost all foreign businesses in Chile have benefited from Pinochet's economic policies.

Pinochet's political strategies were based on rule by terror. His economic policies created the freest market in Latin America for U.S. investments and U.S. MNCs (Price Waterhouse, 1991). Pinochet reduced the role of the state in Chile's economy, dismantled state-owned enterprises, and opened Chile to international market forces. Economists known as the Chicago Boys designed and carried out Pinochet's economic policies.

The Chicago Boys were a dozen intellectuals who had been trained at the University of Chicago; many of them held doctorates in economics from Chicago. Training for Chilean economists at the University of Chicago was made possible by a long-standing student exchange program operated jointly by the University of Chicago and the Catholic University of Santiago. The University of Chicago taught economists the theories of Milton Friedman and Friedrich Von Hayek. The Chicago connection was established by advocates of laissez-faire economics and monetary policy to combat the influence in Chile of Prebisch and the structuralists at the ECLA (O'Brien and Roddick, 1983: 57).

The Chicago Boys ended government price controls, dropped barriers to imports, freed interest rates, ended deficit spending, cut government employment by one-third, and reduced the federal deficit by one-quarter (Kline, 1992: 14). This shock treatment for Chile's economy also included liberalization of foreign investment. Chile's 1974 law on foreign investment (Decree Law 600) created "one of the most liberal investment regimes in the developing countries" (1992: 24). MNCs are guaranteed open and nondiscriminatory treatment in Chile. A Foreign Investment Committee was established to grant *pro forma* approval for DFI requests. MNC contracts are also shielded from any future changes in DFI regulations. However, this last bit of protection for MNCs is hardly necessary. DFI regulations in Chile have only become more generous since 1974.

Chile's Foreign Investment Statute of 1977, an amendment to the 1974 law, allows foreign ownership by MNCs up to 100 percent for almost all business enterprises. MNCs are not required to sell any equity in their plants to Chilean nationals (Price Waterhouse, 1991). Profits and capital owned by foreign investors can be repatriated without quantitative limits. Foreign MNCs are also guaranteed national treatment. Foreign investment is treated just like local investment, and no discrimination is allowed against foreign corporations. Chile withdrew from ANCOM in 1976 because the Chicago Boys found the common market's policies on foreign investment to be too restrictive. Chile's investment laws since 1974 have guaranteed "fairness and equality . . . stability and security" to U.S. MNCs (Kline, 1992: 27).

Pinochet also moved quickly to repair the damage done to Chile's image among MNCs by Allende's nationalizations. Pinochet authorized $125 million in compensation to ITT. Most other MNCs had their nationalized properties returned. Pinochet kept control of the copper mines, but agreed to pay $300 million in compensation to the copper MNCs because "settlement of the nationalization/compensation controversies was a necessary if not a sufficient condition for the resumption of new foreign investment flows to Chile" (Kline, 1992: 12–15).

The economic policies of Pinochet and the Chicago Boys were not without social costs. These policy changes emphasized the interests of the upper classes and state elites (Silva, 1993). Hardest hit were the poor and the labor unions. Wages fell, and unemployment rose to almost 20 percent (O'Brien and Roddick, 1983). The Chilean labor movement lost 11,000 workers to Pinochet's terror. Most of these workers were killed, tortured, or became victims of politically motivated disappearances. After the coup, factory owners had complete control over the workers. Labor rights were suspended and collective bargaining was outlawed (Lear and Collins, 1995). A pro-labor Group of Ten formed in 1977 to fight for workers' rights, but members of the group were either jailed or exiled by Pinochet.

In 1979, Jose Pinera, a member of the Chicago Boys, became Minister of Labor. He pushed through a new Labor Code that allows only nominal workers' rights. The code provides for the existence of unions, but makes these unions as weak as possible. Unions exist only at the level of individual factories. A union cannot coordinate its activities with unions from any other factories. No two unions in the same economic sector are allowed to combine their negotiations during collective bargaining. Solidarity strikes by one union to show support for another union were outlawed. All strikes are limited to 60 days. After that time, strikers can be fired. Management has the right to hire temporary help to substitute for striking workers at any time. Employers can also sack up to 10 percent of their workforce each month without showing cause (O'Brien and Roddick, 1983: 80–81). New factories are protected from all unionization during their first year of operations, and employers have no obligation to provide any fringe benefits to their workforce (Price Waterhouse, 1991).

Local and international protests against denial of labor rights in Chile met with little success. In 1980 the International Labor Organization condemned Pinochet's treatment of workers and called on Chile to provide information regarding the forced dissolution of unions, purges of union leadership, and jailing and disappearances of union members.[56] Labor protests against Pinochet's regime peaked in 1982 and 1983 during a severe economic recession in Chile. Copper workers called a national strike in June 1983, an illegal act under the 1979 Labor Code. Pinochet responded with mass arrests and violence. Four people were killed and 600 were arrested, including Rodolfo Seguel, the head of the Confederation of Copper Workers. Some 3,400 strikers were fired, and state-run copper mines were put under army control.[57]

Labor unrest in the early 1980s was stimulated in part by the county's economic crisis. Heavy private borrowing from foreign banks had undermined Chile's economic stability. Interest rates soared and there was a wave of bankruptcies. A growing trade deficit also threatened Chilean industries and jobs. Pinochet handled the social unrest in his typical fashion with violent repression of the labor force. The Chicago Boys responded to the macroeconomic problems with an uncharacteristic intervention into the national economy. Chile's government moved to take over 85 percent of the foreign debt, converting those private loans into public debts. The Chicago Boys then crafted a five-year austerity program in 1985 that encouraged the International Monetary Fund (IMF) and the World Bank to restructure the Chilean debt portfolio.

Chile's structural adjustment programs meant more hardships for the working class. Wages fell by 20 percent and unemployment rose to more than 30 percent (Meller, 1992). Government expenditures for health and education were reduced 15–20 percent. Chile's structural adjustment policies were praised by the IMF and other international financial institutions and became the model that other LDCs were forced to adopt in order to obtain loans (Kline, 1992: 30; Meller, 1992: 72). While the IMF and MNCs praised Pinochet's austerity measures, Chile's poor suffered. During the adjustment period 1985–90, economic authorities "were more concerned with preserving the assets of private business than with preserving a minimum welfare level" for Chile's workers (Meller, 1992: 90).

Structural adjustment under Pinochet produced new DFI opportunites for MNCs. Chile experienced a boom of direct investment in the late 1980s, spurred on by the new incentive of debt-equity swap schemes (Paus, 1994: 41). Foreign investors and MNCs were encouraged to purchase Chile's international debts and then swap those debt notes for equity in Chilean industries. The debts were offered by Pinochet's administration for purchase at huge discounts. Some of the debts were sold and converted to equity for as little as 30 cents on the dollar (Kline, 1992: 29). Investors also had the option of selling the debt they had purchased to Chile's Central Bank and receiving payment in local currency at close to the full face value of the debt. This option guaranteed an "up-front cash incentive" for foreign investors to put their money into Chile's economy (1992: 29). Investors averaged a 66 percent return on their investments into Chile's debt-equity swaps, and $3.5 billion in debt was converted to equity ownership for foreign investors and foreign MNCs (1992: 29).

Pinochet's legacy to Chile is twofold. His rule by means of state terror left a political legacy of human rights atrocities and a nation in search of truth and reconciliation. His economic policies were built on denials of labor rights and economic peril for the poor, but he eventually produced macroeconomic growth and prosperity. Chile's return to democracy in

1990 required that Pinochet's successors come to terms with his political barbarism and make some hard choices concerning the economic structures built by Pinochet and the Chicago Boys.

Multinational Corporations and Human Rights in the Post-Pinochet Era

The return to democracy in Chile began in 1988. Pinochet conducted a plebiscite, asking voters to approve another eight-year term for him as president. Much to his surprise, Pinochet was rejected by the majority of voters in the 1988 plebiscite, and a free election was scheduled for 1989. A political alliance of parties opposed to Pinochet won the 1989 election and its leader, Patricio Alwyn, was sworn in as president of Chile in 1990. Pinochet stepped down from political office but remained as head of the Chilean military until 1998.

The most striking aspect of Chilean economic policy since 1990 is its basic consistency with the policies of Pinochet and the Chicago Boys (Angell, 1993). Post-Pinochet Chile has been declared the "best managed economy in Latin America, and one of the best in the world."[58] Among newly industrialized countries, it ranks as the fifth-most competitive, trailing Singapore, Hong Kong, Taiwan, and Malaysia but leading Brazil, India, and Mexico.[59] Chile's competitive edge is based on its open markets, attractiveness to MNCs, and liberalization (read repression) of the labor sector. All of these economic structures were established during the reign of the Chicago Boys.

Chile continues to be one of the favorite Third World havens for U.S. MNCs and foreign investment. Direct foreign investment in Chile averaged about $1 billion per year from 1989 to 1993.[60] Total foreign investment jumped to $4.7 billion in 1994.[61] Thousands of U.S. MNCs are now doing business in Chile. Lack of space prevents a full listing here, but some of the most prominent MNCs in Chile are: American Express, Atlantic Richfield, Bank of America, Bankers Trust, Bell South, Bridgestone, Cargill, Chase Manhattan, Chiquita, Ciba-Geigy, Cigna, Citibank, Coca-Cola, Digital, Dole, Dow, Esso, Exxon, Firestone, GE, GM, Goodyear, Kodak, McDonalds, Mellon Bank, Mobil, Motorola, Pepsi, Proctor & Gamble, Ralston Purina, RCA, Texaco, Unisys, Wells Fargo, W. R. Grace, and Xerox.

Rhoda Rabkin points to the ideological foundations of Chilean economic growth to explain why Chile's democratic governments have retained the essential features of the Chicago Boy model. Rabkin believes that Pinochet and the Chicago Boys successfully transformed the economic ideology of Chile. Pinochet's economic reforms have endured beyond his presidency because of this lasting change in ideology: "the changes in the Chilean political economy [created by Pinochet] will endure, because the thinking of Chileans has changed" (Rabkin, 1993: 3). The thinking of Chileans has changed, as compared to the era before 1973, because Pinochet's policies eventually created impressive economic growth. Between 1987 and 1990, Chile's economy grew at a rate of 7 percent per year.[62] This economic success made believers out of some of Pinochet's former critics.

Even Pinochet's political opponents in Chile have adopted his economic assumptions. The center-left political coalition that unseated Pinochet from the presidency in 1989 has stuck to the Chicago Boy economic model because "opposition political leaders were convinced that this was the surest way to win public office and to sustain a governing coalition thereafter" (Rabkin, 1993: 15–16). Further proof of this lasting shift in economic ideology can be found in the lack of meaningful labor law reform since the return to democracy. Rabkin points out that there has been no significant increase in unionization since 1989 and that democratically elected leaders have made no significant changes in the anti-labor statutes imposed during Pinochet's administration.

In the political realm, post-Pinochet governments faced the painful and dangerous question of how to deal with the egregious violations of human rights committed by the authoritarian regime. Pinochet remained as head of the armed forces in order to prevent prosecution of anyone from his administration. As long as Pinochet controlled the military, prosecution was a political impossibility. The military made it clear that they would not allow trials for Pinochet and his associates. As an alternative to putting those responsible for murder and torture on trial, Alwyn's government created the Commission for Truth and Reconciliation. The Truth Commission investigated and documented almost 1,000 disappearances that resulted in death during Pinochet's rule. Exposing the truth about these acts of torture and murder by Pinochet's government was accepted as a "partial substitute for punishment," because punishment of the guilty was not feasible (Donnelly, 1993: 55). Publication of the Truth Commission's findings in its two-volume 1991 report may seem a weak alternative to punishing the guilty, especially in light of the massive suffering caused by Pinochet's atrocities. However, the Truth Commission also became a model that at least one other nation has copied after a similar long-term trauma to its body politic. The Republic of South Africa created its own truth and reconciliation commission, chaired by Archbishop Desmond Tutu, to investigate and publicize human rights atrocities committed by apartheid governments. South Africa, following Chile's example, decided to accept an airing of the truth regarding its past as an alternative to prosecution of crimes against human rights.

To what extent were U.S. MNCs complicitous in the human rights violations committed by the Pinochet regime? Donnelly's case studies of human rights in the Southern Cone (Argentina, Chile, Uruguay) find no evidence that multinational corporations had much influence on Pinochet's choice of policies (1993: 47). Carleton's empirical study, although subject to the aggregation problem, also finds no statistical evidence to support the theory that MNCs in Latin America are drawn to nations that are the most repressive. Carleton's conclusion rejects the repression as cause hypothesis that MNCs are attracted by government repression. He finds no support "for the theory that increased levels of repression attract multinational corporations" (1989: 226).

If MNCs had little influence over Pinochet's policies, and if MNCs were cautious about locating in Chile during the early years of Pinochet's regime because of the "uncertain political and economic environment" there (Kline, 1992: 26), then one can hardly blame MNCs for human rights violations during the coup and the post-coup years. Even the repression of labor in the 1980s, which made it more profitable for U.S. MNCs to be in Chile, was an abuse of human rights for which the Pinochet government must take full responsibility. Surely it is Pinochet himself and his advisors who must take the blame for the horrors committed as they consolidated their power. Surely it is Pinochet and the Chicago Boys who must take the blame for repression of Chile's labor force. Chile is not Mexico. Responsibility for union-busting and denials of workers' rights cannot be laid at the doors of U.S. MNCs in Chile. Clearly, MNCs have indirectly benefitted from low labor costs in Chile, just as they have benefitted from the investment opportunites that opened up because of Chile's structural adjustment programs. However, it would be unfair to the corporations to claim that they caused repression of labor in Chile, or that they caused the social and economic hardships visited on the poor by Chile's austerity programs.

The key explanatory factor for human rights violations in Chile is ideology. Pinochet was determined to do what he did after 1973 not because of considerations about how his policies might affect foreign businesses. His obsession with wiping out Marxism meant that he was going to use as much murder and torture as he deemed necessary to complete the job. Leftists allied to Allende were to be wiped out, whether this policy benefitted MNCs or not. Even if his purges had been harmful to MNC interests, Pinochet would not have hesitated to carry them out. Pinochet's reign of political terror is explained by his anticommunist extremism. Similarly, the economic programs of the Chicago Boys, including their liberalization of the labor market (for example, disempowering unions through outright repression), are best explained by the ideology behind Hayek's economic theories. Even many business leaders found the ideas of the Chicago Boys to be too extreme. Their most ardent belief was that economic liberty is more important than political liberty. The latter had to be sacrificed for the purity of the former (O'Brien and Roddick, 1983: 57). The Chicago Boys were radical economic libertarians whose ideology told them that Chile's unions had to be sacrificed on the altar of laissez-faire economics.

Chile is similar to India and Mexico in that its political economy is geared toward rapid growth by means of multinationalization. All three nations have dropped their barriers to DFI and MNCs. Chile was the first to chart this path in the 1970s. India and Mexico relied on ISI strategies much longer than did Chile, but all three are now embracing globalization of their economies. The significant difference between Chile and the other two cases is the relative lack of complicity in human rights violations for MNCs in Chile. Terrible human rights abuses have occurred in Chile, but MNCs bear little or no direct responsibility, unlike MNCs in Bhopal and in the maquiladora zone. Human rights violations in Chile have been the worst of any nation studied in this chapter. However, the moral culpability of MNCs is also lowest in Chile of the three cases.

The fact that MNCs cannot be blamed for human rights abuses in Chile does not mean that U.S. private and public actors have no role to play in promoting rights in Chile. Mild economic and military sanctions were imposed on Chile by the United States in response to Pinochet's crimes. The Kennedy Amendment of 1976 cut off U.S. military aid to Pinochet. In 1987, Chile was dropped from U.S. preferential trade arrangements contained in the Generalized System of Preferences (GSP). The GSP provides tariff-free access to U.S. markets for selected goods from developing countries. Congress amended the GSP program in 1984 to attach new conditions that Third World countries must meet in order to qualify for GSP trade advantages. To be a beneficiary of the GSP, a nation must be "taking steps to afford workers internationally recognized workers' rights, including freedom of association, the right to organize and bargain collectively, freedom from forced labor, a minimum age of work for children, and acceptable conditions at work relating to hours, wages, and health and safety."[63] Chile was excluded from the GSP program in 1987 because of violations of workers' rights under Pinochet. This action was "an important element in putting pressure on Chile at the time of the ending of the

Pinochet government."[64] Chile was readmitted to the GSP program in 1990, but not until there had been a return to democracy and Chile's government had made some nominal reforms in its labor laws.

GSP sanctions against Chile for violations of labor rights are an important example of a relatively new tool that can be employed by U.S. foreign policy to promote and protect human rights. Along with the older policies of Section 502B governing military aid and the Harkin Amendment on economic aid,[65] the GSP requirements for respecting labor rights are likely to find numerous potential targets for human rights leverage. U.S. policy in the twenty-first century is going to need refinement, extension, and expansion of these laws if the United States is to have a positive impact on rights around the world.

International affairs in the 1990s have included a great deal of public attention to violations of human rights by MNCs. Sweatshops in Central America that turn out clothing for U.S. department stores have been front-page news in the United States. Alleged physical abuse and economic exploitation of workers in Nike factories in Indonesia and Vietnam have been the focus of investigative journalists and human rights activists. Use of child labor by U.S. MNC subcontractors in southern Asia has also raised the concerns of politicians and children's rights advocates. U.S. foreign policies and NGO strategies to combat these widely publicized abuses are among the final topics to be considered in this book. Those issues help to frame the discussion of MNCs, human rights, and public policy in the concluding chapter.

NOTES

1. Winston was kind enough to provide me with a copy of his address to Mobil.
2. Morton E. Winston, "Multinational Corporations and Human Rights," public address presented to the Mobil Corporation World Affairs meeting, summer, 1996.
3. Winston's work as Chair of Amnesty International USA's Board of Directors has included drafting a code of ethics for corporate behavior. In addition to drafting these recommendations regarding ethical and social responsibilities of corporations, Amnesty has also worked hard to develop a wide range of strategies for encouraging corporate behavior that respects, promotes, and protects human rights. Corporate codes of behavior and NGO activities regarding corporations and human rights will be discussed in Chapter 6.
4. "Bhopal: The Second Tragedy," a documentary about the long-term human and environmental impact of the disaster from Films for the Humanities and Sciences, Princeton, New Jersey.

5. Bogard also discusses, in less detail, hazards in other Third World nations regarding the nuclear power industry and deforestation (1989: 54–55, 85).

6. "Ex-Union Carbide Chief Targeted," *Wilmington News Journal*, March 28, 1992.

7. "10 Years Later, Bhopal Recalls Day of Tragedy," *Wilmington News Journal*, December 4, 1994.

8. "First Major Medical Survey on Bhopal Gas Victims," *India Now*, June 1985.

9. "Judges May Free India to Renew Battle over Bhopal," *New Scientist*, January 12, 1991.

10. Ibid.

11. "Health for None: The Bhopal Saga," *India Now*, June 1985.

12. "First Major Medical Survey," *India Now*, June 1985.

13. *Facts on File*, December 12, 1992: 1000.

14. Quoted in *India Now*, April 1985.

15. "Markets: Report Advises Increase in Foreign Direct Investment," *India Abroad* (On-line), April 12, 1996, http://www.indiaabroad.com.

16. "India Congress, Leftwing Party Skirmish on Economy," *India Net Digest* (On-line), April 19, 1996, http://www.digest@indnet.bgsu.edu.

17. (On-line) http://www.spectrum.ieee.org/public access/9511 teaser/whatsn.html

18. "Leader Commits BJP to Economic Reform," *India Abroad* (On-line), December 22, 1995, http://www.indiaabroad.com.

19. Ibid.

20. Ibid.

21. Ibid.

22. Exceptions were made. Between 1973 and 1980, 1,724 proposals for DFI were approved by the Mexican government. Of these, 171 (or roughly 10 percent) were wholly-owned foreign subsidiaries that geared 100 percent of their production for export. In addition to these 171 enterprises, there were only 44 others in which foreign MNCs were allowed to own more than 50 percent of equity (Marton, 1986: 261).

23. Marton notes that export-oriented assembly plants on the border were exempted from the Echeverria laws (1986: 267).

24. *National Geographic*, August 1996.

25. "Officials Accused of Intimidation," *New York Times*, August 15, 1993.

26. Ibid.

27. *Business Week*, April 19, 1993.

28. "Blacklist Charged at Border Plants," *New York Times*, August 15, 1993.

29. "The Mexican Worker," *Business Week*, April 19, 1993.

30. "How Will NAFTA Affect Safety in Mexico?" *Safety and Health*, June 1994.

31.	"Rate of Rare Birth Defects Soars Near Border Factories," *Trial*, October 1992.

32.	Ibid.

33.	Ibid.

34.	Ibid.

35.	U.S. Department of Labor, *NAFTA: The Supplemental Agreements* (Washington, D.C.: Government Printing Office, 1993).

36.	U.S. Department of Labor, *Mexico and NAFTA Report* (Washington, D.C.: Government Printing Office, 1995).

37.	"Mexico Plants Accused of Discrimination," *Wilmington News Journal*, August 18, 1996.

38.	"Paltry Resources," *New York Times*, August 19, 1993.

39.	"Mexico May Renege on Cleanup," *Wilmington News Journal*, May 16, 1995.

40.	"Report Rips Mexico-U.S. Border Plan," *Wilmington News Journal*, April 8, 1996.

41.	"How NAFTA Jeopardizes Health, Safety and Environmental Standards," *Multinational Monitor*, October 1993.

42.	Ibid.

43.	Ibid.

44.	"Treaty Partners Study Fate of Birds at Polluted Mexican Lake," *New York Times*, August 1, 1995.

45.	Ibid.

46.	"Environment Tests NAFTA," *Multinational Monitor*, July/August 1995.

47.	Ibid.

48.	"NAFTA Foes Say Pact Hurts Environment," *Wilmington News Journal*, January 2, 1996.

49.	"Environment Tests NAFTA."

50.	Ibid.

51.	Mickey Kantor, "NAFTA Maintains U.S. Environmental Standards," *New York Times* (letter to the editor), September 23, 1993.

52.	"Some Pray the Pact Will Bring Converts," *New York Times*, August 16, 1993.

53.	"Good NAFTA? The Widely Reviled Pact May Actually Be Benefitting Mexico," *Utne Lens* (On-line), http://www.webkeeper@utne.com.

54.	Ibid.

55.	Ibid.

56.	"ILO to Intensify Work in Field of Human Rights," *UN Chronicle*, May 1980.

57.	"Out of the Frying Pan and into the Fire," *Newsweek*, June 27, 1983.

58.	"Chile Shows the Way," *Economist*, November 13, 1993.

59.	Ibid.

60.	"The Tequila Hangover," *Economist*, April 8, 1995.

61. "No Going Back," *Economist*, June 3, 1995.

62. "Key Macroeconomic Indicators," *Chile Business Update* (On-line), February 1996, http://www.beachnet.org/chiletrade.

63. "Working for Labor Rights," *Multinational Monitor*, December 1993.

64. Ibid.

65. See Chapter 2 in this book.

6

Conclusion

MULTINATIONAL CORPORATIONS AND HUMAN RIGHTS: POSITIVE VERSUS NEGATIVE EFFECTS

International economic inputs have a profound effect on human rights in Third World nations. This is especially true of the economic factors studied in this book — foreign investment, foreign aid, and multinational corporations (MNCs). The research presented in Chapters 3, 4, and 5 produced mixed results. The time has come to summarize my findings and to make some sense out of what may seem to be inconsistent results. This exercise will lead to related discussions about the nature of theory-building in the social sciences and recent efforts to improve the behavior of MNCs. I will also offer some final thoughts about the likely course of future debates on the proper relationship between culture and human rights.

At the broadest level of the global political economy, there is a positive relationship between direct foreign investment by MNCs and better human rights in Third World nations. Increased investment by MNCs is associated with better first and second generation rights in the Third World as a whole. There was no evidence from the aggregate studies of Chapter 3 to support theories that accuse MNCs of human rights abuses in less developed countries (LDCs). LDCs that receive more economic aid from the United States were also found to have better first and second generation human rights. The results of Chapter 4 suggest that, as economic aid goes up across Third World nations, civil-political rights and the physical quality of life both tend to improve. MNC investment, economic growth, and U.S. economic aid all tend to have a similar impact on rights at the broadest international level. As these economic inputs increase, we find associated improvements in human rights.

Turning to military aid, I found that nations receiving higher levels of security assistance also tend to have lower levels of civil and political rights. Similarly, I found that increased military aid was inversely related to the physical quality of life index. Measures in this index tend to go down as military aid goes up across the sample of Third World nations receiving substantial military assistance (more than $1 million per year).

At the broadest levels, MNCs as a group have a net beneficial impact on rights. At a lower level, however, I also found evidence of human rights abuses by particular MNCs in particular LDCs. The violations of human rights by MNCs reviewed in Chapter 5 were more than isolated or anecdotal instances. There is a clear pattern of direct anti-union activities by many of the MNCs in northern Mexico. The environmental destruction unleashed in Bhopal and in the maquila zone is evidence of a further human rights problem caused by the direct actions of U.S. MNCs. MNCs in India and Mexico have violated second generation labor rights and third generation rights to a clean environment.[1]

Women and children tend to suffer most from these patterned abuses of rights. Women and children were the primary victims of the Bhopal catastrophe. Because they represent the bulk of the labor force in the maquila zone, women are the primary targets of anti-union activities and work-related injuries. Sexual harassment and discrimination also remain as prevalent problems in the Third World MNC workplace.

At the international level, I found MNCs to be beneficial to human rights. At the national level, I found patterned behavior by many MNCs that is inimical to rights. This mixed bag of results is not surprising, however, given the nature of the theories with which I started, and given the nature of theory testing in the social sciences. Imre Lakatos has offered a useful description of scientific theories and scientific testing.[2] All theories, according to Lakatos, have a similar structure. They are made up of long chains of empirical assumptions and scientific hypotheses. These elements are connected to each other and display some degree of internal logical consistency. A broad theory, such as the Hymer thesis or the engines of growth view, is best understood as a research program. A research program exists on at least two levels. At its center is the hard core of the theory. This hard core represents the theory's most basic assumptions. For example, at the hard core of the Hymer thesis are the assumptions that poor nations are exploited by wealthy countries and that the organizational structure of MNCs causes inequality amongnations. Beyond the hard core of each theory is a protective belt of less important assumptions and hypotheses that are related to the core but which can be refuted or jettisoned without requiring changes to the hard core assumptions.

Social scientists frequently test a theory by comparing hypotheses derived from that theory to empirical data. This was the methodology used in Chapters 3 and 4. Lakatos argues that empirical testing of this sort may corroborate or falsify elements of a theory's protective belts but not its hard core assumptions. In fact, for Lakatos, the hard core itself can never be proven to be correct or incorrect, because "all theories are equally unprovable" (1970: 95). Well-developed theories are very complex. Any test of a complex theory can only hope to assess the accuracy or validity of some limited part of that theory. Therefore, "we cannot prove theories and we cannot disprove them either" (1970: 100), because this would require an infinite number of tests to fully assess the many parts of a broad and complex theory.

Lakatos develops this description of scientific theories not because he thinks theory testing is a waste of time. The fact that we cannot prove or disprove the truth of a theory in any final sense does not make theory testing and theoretical debate any less important. On the contrary, theory testing becomes even more important precisely because the truth value of the hard core is indeterminable. Lakatos favors "methodological tolerance" and "theoretical pluralism" (1970: 155–57). He wants to see a proliferation of theories within scientific disciplines. He believes that when there are many theories to advance conflicting truth claims, then scientific progress is more likely to occur.

When one tests a theory, what one is most likely to be testing are the protective belts of the theory and not its hard core of assumptions. Therefore, when we find that empirical evidence is not consistent with hypotheses derived from the theory, we have not refuted or falsified the theory as a whole.[3] Rather, scientific testing of a theory at best may call into question the protective belts and probably requires that defenders of the theory rethink some of their ancillary hypotheses. However, the hard core basic assumptions of the theory have not been disproven.

Foreign investment by MNCs is associated with better human rights at the international level. However, this finding from Chapter 3 does not, in and of itself, falsify the Hymer thesis. Some MNCs try to destroy labor unions. Many MNCs do harm to the environment. These findings at the national level are consistent with the Hymer thesis. However, these lower level findings do not negate the validity of the engines of growth theory at the higher level.

Lakatosian philosophy of science reveals why the conclusions from Chapter 3 are inconsistent with the conclusions from Chapter 5, yet both sets of results remain valid. The Lakatosian view of theory, if properly applied to theory-building in the social sciences, would predict precisely this type of outcome from extensive testing of a theory as broad and vague as the Hymer thesis (or the engines of development view). Both theories are painted with incredibly broad strokes. One theory predicts harm to rights from MNCs, and the other predicts a beneficial impact of MNCs on rights. Either one or both could be an accurate description of MNCs and rights under certain conditions. The engines of development view is the most valid description at the international level, where the good done by the majority of MNCs outweighs the harm done by other MNCs. At this level, the random errors cancel out, as a statistician would say, and what we are left with is the good done by MNCs in the aggregate. At this level, Hymer's thesis does not hold.

To the contrary, when one seeks evidence at a lower level that human rights have been abused by specific MNCs, such evidence is not hard to find. Hymer's thesis stands confirmed at that lower level of analysis. The larger, crucial, theoretical point in all of this is that neither theory has been proven false in any final sense. Both have evidence in their support at different levels of analysis and in different contexts.

Concomitantly, both theories have been weakened to some extent. Neither can claim to be an accurate description of the impact of MNCs on rights in all contexts. Each theory has only limited validity; a kernel of truth. Each kernel of truth is accurate in some contexts and erroneous in others. However, to show that either theory has holes in its intellectual fabric is insufficient proof to justify dimissing that theory *in toto*. What my tests have done is to expose the weaknesses of each theory at different levels of analysis. A more fundamental test of either theory would require going to its hard internal core. Again, Lakatos gives us the best account of how that must be done. To reject an entire theory requires what Lakatos calls "sophisticated methodological falsification."[4] Sophisticated falsification of a theory happens only when an old theory is replaced by a new, full-blown, alternative theory. The new theory must explain the same facts that were accounted for by the old theory. The new theory must also account for additional facts that the old theory could not explain.

In order to refute either the Hymer thesis or the engines of development theory, once and for all time, one would have to develop a new grand theory of human rights and MNCs. This new theory would have to explain why MNCs are beneficial to rights at the international level and also account for conditions under which MNCs will be harmful to rights at lower levels of analysis. No such grand theory of rights and MNCs will be attempted by this author is this book. My goal is not to create new theories of rights and MNCs. Rather, my goal is to present empirical evidence that is directly related to the validity of existing theory. I also hope that my research, rather than leading to new theory, could inform the debates on human rights that are now taking place in policy circles and in activist organizations.

There have long been allegations of human rights abuses on the part of MNCs in Chile, India, and Mexico. These nations were selected as case studies for Chapter 5 in part because they are among the most publicized cases.[5] Someone or some group cared enough and was committed enough to investigate the behavior of MNCs in these nations. Rights activists and human rights nongovernmental organizations (NGOs) deserve most of the credit for bringing specific abuses by MNCs to the attention of scholars. Activists can help to set academic research agendas by their documentation of human rights abuses. Social science research, for its part, must be tied closely to ongoing policy debates. Political activism and basic research both have a necessary role to play regarding international human rights. Scholars must produce research that informs debate and ties into salient policy issues. Human rights activists can help to point students of human rights in certain directions rather than others.

For U.S. politics in the 1990s attention to human rights violations by MNCs has centered around a few particular cases. These are the same cases that led the Clinton administration and NGOs to create new methods for pressuring MNCs to respect human rights. A review of these cases and recent policy innovations follows. That review will lead me to a final consideration of the utility of political and philosophical research for international human rights.

SWEATSHOPS VERSUS CODES OF CONDUCT

Sweatshops

Much media attention and considerable NGO activity have been devoted to investigating the alleged use of Third World sweatshops by U.S. MNCs. Nike manufactures in Indonesia and Vietnam. Wal-Mart has contracted with textile plants in Honduras. Goods for the Disney stores are sewn in Haiti. Clothes for the Gap come from maquiladoras in El Salvador. These are just a few examples from the scores of U.S.

multinationals that employ a total of 1 million garment workers in LDCs. The high profiles of pop-culture icons like Michael Jordan and Kathie Lee Gifford, who endorse goods for Nike and Wal-Mart, guarantee media attention. As charges of abuse in sweatshops have grown, many human rights organizations have mounted worldwide campaigns to eliminate sweatshop conditions. A minor scandal involving alleged sweatshops and Wal-Mart's Kathie Lee line of clothing became important enough in 1996 for President Clinton to appoint a task force on sweatshops. The recommendations from the task force, as well as NGO strategies for fighting sweatshops, will be reviewed later; but first let us look at the charges against MNCs. Two cases are especially instructive. Wal-Mart operations in Honduras and Nike's plants in Indonesia are good examples of the international political economy of sweatshops.

Philip Knight, co-founder of Nike, was a graduate student at Stanford's business school in the 1960s when he wrote a paper on the potential profits to be made by manufacturing sneakers in Asia. Today, Nike is the world's largest athletic shoe manufacturer, with annual sales of more than $6 billion and profits exceeding $500 million in 1996.[6] Nike achieved this success by putting Knight's Stanford theory into practice. Nike began manufacturing in Asia during the 1970s with plants in South Korea and Taiwan. As unions were formed and wages rose in those countries, Nike shifted its production to Indonesia in 1986 and later expanded into China and Vietnam.

Indonesia is controlled by an authoritarian government under President Suharto. The U.S. State Department and Amnesty International have documented a long history of human rights abuses by Suharto's regime, not the least of which involves the brutal invasion, annexation, and subsequent repression of the independent nation of East Timor.[7] Indonesia is also a haven for MNCs and foreign investment. Only one union is allowed to exist under Indonesian labor laws. That union is government controlled. Independent unionization is not allowed. Recent State Department reports have singled out Indonesia's repression of labor rights for special criticism.[8]

Adidas, Converse, Nike, Reebok, and many other athletic equipment manufacturers have operations in Indonesia. Nike is the largest by far, employing 120,000 workers in Indonesia. Women make up 90 percent of the apparel industry workforce. Indonesia produces the largest percentage of Nike products of any nation, approximately 36 percent.[9] Nike, like other MNCs in Indonesia, does not have direct ownership of the factories. Rather, they hire subcontractors who own the plants. Journalists and human rights activists have documented the following abuses by MNC subcontractors in Indonesia: verbal, physical, and sexual abuse of workers; use of child labor; sexual discrimination; and corporal punishment used against workers. Anyone who attempts to organize the workers and workers who merely speak out against low wages or unsafe working conditions are arrested, fired from their jobs, and sometimes murdered.

Violence has been used routinely to control workers. One union organizer was kidnapped, raped, and killed in 1996, allegedly by the military.[10] Police have been brought in to break strikes, interrogate labor leaders, and intimidate workers.[11] Workers often go on strike simply to protest the fact that they are not being paid the minimum wage required under Indonesian law. Twenty-three strikers who protested against subminimum wages in 1992 were fired. Similar firings, for the same reason, took place at other Nike plants in 1996. A riot at one plant in 1997 forced a three-day shutdown. Some 5,000 workers went on a rampage, burning cars and destroying the factory's offices. Workers claimed they were not being paid an increase in the minimum wage that had been mandated by law weeks before. In this instance, the plant had to give in and agree to a 10 percent pay raise.[12]

Workers in Nike production facilities also claim they have been forced to work overtime, and child labor is common. Indonesian law requires that workers be at least 15 years old, but girls as young as 13 have been hired in many plants. Children as young as 11 stitch together soccer balls for Nike and Reebok subcontractors in Pakistan.[13] Documented physical abuse against workers includes: kicking, hitting, slapping, striking on the buttocks, and women being forced to run around one plant in the hot sun until they fainted. Twelve of these women had to be taken to an emergency room; their crime was wearing the wrong kind of shoes to work.[14] A spokeswoman for Nike's corporate headquarters condemned this last incident, saying the company was outraged and horrified by what had happened to the 12 women.[15]

Because all MNCs, including Nike, are sensitive to public pressure and want to avoid a bad image in the media, many have taken steps to counter the bad press caused by sweatshop allegations. Levi Strauss pulled its production out of Indonesia altogether when subcontractors were accused of strip searching their employees in 1994. In 1992, Nike adopted a code of conduct for its 35 plants throughout Asia. According to Nike's corporate officers, all subcontractors are required to adhere to the code. It requires compliance with all local laws, including minimum wage statutes. Forced labor and use of child labor are prohibited. The Nike code also requires provision of worker insurance and compliance with local health and safety regulations.[16]

Nike even went so far as to hire Andrew Young, former Ambassador to the United Nations (UN), and his consulting firm to do an independent audit of conditions in Nike's Asian plants. Young announced the results of his investigations in June 1997. He said he found no evidence of widespread or systematic abuse of workers at Nike's factories. Nike's critics questioned the objectivity of Young's assessment, pointing out that his firm, Goodworks International, was on the Nike payroll. Young's report clearing Nike of any responsibility quickly lost credibility. The same week that Young's favorable report was released, a manager at one of Nike's subcontractors was convicted of physically abusing workers.[17]

Nike claims to be a force for positive changes in the Third World. If Nike receives complaints about worker abuse, company policy says that the subcontractor must rectify the situation or Nike will consider termination of the business. Knight is fond of pointing out that there are always long lines to apply for jobs at every one of Nike's Asian plants, implying that people are eager to work for his company. He also believes that MNCs lead LDCs out of poverty. He claims to have the "best factories in the world," factories that have (in his opinion) the "best conditions" for their workers. Knight and his associates also warn that if wages go too high, it could wreck the economies of Third World nations.[18] Nike spokesman Jim Small cautioned that the 10 percent raise forced on Nike's subcontractor by the 1997 riot could cause the labor force in Indonesia to "price itself out of the market."[19] Nike, the Indonesian government, and economists from the World Bank all claim that low wages are a necessary condition for sustained economic growth in Indonesia.[20]

Growth in Indonesia has been impressive during the last three decades. No doubt part of this growth is due to the presence of foreign MNCs. Economic output has increased by an average of 7 percent per year for the last 30 years.[21] GNP per capita has tripled over the last 20 years.[22] Perhaps Nike's workers in Indonesia are happy, as Knight would like us to believe. According to at least one survey, most of the workers in Nike subcontractor factories say they like working there. However, the survey showing worker satisfaction at Nike plants conducted its interviews while management was present, calling into question the candor of the employees' comments. According to the same study, "Indonesia is booming and poverty is falling, relative to its impoverished past, and much of the boom has come since American companies began investing there a decade or so ago."[23]

It is evident, however, that many of Nike's workers have not shared in Indonesia's recent economic prosperity. Minimum wages are not always paid by Nike subcontractors, a violation of Indonesian law and contrary to

Nike's own code of conduct. Even when the minimum wage is paid, it is equal to only 90 percent of the cost of living for one person in Southeast Asia. The retail price for one pair of Nike sneakers in the United States is roughly equivalent to a month's wages for a worker at one of their plants in Indonesia. Nike's critics want the corporation to guarantee workers not just the below-subsistence-level minimum wage. They believe that the number one maker of athletic shoes is wealthy enough to provide a living wage to all of its employees.

Similar charges of abuse and similar demands for redress have been brought against Wal-Mart for its operations in Honduras. Early in 1996 sweatshop allegations regarding Wal-Mart became a media event because of the role played by Gifford. Accusations that the Kathie Lee line of clothing was produced by women working under sweatshop conditions first brought a defensive denial from the talk show celebrity. Congress quickly scheduled hearings on the matter, and labor activists substantiated the charges against Wal-Mart's suppliers. Testimony before Congress revealed the use of child labor in Honduran maquiladoras. Workers also testified to laboring in extreme heat for up to 20 hours per day, at wages of only 31 cents per hour.[24]

Prior research shows that the conditions exposed during the 1996 Wal-Mart scandal are nothing new. A long history of worker abuse in Honduran export processing zones has been documented by labor activists. Verbal, physical, and sexual abuse have been common in these plants. Workers have been hit, punched, slapped, threatened, and had their heads smashed into sewing machines by managers.[25] One worker even told of having scissors pressed against her face and being threatened with disfigurement if she talked to anyone about the beatings at her plant.[26]

Although 16 is the minimum age for workers under Honduran law, it is not unusual to find girls as young as 12 sewing in the maquila plants. Pregnant women have been fired so the facories can avoid paying maternity benefits. No unions are allowed in the Honduran export processing zones. Workers who attempt to organize unions are fired and blacklisted.[27]

As the investigation into the Wal-Mart case progressed, charges of sweatshops hit much closer to home. As it turns out, some of the Kathie Lee items were sewn in New York City at a "substandard and abusive" factory that mirrored some of the sweatshop conditions of the Honduran plants.[28] Gifford dropped her defensive posture after the New York plant was exposed and became an advocate in the media for labor rights instead. She started to campaign against child labor and sweatshops. When it was revealed that workers in the New York City sweatshop had not been paid, Kathie Lee sent her husband to the plant to hand out $300 in cash to each worker. She appeared at a press conference with Governor George Pataki in support of state legislation allowing seizure of goods made in sweatshops.[29] She met with a 15-year-old girl from Honduras who said she had been abused and sexually harassed at the plant contracted by Wal-Mart. Finally, she appeared at the White House with Secretary of Labor Robert Reich and assisted Clinton's task force on sweatshops.

Corporate Codes of Conduct

Clinton organized the task force on sweatshops in response to the attention generated by the Wal-Mart controversy. Media politics and public pressure persuaded Clinton to create a committee made up of representatives from the MNCs, labor organizations, human rights NGOs, and religious organizations. The Apparel Industry Partnership (AIP) was organized to draft a voluntary code of conduct for the garment industry that would prohibit sweatshops and other forms of worker abuse.

The AIP was not the Clinton administration's first attempt at a corporate code of conduct. In 1995 his administration announced an earlier, voluntary code of conduct for U.S. corporations operating abroad. At that time, Clinton was under pressure from critics who had denounced his 1994 decision to renew China's most favored nation trading status. The Model Business Principles of 1995 were designed to appease people who were concerned about trade and human rights in China. The 1995 principles, however, satisfied neither MNCs nor human rights activists. The code drafted by the White House called on U.S. firms to: respect workers' rights to organize and bargain collectively; promote free expression for workers and prohibit political coercion in the workplace; prohibit child labor, forced labor, and discrimination based on race, gender, or religion; provide a safe and healthy workplace; and adopt responsible environmental practices.[30]

The 1995 code was designed with China in mind but addressed U.S. MNCs in all countries to avoid singling out China. Companies were asked to adopt the code voluntarily, but corporate America was less than enthusiatic. Business leaders, many of whom had already drafted codes for their own firms, criticized the 1995 Model Principles as being too vague and too broadly worded to have any meaningful effect. Corporations were also upset that the White House had drafted the principles without consulting anyone in the business community.[31] Members of Congress called the proposal "weak and ineffectual," and a director for Human Rights Watch said that Clinton's 1995 code fell "far short of what is needed."[32]

The Clinton administration learned from the tepid reponse to their 1995 code and applied this lesson to the drafting of an anti-sweatshop code in 1996. This time, corporate leaders and human rights NGOs were invited to take part in the drafting process itself. After eight months of work the AIP announced its code. The AIP code of conduct incorporated the 1995 model principles, but the anti-sweatshop code also went much farther. In addition to elements carried over from the 1995 principles, the AIP voluntary code sets a maximum 60-hour work week and requires at least one day off per week, bars the use of prison workers, prohibits employment of children younger than 15 except in those countries where the minimum work age is 14, and requires MNCs to pay no less than the local minimum wage.[33]

Manufacturers who promise to adhere to the AIP code are rewarded with a "no sweatshop" label for their products. Nike, Reebok, Liz Claiborne, L.L. Bean, Eddie Bauer, Phillips-Van Heusen, Patagonia, and Nicole Miller were among the first MNCs to sign on to the agreement. Critics argued that the AIP code was little more than a clever way for MNCs to gain a better public image, as corporations wage a public relations campaign to fool consumers into thinking conditions are improving in Third World garment maquiladoras. This naturally raises the question of who will monitor compliance with the agreement and enforce the code. Task force members suggested that local human rights NGOs be used to monitor compliance, but it is much more likely that MNCs will be left to police themselves. A half-dozen human rights organizations that were not parties to the task force denounced the AIP code for not requiring U.S. firms to pay a living wage in the Third World. The code was also criticized for not banning excessive overtime.[34] One critic went so far as to call the AIP code "the goodhousekeeping seal of approval for a kinder, gentler sweatshop."[35]

The 1990s witnessed a proliferation of corporate codes of conduct, some coming from the White House, some coming from the corporations themselves, and the best models coming from non-governmental organizations. NGOs, such as the Coalition for Justice in the Maquiladoras (CJM) and Amnesty International (AI) have produced corporate codes on human rights that are superior to those coming from the White House or from MNCs.

The CJM code is much more detailed than the White House recommendations of 1995 and 1996. The CJM's Maquiladora Standards of Conduct were drafted in 1991 by a coalition of 60 community, environmental, labor, Latino, and women's organizations. The CJM standards are based on existing Mexican and U.S. laws, as well as international labor standards established by the International Labor Organization.[36] The CJM code targets the maquiladoras in northern Mexico, and its provisions are based on CJM's knowledge of the past behavior of the maquilas. The 1991 Standards of Conduct focus on four areas: environmental contamination, health and safety, fair employment practices, and community impact of the maquilas.

The environmental provisions of the CJM code are the most detailed and demanding to be found in any corporate code on rights and responsibilities. This is understandable, given the environmental crises in Mexico caused by the maquiladoras.[37] MNCs are called on to comply with all federal environmental regulations from both the United States and Mexico. Environmental impact statements should be filed for all new MNC operations. MNCs are also to publish all government citations for environmental violations, along with the steps being taken to come into compliance. The CJM standards require full public disclosure of all toxic discharges and of all hazardous materials in storage. Full disclosure is also called for regarding transportation or disposal of any hazardous materials. MNCs are called upon to ensure proper disposal of all spent containers for toxic substances.[38] Finally, the CJM code requires that MNCs undertake remedial action to clean up any past dumping and pay fair compensation to anyone who has been harmed by pollution. None of the maquiladoras has been willing to endorse the CJM code's environmental provisions.

Section II af the CJM code covers health and safety. Corporations are called on to comply with Mexican and U.S. health and safety regulations. Companies must disclose to employees and to the public the identity of all chemicals and all chemical wastes on their premises. Appropriate warning labels must be affixed to each container with instructions in Spanish and English. Employees are to have written explanations of the risks associated with all toxic materials, and MNCs are asked to use the least toxic chemicals available. Corporations must also take steps to limit repetitive strain injuries and other ergonomic problems. Health and safety training and protective clothing and equipment for all workers are additional corporate responsibilities under the CJM standards. Finally, the CJM code calls for regular inspections by both an in-house worker and management safety team and by qualified, outside, independent consultants.

Section III of the Maquiladora Standards of Conduct addresses fair employment practices. Discrimination is prohibited, as is child labor. Equal pay must be provided for equal work. U.S. corporations must recognize Mexican workers' rights to organize and bargain collectively. MNCs are also reminded of Mexican laws that require medical treatment, severence pay, profit sharing plans, and other benefits for workers. Finally, corporations must take positive steps to prevent sexual harassment, including educating employees about what constitutes sexual harassment.

The final section of CJM's Standards of Conduct covers the community impact of maquiladoras. U.S. transnational corporations are reminded of their moral responsibilities to local communities in Mexico. The standards speak out against the barracks style housing that is so common in the maquila zone. Corporations are called on to cease construction of barracks and to take immediate steps to move employees out of existing barracks and into more suitable housing. Corporations are also called upon to establish trust funds for improving infrastructure in the maquila zone. Schools would be one of the primary beneficiaries of these trust funds.

The CJM succeeded in drafting one of the most detailed codes of conduct for U.S. MNCs. If put into effect, this code would have a major impact on improving human rights conditions in Mexico. Alas, calls for MNCs to endorse and comply with the Maquiladora Standards of Conduct have largely fallen on deaf ears in the corporate sector.

Amnesty International has developed the most comprehensive approach to improving MNC behavior regarding human rights. AI has drafted its own code of conduct for MNCs, but its policies on MNCs and rights include much more than just the code. AI does not do any independent monitoring of corporate behavior. AI also takes no position regarding sanctions or boycotts against particular MNCs.[39] They do, however, "in some cases, expose, publicize and campaign against corporations which are engaged in verifiable patterns of conscious collusion or unconscious collaboration with human rights violations by governments."[40] AI has identified three types of MNCs that are a threat to human rights. First are those MNCs that produce products or services that others use to violate human rights. Second are those MNCs that knowingly cooperate with human rights abuses committed by others. Third, and most serious, are MNCs that directly commit human rights violations themselves.

AI tactics regarding MNCs and rights exist on three levels. First, AI has developed a general set of principles that should be included in any corporate code of conduct. Second, AI urges MNCs to respect and promote the following rights in their own sphere of operations: freedom of speech, freedom of opinion, and freedom of assembly; labor rights; maternity leave and child care; adequate housing and education for employees; and nondiscrimination in the workplace. Finally, AI asks MNCs to be proactive outside their own sphere of operations. MNCs should require that all subcontractors and business partners uphold the rights listed above. MNCs should provide their good offices and resources in support of local human rights NGOs. MNCs should also express due concern for human rights to host governments. AI believes that "human rights are everyone's business," for all corporations large and small, and for all employees "from the factory floor to the corporate boardroom."[41]

AI's "Principles and Recommendations Concerning Corporate Ethical and Social Responsibility in the Field of Human Rights" were completed in 1996.[42] This document was motivated by two concerns. AI wanted to demonstrate its support for adoption of codes of conduct by individual corporations. AI offered its recommendations, which are themselves based on the Universal Declaration of Human Rights, as a model to be followed by MNCs when drafting their own codes of conduct.

Specific recommendations from AI on what to include in each MNC's code of conduct begin with prohibitions against discrimination in hiring and promotions. Next are rights to security of the person. Corporations with private security forces must establish guidelines on the appropriate use of coercion, restraint, and force against employees who are considered a security threat. Companies must ensure that security personnel refrain from all acts that constitute cruel, inhuman, or degrading treatment. Security forces must also refrain from all acts of arbitrary arrest, detention, or exile. Companies that produce a product that can be used in the violation of human rights should keep watch over the end uses of their products, and should discontinue selling to anyone using said products in the violations of rights. To protect rights that prohibit slavery, MNCs must forbid the use of bonded child labor or coerced prison labor.

To ensure the right to work, companies must guarantee free choice of employment, protection from unemployment, and equal pay for equal work. Companies must also enforce policies that prohibit interference with the right to form or join labor unions.

To promote the rights to rest and leisure and the right to subsistence, companies should ensure reasonable hours of work and periodic holidays with pay. MNCs should also provide support for basic subsistence to employees who, because of circumstances beyond their control, lack the ability to continue working. Such arrangements would include medical benefits, insurance, housing allotments, pension plans, and emergency relief funds. Employees should be granted leaves of absence from work in order to care for sick children without jeopardizing their employment.

Finally, AI notes that the right to education can be indirectly supported by MNCs that enforce policies prohibiting child labor. The right to education is also promoted by corporations that facilitate technical training and educational programs for their workers.

For each area of rights, AI calls on all corporations to ensure these freedoms in their own sphere of operations and to promote the same rights in the wider communities in which they operate. AI also encourages individual business men and women to provide support for any persons denied these rights.

The codes of conduct drafted by AI, by CJM, and by the White House are blueprints for MNC behavior that respects and promotes human rights. Codes of conduct, like NGO exposure of specific rights violations, also serve as useful indicators for where to focus research on rights. As we have seen over the course of this book, human rights research can be conducted at several different levels of analysis and by employing many distinct methodologies. The study of international human rights cuts across many dimensions and many academic disciplines. Philosophy, cultural anthropology, policy analysis, international law, developmental theory, and political economy are just a few of the modes of analysis that can contribute to an understanding of the relationship between MNCs and rights.

Because research into human rights is such a diverse field of study, the purposes for that research can also be numerous. David Ricci has identified two of the most common reasons that political scientists engage in research. Political scientists seek either to partake of small conversations or to engage in what Ricci calls the great conversation (Ricci, 1984). Most contemporary political science is content to stay in the realm of small conversations, whereas Ricci wants the discipline to return to its roots in the great conversation. I find Ricci's distinction between small conversations and the great conversation intriguing, and I will use this distinction to make some final comments on my own research.

SMALL CONVERSATIONS VERSUS THE GREAT CONVERSATION: TOWARD A GLOBAL CULTURE FOR HUMAN RIGHTS

Ricci has written an excellent history of political science as an academic discipline. The book's title reflects Ricci's belief that a close look at the discipline reveals *The Tragedy of Political Science*. The history of political science is a tale of tragedy because, in Ricci's opinion, the discipline has lost its way and abandoned its founding principles. The evolution of political science has pushed the discipline away from the great conversation. The great conversation of classical political theory has been replaced with a much more restricted series of small conversations.

The decline of political science began (for Ricci) when it abandoned "the traditional vocabulary of political theory" and adopted instead a more value-neutral vocabulary about empirical political phenomena (Ricci, 1984: 298–99). The old vocabulary used traditional concepts, such as justice, rights, patriotism, and virtue. The purpose of classical political theory was to engage in the great conversation regarding the founding purposes of the discipline. The founding principles of the discipline were the moral development of individuals; pointing the way toward a better society; and promoting the values of democracy, citizenship, and tolerance. The new vocabulary claims to be more scientific than the traditional discourse on politics. The new vocabulary seeks scientific precision and tries to avoid value judgments by employing words like attitude, interaction, cognition, socialization, and system. However, as the new vocabulary tries to make the study of politics more scientific and more empirical, it also precludes the great conversation. Political science has replaced the great conversation with a series of more limited and limiting small conversations.

"Small conversations take place in many learned disciplines, when members of a scholarly community speak mainly to one another, in language so specialized and full of jargon that it is largely unintelligible to the public or to their colleagues in other university departments across the campus mall" (Ricci, 1984: 299). This is the point at which political science becomes a tragedy. The tragedy is that a purely empirical "science of politics" cannot produce the type of knowledge required for "good citizenship and better government" (1984: 70). As political research has become more scientific, it has also become more threatening to values the discipline once upheld. For example, empirical political scientists have studied the role of elites and the impact of public apathy on U.S. politics. The conclusions reached in the course of these small conversations were that political control in the hands of elites, and political apathy on the part of the masses, were good for U.S. politics (1984: 153). Research by Lipset, Truman, and others argued that low voter turnouts, combined with greater power in the hands of privileged elites, were "somewhat desirable" factors for U.S. politics because "people who are relatively privileged are more likely than the masses to support democracy itself" (1984: 153).

Professional political scientists become so caught up in their small conversations that they fail to see the larger implications of their research. In the case of research on masses and elites, the investigators failed to appreciate the truly antidemocratic nature of their conclusions. For Ricci, a return to the great conversation is needed to reveal the antidemocratic bias hidden in the scientific conclusions drawn by Lipset, Truman, and other political empiricists. For Ricci, the larger issue is that political science as an institution needs to adopt new approaches that could counter apathy among the masses and reduce the concentration of political power in the hands of elites. To raise such issues, however, would be contrary to the objectivity that most contemporary political scientists believe is required for doing true scientific work. Most research by professional political scientists is confined to the realm of empirical and objective science. This is the realm of the small conversations. The great conversation is value-laden and inherently normative, hence it is avoided by empiricists who engage in small conversations.

No doubt Ricci would classify the research presented in Chapters 3, 4, and 5 as small conversations. Given the way he defined small conversations, I would have to agree. My purpose in presenting the research from my empirical chapters was not to create "good citizenship and better government"; therefore, I was not engaged in the great conversation. Research in Chapter 3 is engaged in the small conversation established by theories of rights and development. Chapter 4 was a discourse in the small conversation of theories on rights and foreign aid. However, unlike Ricci, I do not think that one can ultimately separate the great conversation from the smaller ones.

It seems to me that the great conversation will go nowhere unless its debate over weighty moral issues is based on an accurate understanding of the world around us. In order to get to the great conversation, and in order for the great conversation to produce results that could effectively change the world, a lot of less glamorous work needs to be done at the level of the small conversations. There is no way around this. We need to be clear on the nitty-gritty details of our world before we can hope to effectively reform political or economic structures. We need to know exactly how, and exactly to what extent, MNCs violate human rights before we can hope to ensure greater international justice by forcing a change in MNC behavior. We need to be clear on the good done by MNCs, as well as the bad, if we want to make them better. We need to go down to the level of the small conversations frequently if we want to make the great conversation something more than just a debate about preferences and passions.

The one point at which this book rose to the level of the great conversation, as defined by Ricci, was in Chapter 1. The international debate over the proper relationship between culture and rights is a good example of what Ricci must have had in mind when he made his distinction between small and great conversations.[43] What could be more important to the moral development of individuals or to the creation of a better polity than deciding which rights are to be universal human rights? I want to return now to this great conversation concerning a cross-cultural standard of human rights that is applicable to all societies.

In my conclusion to Chapter 1, I spoke of a possible synthesis of the conflicting views on rights and culture. I outlined the content of this synthesis, but I did not say anything about the process by which the synthesis would be achieved. The substance of a synthesis combining normative hegemony and cultural relativism began with an emphasis on individual rights and on first generation civil and political rights. Then, I argued, first generation rights of individuals would have to be supplemented by second and third generation rights and by a sensitivity to group rights. I also argued that attention to rights abuses by governments had to be supplemented by attention to MNCs that violate rights. My best guess is that the great global conversation on culture and rights must evolve in the direction of such a synthesis. My reasons for optimism and my hopes for cross-cultural agreement on rights are based on my predictions of how this compromise will be produced.

How will the synthesis of international views on culture and rights be achieved? Will it be done by philosophers or political theorists who define human rights for us? I doubt it. Will it be done by international laws that declare universal human rights? I think not, at least not as a first step. International agreement on basic human rights can be established only through a political process, through international political dialogue. This political process will take place and is already taking place within the context of an emerging global culture.

A truly global culture would have to have certain necessary elements. It would include a set of institutions that could claim moral and political legitimacy at the international level (perhaps a strengthened United Nations and World Court). It would include patterned interactions among its members (for example, global transportation and communication networks). It would include a global economic structure that unites its various parts under a shared set of guidelines and common use of the same economic instruments (most likely to be free markets, the World Trade Organization, and the U.S. dollar). It would include a set of globally recognizable symbols (such as the "$," the "golden arches," and the Coke logo). Finally, a global culture must necessarily include a set of shared norms, a universally applicable set of human rights standards. Although many would debate the extent to which a global culture currently exists, I take it to be irrefutable that business, economic, political, and social trends are at least moving us in the direction of an emergent global culture. My interests lie with those elements of the nascent global culture that are most closely related to human rights and a global political community.

According to Glenn Tinder, "community is inquiry," and inquiry "takes place through communication" (1980: 30–31). Therefore, a political community can be conceptualized as a space within which communication takes place. A global community, then, would be a global space within which global inquiry and global communication take place. A global human rights community would be a space for communication and inquiry into a set of shared norms. A global political community is defined by Henry Nau "in terms of how states chose to identify rights. . . . The degree of similarity in national conceptions of the good political life defines the boundaries of shared international political community" (1990: 56). I would suggest that by means of a global dialogue on human rights, we are indeed seeking out the boundaries of a shared political community. At the same time we are furthering the growth of the normative underpinnings for a global culture.

Universal human rights, in this sense, represent nothing less than the ethical dimensions of the emerging global culture. Human rights are, therefore, the "primary values of international relations" (Forsythe, 1991: 7). A global culture is in the making; the evidence of this abounds. Perhaps the greatest steps forward to date have been in the areas of communications and transportation. Global media networks are now commonplace. Satellite linkages allow for instantaneous transmission and reception of news, information, telephone, and economic exchanges. Computerized international currency exchange alone now exceeds $650 billion per day (Denemark, 1992: 4). This expanding global communication-transportation-economic space has a direct impact on normative international affairs. The fall of the Eastern bloc that began in 1989 constituted a victory for the spread of civil and political rights by means of the demonstration effect. The demonstration effect itself was created by economic interactions and by media outputs from the West to the East.[44]

My point here is simply that a global communication space already exists, and this has certain direct, normative effects. A global ethical space is still evolving. Movement toward this shared international ethical space is inevitable and irreversible. It is an unstoppable movement if only because of the exponential expansion of the global communication-information net.

How is this global ethical space (a normative global culture) being established? How will a universally applicable set of human rights standards be achieved? Not via philosophy and not via international law, at least not the crucial next steps. Development of new international laws and legal instruments (treaties, enforcement mechanisms, and so forth) are important for the creation of a global moral culture. Law, however, like philosophy, cannot be the prime mover. Defining and applying global standards of human rights are ultimately political acts. Politics is the primary sphere for future normative synthesis at the global level. The three categories from Chapter 1 regarding the relationship between culture and rights can help us to understand the essential political nature of this process.

Normative hegemony and strong cultural relativism stake out positions of confrontation and exclusion regarding definitions of human rights. Normative hegemony says that rights have a certain restricted definition, and if you are not talking about that particular definition, then you are not talking about human rights. Instead you are merely referring to human dignity or some other such conceptual category. Strong cultural relativism counters with claims that normative hegemony is culturally biased and ethically deficient for non-Western societies. Strong cultural relativism says that non-Western standards are often superior to the allegedly non-applicable Western conceptions of human rights. Both normative hegmony and strong cultural relativism construct arguments designed to exclude each other's position.

To develop a cross-cultural definition of human rights requires that we develop a multicultural definition of human rights. No one set of cultural norms should be given necessary priority in all cases. The political process requires that we seek consensus. The process should be such that it facilitates the building of consensus. The process requires tolerance and a willingness to let all voices be heard. On the other hand, Americans have no need to apologize for sticking up for the values of our culture. The process requires tolerance of opposing views, as well as the responsibility for strong advocacy of our own norms. It is in the nature of the international human rights movement to establish a core set of norms. International human rights can never be a matter of anything goes. Some things are simply beyond the pale. Which values are to be excluded? Again, this is more of a political question than it is a matter of having the proper philosophical definition for rights. Those norms will be excluded that the global dialogue determines to be beyond the pale for a shared set of standards. Like any observer, I have my own personal aversions to practices that I believe are inconsistent with a shared global standard. These include the obvious candidates of genocide and slavery, along with others that remain controversial to this day: inequality between the sexes, female genital mutilation, and use of child labor. The inherent strength of normative hegemony is that, of all views, it most clearly excludes such practices as being contrary to human rights and fundamental freedoms. However, the inherent weakness of normative hegemony is that, if not tempered by some degree of cultural relativism, it tends to exclude too much. It seeks to silence the voices of other parties to the international dialogue by means of a priori definitions of what properly constitutes the legitimate denotation of the term "human rights."

Just exactly where do we draw the line then? The line between normative hegemony and cultural relativism will be determined by those who are involved in the efforts to build a global community and a global culture. Politics remain primary. Nation-states, human rights NGOs, and individual rights activists all have roles to play. Whether we like it or not, key players will come from the United States. U.S. foreign policies and U.S. corporations will continue to have a disproportionate share of influence and responsibilities. Perhaps this is as it should be. The only way to influence the course of events in this realm is to get into the game.

Strong cultural relativists who opt out of the human rights dialogue, as Islamic fundamentalism and China's government have come dangerously close to doing, will find that they have little or no influence over the creation of international normative standards. Such a lack of influence would almost certainly carry over into other spheres of global interaction (media, diplomatic influence, economic power, and so forth). In the terminology popularized by Nye (1990), nations or cultures that opt out of the human rights dialogue will have no "soft power." Their lack of influence regarding normative and cultural debates will necessarily carry over into a lack of influence over other social, political, and economic developments as well. Futhermore, those who are a party to the ongoing human rights debate are likely to find themselves transformed by the process. Moderate Islamic states are a good example of cultures undergoing slow but significant transformation of their policies on rights.

Global trends in international political economy are further indications that economic power and normative influence will go hand-in-hand in the twenty-first century. U.S. foreign economic policy takes the position that all future trade agreements must include minimal standards for labor rights and environmental protections. In the future, expansion of the North American Free Trade Agreement and of the World Trade Organization will require that violations of labor rights or lack of vigorously enforced environmental standards are to be classified as unfair trade practices.[45] Because the United States is the number one player in the game of international trade, its norms regarding labor and environmental rights carry the most weight. The common market members of the European Union also support this view. Therefore, as Third World nations become more fully integrated into free trade regimes with the Organization for Economic Cooperation and Development nations (another inevitable trend), then LDCs will be forced to drop their cultural reservations against protecting all three generations of human rights. To do anything less would exclude LDCs from the free trade agreements of the twenty-first century, something that they cannot afford.

At their most basic levels, international economic power and global normative influence are indivisible. U.S. foreign policies and U.S. MNCs are destined to be major players in both areas. However, no one can determine the outcome of the debate over culture and rights in advance by defining human rights prior to the international political dialogue. Likewise, expanding the political and legal frameworks that protect human rights to include MNCs (as well as governments) will not be a quick or easy task. Unfortunately, it will be a long time, perhaps generations, before these issues are resolved. As Max Weber once said of politics itself, creating universal standards of human rights, and enforcing human rights obligations on MNCs, will be analogous to the "slow boring of hard boards" (1946: 128).

NOTES

1.   There is also evidence from Chile that MNCs are enhancing environmental problems there. See Kline, 1992: 264–65. See also Collins and Lear, 1994; "Chile's Environment Pays Price of Development," *Wilmington News Journal*, March 29, 1992.

2.   I must note in all fairness that Lakatos explicitly excludes social science theories from those theories he says he is describing. Lakatos would say that the theories I reviewed in Chapter 3 (the Hymer thesis and the engines of growth theory) are not worthy of being called scientific theories. Lakatos himself finds all social science theories to be "pseudo-intellectual garbage" and takes his examples of true theory from the hard sciences (physics) (1970: 176). The theory testing methods that I used in Chapter 3 (perhaps the most common statistical techniques used in contemporary political science) are also denounced by Lakatos. He feels that all social science theory and all social science statistical procedures are nothing more than ad hoc attempts. They produce little more than "intellectual pollution" (1970: 176).

3.   Popper (1965) built an elaborate philosophy of science based on the assumption that theory testing can refute or falsify theories. Much of Lakatos' work is an effort to correct what he saw as Popper's mistakes in this area.

4.   Lakatos favors sophisticated methodological falsification as opposed to Popper's naive or dogmatic falsification.

5.   The squeaky wheel gets the grease.

6. "U.S. Industry Overseas: Sweatshops or Job Source?" *Washington Post*, July 28, 1996.

7. Indonesia invaded East Timor in 1974. The ensuing occupation and military repression of Timorese self-determination has caused more than 200,000 deaths. This genocide has killed roughly one-third of the island's population. See "A Victim's Plea for Justice," *Los Angeles Times*, November 15, 1996.

8. "U.S. Officials Exhibit Dichotomy in Policy on Indonesia and Human Rights," *Washington Post*, March 18, 1995.

9. "U.S. Industry Overseas."

10. "Indonesia Goes for Gold in Sweatshops," *Los Angeles Times*, July 28, 1996.

11. "An Indonesian Asset Is Also a Liability: Low Wages Woo Foreign Business, But the Price Is Worker Poverty," *New York Times*, March 16, 1996.

12. "Indonesian Plant that Makes Sneakers for Nike Settles Pay Dispute after Melee," *Wall Street Journal*, April 28, 1997.

13. "An Indonesian Asset."

14. "Brutality in Vietnam," *New York Times*, March 28, 1997.

15. Ibid.

16. "An Indonesian Asset."

17. "Manager for Nike Contractor Convicted," *Wilmington News Journal*, June 28, 1997.

18. "Trampled Dreams," *New York Times*, July 12, 1996.

19. "Indonesian Plant Settles Pay Dispute."

20. "For Indonesian Workers at Nike Plant: Just Do It." *New York Times*, August 9, 1996.

21. "Indonesia Goes for Gold in Sweatshops."

22. "U.S. Industry Overseas."

23. Ibid.

24. "Kathie Lee's Misstep Exposes Sweatshops," *Wilmington News Journal*, June 13, 1996.

25. "Women and Children First: Labor Rights Abuses in Honduran Maquiladoras," *Multinational Monitor*, January/February 1993.

26. Ibid.

27. Ibid.

28. "Kathie Lee's Misstep."

29. Ibid.

30. "Code of Conduct Draft Assailed," *Washington Post*, March 28, 1995.

31. "White House Unveils Its Overseas Code of Corporate Conduct," *Los Angeles Times*, March 28, 1995.

32. Ibid.

33. "Apparel Industry Gets Conduct Code," *Wilmington News Journal*, April 15, 1997.

34. "Anti-sweatshop Code Gets Clinton Blessing," *Wilmington News Journal*, April 13, 1997.

35.   Ibid.

36.   The full text of the CJM code of conduct can be found in the *CJM Newsletter*, 2(1): 1992.

37.   See the discussion of Mexico in Chapter 5.

38.   All too often these dangerous containers that once held hazardous chemicals are used to transport and store water for poor people living around the maquilas.

39.   For example, in the 1980s and 1990s, an international boycott was organized against Nestle Corporation. The Nestle boycott was in protest against the way they marketed their infant formula in the Third World. Critics charged that Nestle used high pressure tactics and misleading information to increase sales of their products. These tactics allegedly led to improper use of the formula by Third World mothers and may have caused the deaths of millions of babies. See "Boycott Retargets Multinational," *The Interdependent*, 16(3): 1990.

40.   Morton E. Winston, "Multinational Corporations and Human Rights," public address to Mobil Corporation's World Affairs meetings, summer 1996.

41.   Ibid.

42.   I am indebted to Winston for providing me with a draft of AI's code for corporate conduct.

43.   Ricci does not discuss debates over culture and human rights in his book. Instead, he points to the book by John Rawls (1971), *A Theory of Justice*, as an example of the "way out of political science's dilemma"; the dilemma being the need to choose between great versus small conversations (Ricci, 1984: 320).

44.   For a discussion regarding the impact of a media demonstration effect on international cultural changes, see Meyer, 1988: chap. 4.

45.   "Son of GATT: The New World Trade Organization Needs the Right Priorities and the Right Boss," *Economist*, August 6, 1994.

Selected Bibliography

Aboulmagd, A. Kamal. (1990). "Human Rights in Islam." *Salzburg Seminar Newsletter*, 18: 4–6.

Access Information Service. (1994). "US Troops in Somalia." *Resource Brief*, 8(4).

Alexander, Robin, & Gilmore, Peter. (1994). "The Emergence of Cross-Border Solidarity." *NACLA Report of the Americas*, July/August 1994: 42–49.

Amin, Samir. (1979). "Toward an Alternative Strategy for Auto-centered Development." In George Modelski (ed.), *Transnational Corporations and World Order*, pp. 404–13. San Francisco, Calif.: W. H. Freeman.

Amnesty International. (1995). *Human Rights and US Security Assistance*. New York: Amnesty International USA Publications,

Angell, Alan. (1993). "The Transition to Democracy in Chile: A Model or an Exceptional Case?" *Parliamentary Affairs*, October 1993, pp. 1–15.

Banks, David L. (1986). "The Analysis of Human Rights Data Over Time." *Human Rights Quarterly*, 8(4): 654–80.

Bedau, Hugo Adam. (1979). "Human Rights and Foreign Assistance Programs." In Peter G. Brown and Douglas MacLean (eds.), *Human Rights and U.S. Foreign Policy*, pp. 29–44. Lexington, Mass.: D. C. Heath.

Beinart, Peter. (1996). "Out of Africa." *World Politics Annual Editions 96/97*: 156–59.

Bergsten, C. Fred, Horst, Thomas, & Moran, Theodore H. (1978). *American Multinationals and American Interests*. Washington, D.C.: Brookings Institution.

Black, Naomi. (1989). *Social Feminism*. Ithaca, N.Y.: Cornell University Press.

Bogard, William. (1989). *The Bhopal Tragedy: Language, Logic and Politics in the Production of a Hazard.* Boulder, Colo.: Westview.

Boyd, Andrew. (1990). *Atlas of World Affairs.* New York: Routledge.

Brecher, Jeremy. (1993). "Global Village or Global Pillage?" *The Nation,* December 6, 1993, p. 685.

Brems, Eva. (1997). "Enemies or Allies? Feminism and Cultural Relativism as Dissident Voices in Human Rights Discourse." *Human Rights Quarterly,* 19(1): 136–64.

Brown, Peter G., & MacLean, Douglas (eds.). (1979). *Human Rights and U.S. Foreign Policy.* Lexington, Mass.: D. C. Heath.

Bunch, Charlotte. (1990). "Women's Rights as Human Rights: Toward a Re-Vision of Human Rights." *Human Rights Quarterly,* 12(3): 486–98.

Calvocoressi, Peter. (1987). *World Politics since 1945.* New York: Longman.

Caporaso, James A. (1987). *A Changing International Division of Labor.* Boulder, Colo.: Lynne Reiner.

Cardoso, Fernando Henrique, & Faletto, Enzo. (1971). *Dependency and Development in Latin America.* Berkeley: University of California.

Carleton, David. (1989). "The New International Division of Labor, Export-Oriented Growth, and State Repression in Latin America." In George A. Lopez and Michael Stohl (eds.), *Dependence, Development, and State Repression.* Westport, Conn.: Greenwood.

Carleton, David. (1985). "The Foreign Policy of Human Rights." *Human Rights Quarterly,* 7(2): 205–29.

Carleton, David, & Stohl, Michael. (1987). "The Role of Human Rights in U.S. Foreign Assistance Policy." *American Journal of Political Science,* 31(4): 1002–18.

Carr, E. H. (1939). *The Twenty-Years' Crisis.* New York: Harper.

Chandler, Alfred D., & Redlich, Fritz. (1961). "Recent Developments in American Business Administration and Their Conceptualization." *Business History Review,* Spring 1961, pp. 103–28.

Chomsky, Noam. (1988). *The Culture of Terrorism.* Boston, Mass.: South End.

Chomsky, Noam. (1979). *The Political Economy of Human Rights.* Boston, Mass.: South End.

Chomsky, Noam, & Herman, Edward S. (1979). *The Washington Connection and Third World Fascism.* Boston, Mass.: South End.

Cingranelli, David Louis. (1993). *Ethics, American Foreign Policy, and the Third World.* New York: St. Martin's.

Cingranelli, David Louis (ed.). (1988). *Human Rights: Theory and Measurement.* London: Macmillan.

Cingranelli, David Louis & Pasquarello, Thomas E. (1985). "Human Rights and the Distribution of U.S. Foreign Aid to Latin American Countries." *American Journal of Political Science,* 29(3): 539–63.

Claude, Richard P., & Jabine, Thomas B. (eds.). (1992). *Human Rights and Statistics.* Philadelphia: University of Pennsylvania Press.

Claude, Richard P., & Jabine, Thomas B. (1986). "Editor's Introduction." *Human Rights Quarterly*, 8(4): 551–66.

Coalition for Justice in the Maquiladoras. (1995). "Ford Workers Strike for a Living Wage!" *CJM Newsletter*, Summer 1995, pp. 1–2.

Coalition for Justice in the Maquiladoras. (1993). "Stepan Chemical Company: The Poisoning Continues." *CJM Newsletter*, Spring 1993, pp. 1–6.

Cobbah, Josiah A. M. (1987). "African Values and the Human Rights Debate: An African Perspective." *Human Rights Quarterly*, 9(3): 307–31.

Cohen, Stephen D. (1994). *The Making of United States International Economic Policy*. Westport, Conn: Praeger.

Collier, David. (1993). "The Comparative Method." In Ada Finifter (ed.), *Political Science: The State of the Discipline*. Washington, D.C.: American Political Science Association.

Collins, Joseph, & Lear, John. (1994). *Chile's Free-Market Miracle: A Second Look*. San Francisco, Calif.: Institute for Food and Development Policy.

Conteh-Morgan, Earl. (1990). *American Foreign Aid and Global Power Projection*. Brookfield, Vt.: Gower.

Copper, John. (1985). *Human Rights in Post-Mao China*. Boulder, Colo.: Westview.

Cranston, Maurice. (1973). *What Are Human Rights?* New York: Taplinger.

Danaher, Kevin, Berryman, Phillip, & Benjamin, Medea. (1987). *Help or Hindrance? United States Economic Aid in Central America*. San Francisco, Calif.: Institute for Food and Development Policy.

Das, Tarun. (1997). "The Equation of Eight P's: A New Economic Direction for India." *World Affairs*, 1(2): 104–13.

Denemark, Robert A. (1992). "Finance and Fads in International Political Economy." Paper presented to the Annual Meetings of the International Studies Association, Atlanta, March 1992.

Department of State (1990). "Caribbean Basin Initiative." *Gist*, April 1990. Washington, D.C.: Bureau of Public Affairs.

Doherty, Carroll J. (1994). "GOP Sharpens Budgetary Knife over International Programs." *Congressional Quarterly*, December 17, 1994, pp. 3566–69.

Doherty, Carroll J. (1993). "Sending Aid Abroad." *Congressional Quarterly*, December 11, 1993, pp. 74–93.

Dominquez, Jorge I. (1979). *Enhancing Global Human Rights*. New York: McGraw-Hill.

Donaldson, Gary A. (1996). *America at War Since 1945*. Westport, Conn.: Praeger.

Donaldson, Thomas. (1982). *Corporations and Morality*. Englewood Cliffs, N.J.: Prentice-Hall.

Donnelly, Jack. (1993). *International Human Rights*. Boulder, Colo.: Westview.

Donnelly, Jack. (1989a). *Universal Human Rights in Theory and Practice*. Ithaca, N.Y.: Cornell University Press.

Donnelly, Jack. (1989b). "Repression and Development: The Political Contingency of Human Rights Tradeoffs." In David P. Forsythe (ed.), *Human Rights and Development*, pp. 305–28. New York: St. Martin's.

Donnelly, Jack. (1986). "International Human Rights: A Regime Analysis." *International Organization*, 40(3): 599–642.

Donnelly, Jack. (1982). "Human Rights and Human Dignity: An Analytic Critique of Non-Western Conceptions of Human Rights." *American Political Science Review*, 76(1): 303–16.

Donnelly, Jack, & Howard, Rhoda E. (1986). "Human Dignity, Human Rights, and Political Regimes." *American Political Science Review*, 80(3): 801–17.

Doran, Charles. (1994). "North-South Relations and Foreign Aid Reform: A Realistic Approach." In Richard S. Belous and Sheila M. Cavanagh (eds.), *New Views on North-South Relations and Foreign Assistance*. Washington, D.C.: National Planning Association.

Doran, Charles. (1978). "U.S. Foreign Aid and the Unstable Polity." *Orbis*, 22(2): 435–52.

Doran, Charles, with Modelski, George, & Clark, Cal. (1983). *North-South Relations: Studies in Dependency Reversal*. New York: Praeger.

Dougherty, James E., & Pfaltzgraff, Robert L., Jr. (1990). *Contending Theories of International Relations*. New York: Harper & Row.

Dworkin, Ronald. (1977). *Taking Rights Seriously*. Cambridge, Mass.: Harvard University Press.

Ebenstein, William. (1969). *Great Political Thinkers: Plato to the Present*. Hinsdale, Ill.: Dryden.

Eckstein, Harry. (1975). "Case Study and Theory in Political Science." In Fred Greenstein and Nelson Polsby (eds.), *Handbook of Political Science*. Reading, Mass.: Addison-Wesley.

Encarnation, Dennis J. (1989). *Dislodging Multinationals: India's Strategy in Comparative Pespective*. Ithaca, N.Y.: Cornell University Press.

Enloe, Cynthia. (1990). *Bananas, Beaches and Bases: Making Feminist Sense of International Politics*. Los Angeles: University of California Press.

Falk, Richard. (1981). *Human Rights and State Sovereignty*. New York: Holmes and Meier.

Feinberg, Joel. (1973). *Social Philosophy*. Englewood Cliffs, N.J.: Prentice-Hall.

Feinberg, Joel. (1970). "The Nature and Value of Rights." *Journal of Value Inquiry*, 4 (Winter): 243–60.

Fernandez-Kelly, Maria Patricia. (1983). *For We Are Sold, I and My People*. Albany: State University of New York Press.

Forsythe, David P. (1991). *The Internationalization of Human Rights*. Lexington, Mass.: D. C. Heath.

Forsythe, David P. (1989). *Human Rights and World Politics*. Lincoln: Nebraska University Press.

French, Peter. (1984). *Collective and Corporate Responsibility*. New York: Columbia University Press.

General Accounting Office. (1993). *Foreign Assistance: AID Strategic Direction and Continued Management Improvements Needed*. Washington, D.C.: General Accounting Office.

Gerner, Deborah J. (1988). "Weapons for Repression? U.S. Arms Transfers and the Third World." In Michael Stohl and George Lopez (eds.), *Terrible Beyond Endurance: The Foreign Policy of State Terrorism*. Westport, Conn.: Greenwood.

Goldstein, Robert Justin. (1986). "The Limitations of Using Quantitative Data in Studying Human Rights Abuses." *Human Rights Quarterly*, 8(4): 607–27.

Goodman, Ellen. (1993). "Women's Rights Are Human Rights." *Wilmington News Journal*, June 22, 1993, p. 11.

Guendelman, Sylvia, & Silberg, Monica Jasis. (1993). "The Health Consequences of Maquiladora Work: Women on the US-Mexico Border." *American Journal of Public Health*, January 1993, pp. 37–45.

Hadar, Arron. (1981). *The U.S. and El Salvador*. Berkeley, Calif.: US-El Salvador Research and Information Center.

Haniffa, Aziz. (1996). "Record Foreign Direct Investment Reported." *India Abroad* (On-line), March 22, 1996, http://www.indiaabroad.com.

Henderson, Conway W. (1993). "More Murder in the Middle: Life-Integrity Violations and Democracy in the World, 1987." *Human Rights Quarterly*, 17(1): 170–91.

Henderson, Conway W. (1991). "Conditions Affecting the Use of Political Repression." *Journal of Conflict Resolution*, 35(1): 120–42.

Hofrenning, Daniel J. B. (1990). "Human Rights and Foreign Aid." *American Politics Quarterly*, 18(4): 514–26.

Holsti, Ole R. (1996). "Public Opinion on Human Rights in American Foreign Policy." *American Diplomacy* (On-line), 1(1): http://www.unc.edu/depts/diplomat/Holsti.

Hook, Steven W. (1995). *National Interest and Foreign Aid*. Boulder, Colo.: Lynne Reinner.

Howard, Rhoda E. (1986). *Human Rights in Commonwealth Africa*. Totowa, N.J.: Rowman and Littlefield.

Howard, Rhoda E. (1983). "The Full-Belly Thesis: Should Economic Rights Take Priority Over Civil and Political Rights? Evidence from Sub-Saharan Africa." *Human Rights Quarterly*, 5(4): 467–90.

Human Rights Watch. (1995). "Bosnia-Hercegovina." *Human Rights Watch/Helsinki Report*, 7(13).

Human Rights Watch. (1991). *El Salvador's Decade of Terror*. New Haven, Conn.: Yale Unversity Press.

Huntington, Samuel P., & Nelson, Joan. (1976). *No Easy Choice: Political Participation in Developing Countries*. Cambridge, Mass.: Harvard University Press.

Hymer, Stephen. (1979). "The Multinational Corporation and the Law of Uneven Development." In George Modelski (ed.), *Transnational Corporations and World Order*, pp. 386–403. San Francisco, Calif.: W. H. Freeman.

Jentleson, Bruce W. (1997). "Who, Why, What and How: Debates over Post–Cold War Military Intervention." In Robert J. Lieber (ed.), *Eagle Adrift*. New York: Longman.

Juffer, Jane. (1988). "Dump at the Border: U.S. Firms Make Mexico a Wasteland." *Progressive*, October 1988, pp. 24–29.

Kinder, Hermann, & Hilgemann, Werner. (1978). *Anchor Atlas of World History*. New York: Doubleday.

Kirkpatrick, Jeane. (1981). "Establishing a Viable Human Rights Policy." *World Affairs*, Spring 1981, pp. 317–27.

Kirkpatrick, Jeane. (1979). "Dictatorships and Double Standards." *Commentary*, November 1979, pp. 34–45.

Kline, John M. (1992). *Foreign Investment Strategies in Restructuring Economies: Learning from Corporate Experiences in Chile*. Westport, Conn.: Quorum.

Knight, C. Foster. (1995). "NAFTA Promises Payoff in Environmental Benefits." *Forum for Applied Research and Public Policy*, Summer 1995, pp. 29–33.

Koechlin, Tim. (1995). "NAFTA's Footloose Plants Abandon Workers." *Multinational Monitor*, April 1995, pp. 25–27.

Kowalewski, David. (1989). "Asian State Repression and Strikes against Transnationals." In George A. Lopez and Michael Stohl (eds.), *Dependence, Development and State Repression*. Westport, Conn.: Greenwood.

Kowalewski, David. (1982). *Transnational Corporations and Caribbean Inequalities*. New York: Praeger.

LaBotz, Dan. (1993). "Manufacturing Poverty: Maquiladorization of Mexico." *Multinational Monitor*, May 1993, pp. 18–23.

LaFeber, Walter. (1997). *America, Russia and the Cold War*. New York: McGraw-Hill.

Lakatos, Imre. (1970). "Falsification and the Methodology of Scientific Research Programmes." In Imre Lakatos and Alan Musgrave (eds.), *Criticism and the Growth of Knowledge*. Cambridge: Cambridge University Press.

Lappe, Frances Moore, Collins, Joseph, & Kinley, David. (1980). *Aid as Obstacle: Twenty Questions about Our Foreign Aid and the Hungry*. San Francisco, Calif.: Institute for Food and Development Policy.

Lear, John, & Collins, Joseph. (1995). "Working in Chile's Free Market." *Latin American Perspectives*, 22(1): 10–27.

Lerner, Daniel. (1964). *The Passing of Traditional Society: Modernizing the Middle East*. New York: The Free Press.

Levinson, Jerome I. (1993). *The Labor Side Agreement to NAFTA: An Endorsement of Abuse of Labor Rights In Mexico*. Washington, D.C.: Economic Policy Institute.

Lewis-Beck, Michael S. (1980). *Applied Regression: An Introduction*. Beverly Hills, Calif.: Sage.

Lijphart, Arend. (1971). "Comparative Politics and Comparative Method." *American Political Science Review*, 65(2): 682–93.

Lippmann, Matthew. (1985). "Multinational Corporations and Human Rights." In George W. Shepherd, Jr. and Ved P. Nanda (eds.), *Human Rights and Third World Development*, pp. 249–72. Westport, Conn.: Greenwood.

Lumsdaine, David Halloran. (1993). *Moral Vision in International Politics: The Foreign Aid Regime, 1949–1989*. Princeton, N.J.: Princeton University Press.

MacDonald, Hamish. (1992). "Rao's New Dowry: New Dehli Dismantles More Barriers to Foreign Ventures." *Far Eastern Economic Review*, February 20, 1992, pp. 40–41.

Machiavelli, Niccolo. (1952). *The Prince*. New York: New American Library.

MacLean, Douglas. (1979). "Constraints, Goals, and Moralism in Foreign Policy." In Peter G. Brown and Douglas MacLean (eds.), *Human Rights and U.S. Foreign Policy*, pp. 93–108. Lexington, Mass.: D. C. Heath.

Manning, Robert. (1985). "Deadlock Over Bhopal." *Far Eastern Economic Review*, July 11, 1985, pp. 49–54.

Martin, Rex. (1980). "Human Rights and Civil Rights." *Philosophical Studies*, 37(4):391–403.

Marton, Katherin. (1986). *Multinationals, Technology, and Industrialization: Implications and Impact in Third World Countries*. Lexington, Mass.: D. C. Heath.

Marx, Karl, & Engels, Frederich. (1848). *The Communist Manifesto*. New York: International Publishers.

May, Larry. (1987). *The Morality of Groups*. South Bend, Ind.: University of Notre Dame Press.

McCamant, John F. (1981). "A Critique of Present Measures of 'Human Rights Development' and an Alternative." In Ved P. Nanda, James Scarritt, and George W. Shepherd, Jr. (eds.), *Global Human Rights: Public Policies, Comparative Measures, and NGO Strategies*. Boulder, Colo.: Westview.

McCartney, Laton. (1988). *Friends in High Places, The Bechtel Story: The Most Secret Corporation and How It Engineered the World*. New York: Simon and Schuster.

McLaren, Ronald. (1984). "Kawaiso, Justice and Reciprocity." *Philosophy East and West*, 34(1): 53–66.

McNeill, Desmond. (1981). *The Contradictions of Foreign Aid*. London: Croom Helm.

Meeker-Lowry, Susan. (1992). "Maquiladoras: A Preview of Free Trade." *Z Magazine*, October 1992, pp. 25–30.

Meisenhelder, Tom. (1994). "The Decline of Socialism in Zimbabwe." *Social Justice*, 21(4): 83–100.

Meller, Patricio. (1992). *Adjustment and Equity in Chile*. Paris: Organization for Economic Cooperation and Development.

Meyer, William H. (1988). *Transnational Media and Third World Development*. Westport, Conn.: Greenwood.

Modelski, George (ed.). (1979). *Transnational Corporations and World Order*. San Francisco, Calif.: W. H. Freeman.

Moon, Bruce E., & Dixon, William. (1985). "Politics, the State and Basic Human Needs: A Cross National Study." *American Journal of Political Science*, 29(4): 661–94.

Morgenthau, Hans J. (1985). *Politics among Nations: The Struggle for Power and Peace*. New York: Knopf.

Morris, M. D. (1979). *Measuring the Conditions of the World's Poor: The Physical Quality of Life Index*. New York: Pergamon.

Muller, Ronald. (1979). "Poverty is the Product." In George Modelski (ed.), *Transnational Corporations and World Order*, pp. 245–62. San Francisco, Calif.: W. H. Freeman.

Nau, Henry R. (1990). *The Myth of America's Decline*. New York: Oxford University Press.

Nayyer, D. (1978). "Transnational Corporations and Manufactured Exports from Poor Countries." *Economic Journal*, 88(1): 549–84.

Nullis, Claire. (1993). "WHO Calls for Halt to Female Circumcision." *Wilmington News Journal*, May 13, 1993, p. 2.

Nye, Joseph S., Jr. (1990). *Bound to Lead*. New York: Basic Books.

O'Brien, Phil, & Roddick, Jackie. (1983). *Chile: The Pinochet Decade*. London: Latin America Bureau.

Overseas Private Investment Corporation. (1996). *Investor Services Handbook*. Washington, D.C.: Overseas Private Investment Corporation.

Page, Sheila. (1987). "Developing Country Attitudes Toward Foreign Investment." In Vincent Cable and Bishnodat Persaude (eds.), *Developing with Foreign Investment*, pp. 28–43. New York: Croom Helm-Methuen.

Panichas, George A. (1977). *The Simone Weil Reader*. New York: David McKay.

Panikkar, R. (1982). "Is the Notion of Human Rights a Western Concept?" *Diogenes*, 120 (Winter): 75–102.

Park, Han S. (1987). "Correlates of Human Rights: Global Tendencies." *Human Rights Quarterly*, 9(4): 405–13.

Paus, Eva A. (1994). "Economic Growth through Neoliberal Restructuring? Insights from the Chilean Experience." *Journal of Developing Areas*, 28(4): 31–56.

Pennock, J. Roland. (1981). "Rights and Citizenship." *News for Teachers of Political Science*, 31 (Fall).

Peterson, V. Spike. (1990). "Whose Rights? A Critique of the 'Givens' in Human Rights Discourse." *Alternatives*, 15(3): 303–44.

Pindyke, Robert S., & Rubinfeld, Daniel L. (1981). *Econometric Models and Economic Forecasts*. New York: McGraw-Hill.

Poe, Steven C. (1990). "Human Rights and U.S. Foreign Aid: A Review of Quantitative Studies and Suggestions for Future Research." *Human Rights Quarterly*, 12(3): 499–509.

Poe, Steven C. with Pilatovsky, Suzanne, Miller, Brian, & Ogundele, Ayo. (1994). "Human Rights and U.S. Foreign Aid Revisited: The Latin America Region." *Human Rights Quarterly*, 16(3): 539–58.

Poe, Steven C., & Sirirangsi, Rangsima. (1994). "Human Rights and U.S. Economic Aid to Africa." *Social Science Quarterly*, 75(3): 494–509.

Poe, Steven C., & Tate, Neal. (1994). "Repression of Human Rights to Personal Integrity in the 1980s: A Global Analysis." *American Political Science Review*, 88(4): 853–72.

Popper, Karl. (1965). *The Logic of Scientific Discovery*. New York: Harper & Row.

Price Waterhouse. (1991). *Doing Business in Chile*. Santiago: Price Waterhouse.

Pritchard, Kathleen. (1989). "Human Rights and Development: Theory and Data." In David P. Forsythe (ed.), *Human Rights and Development*, pp. 329-347. New York: St. Martin's.

Pye, Lucian. (1965). "The Concept of Political Development." *Annals of the American Academy of Political and Social Science*. Washington, D.C.: American Academy of Political and Social Science.

Rabkin, Rhoda. (1993). "How Ideas Become Influential: Ideological Foundations of Export-Led Growth in Chile (1973–1990)." *World Affairs*, 156(1): 3–25.

Ram, Mohan. (1984). "Counting the Cost." *Far Eastern Economic Review*, December 20, 1984, pp. 10–11.

Rawls, John. (1971). *A Theory of Justice*. Cambridge, Mass.: Harvard University Press.

Reich, Simon. (1989). "Roads to Follow: Regulating Direct Foreign Investment." *International Organization*, 43(4): 543–84.

Renteln, Alison Dundes. (1990). *International Human Rights: Universalism versus Relativism*. Newbury, Conn.: Sage.

Ricci, David M. (1984). *The Tragedy of Political Science: Politics, Scholarship, and Democracy*. New Haven, Conn.: Yale University Press.

Robertson, A. H., & Merrills, J. G. (1992). *Human Rights in the World*. New York: Manchester University Press.

Rose, Loretta Lynn. (1988). "Foreign Aid and Human Rights." *International Perspectives*, July/August 1988, pp. 23–25.

Sachs, Jeffrey. (1989). "Making the Brady Plan Work." *Foreign Affairs*, 68(3): 87–104.

Schifter, Richard. (1990). *Country Reports on Human Rights Practices for 1989*. Washington, D.C.: Government Printing Office.

Schifter, Richard. (1988). "The Semantics of Human Rights." *The Department of State Bulletin*. Washington, D.C.: Bureau of Public Affairs.

Schoultz, Lars. (1981). *Human Rights and United States Policy toward Latin America*. Princeton, N.J.: Princeton University Press.

Schoultz, Lars. (1980). "U.S. Foreign Policy and Human Rights." *Comparative Politics*, 13(1): 149–70.

Selcraig, Bruce. (1994). "Border Patrol." *Sierra*, May/June 1994, pp. 58–81.

Shaiken, Harley. (1993). "Two Myths about Mexico." *New York Times*, August 23, 1993.

Sieghart, Paul. (1983). "Economic Development, Human Rights and the Omelette Thesis." *Development Policy Review*, 1(1).

Silva, Eduardo. (1993). "Capitalist Coalitions, the State, and Neoliberal Economic Restructuring: Chile 1973–1988." *World Politics*, 45 (July): 526–59.

Singh, N. K. (1985). "Bhopal Eight Months Later." *World Press Review*, August 15, 1985, p. 56.

Skogly, Sigrun I. (1994). "Human Rights and Economic Efficiency: The Relationship between Social Cost of Adjustment and Human Rights Protection." In Peter Baehr, Hilde Hey, Jaqueline Smith, and Theresa Swinehart (eds.), *Human Rights in Developing Countries Yearbook 1994*. Boston, Mass.: Kluwer Law and Taxation Publishers.

Skogly, Sigrun I. (1993). "Structural Adjustment and Development: Human Rights — An Agenda for Change." *Human Rights Quarterly*, 15(4).

The South Commission. (1990). *The Challenge to the South*. New York: Oxford University Press.

Spero, Joan Edelman. (1990). *The Politics of International Economic Relations*. New York: St. Martin's.

Stohl, Michael with Carleton, David, & Johnson, Steven E. (1984). "Human Rights and U.S. Foreign Assistance from Nixon to Carter." *Journal of Peace Research*, 21(3): 215–26.

Strouse, James C., & Claude, Richard P. (1976). "Empirical Comparative Rights Research: Some Preliminary Tests of Development Hypotheses." In Richard P. Claude (ed.), *Comparative Human Rights*, pp. 51–68. Baltimore, Md.: Johns Hopkins University Press.

Subhash, C. Jain. (1993). *Market Evolution in Developing Countries: The Unfolding of the Indian Market*. New York: International Business Press.

Sunkel, Osvaldo. (1979). "Big Business and 'Dependencia'." In George Modelski (ed.), *Transnational Corporations and World Order*, pp. 216–25. San Francisco, Calif.: W. H. Freeman.

Thurow, Lester. (1992). *Head to Head: The Coming Economic Battle among Japan, Europe, and America*. New York: William Morrow.

Tiano, Susan. (1994). *Patriarchy on the Line*. Philadelphia, Pa.: Temple University Press.

Timerman, Jacobo. (1981). *Prisoner without a Name, Cell without a Number*. New York: Random House.

Tinder, Glenn. (1980). *Community: Reflections on a Tragic Ideal*. Baton Rouge: Louisiana State University Press.

Tolchin, Martin, & Tolchin, Susan J.. (1992). *Selling Our Security*. New York: Penguin Books.

Tonelson, Alan. (1982). "Human Rights: The Bias We Need." *Foreign Policy*, 78 (Winter): 52–74.

Unger, Sanford J., & Vale, Peter. (1985). "South Africa: Why Constructive Engagement Failed." *Foreign Affairs*, 64(2): 234–58.

United Nations Centre on Transnational Corporations. (1992). *Foreign Direct Investment and Technology Transfer in India*. New York: United Nations Centre on Transnational Corporations.

United Nations Development Program and The World Bank (1992). *African Development Indicators*. Washington, D.C.: International Bank for Reconstruction and Development/World Bank.

U.S. Department of Labor. (1993). *Comparison of Labor Law in the United States and Mexico: An Overview*. Washington, D.C.: U.S. Department of Labor.

U.S. Senate. (1979). "The International Telephone and Telegraph Company and Chile, 1970–1971." In George Modelski (ed.), *Transnational Corporations and World Order*, pp. 226–44. San Francisco, Calif.: W. H. Freeman.

Vance, Cyrus. (1977). "Human Rights and Foreign Policy." *Georgia Journal of International and Comparative Law 7*, Supplement, pp. 223–30.

Van Dyke, Vernon. (1977). "The Individual, the State, and Ethnic Communities in Political Theory." *World Politics*, 29 (April): 343–69.

Van Dyke, Vernon. (1970). *Human Rights, The United States, and World Community*. New York: Oxford University Press.

Van Hook, Mary P. (1994). "The Impact of Economic and Social Change on the Roles of Women in Botswana and Zimbabwe." *Affilia*, 9(3): 288–307.

Vasquez, John A. (1987). *Classics of International Relations*. Englewood Cliffs, N.J.: Prentice-Hall.

Wallerstein, Immanuel. (1979). "Underdevelopment and Phase B: Effect of Seventeenth Century Stagnation on Core and Periphery of the European World Economy." In Walter L. Goldfrank (ed.), *The World System of Capitalism: Past and Present*. Beverly Hills, Calif.: Sage.

Walters, Robert S., & Blake, David H. (1992). *The Politics of Global Economic Relations*. Englewood Cliffs, N.J.: Prentice-Hall.

Walzer, Michael. (1977). *Just and Unjust Wars: A Moral Argument with Historical Illustrations*. New York: Basic Books.

Weber, Max. (1946). "Politics as a Vocation." In H. H. Gerth and C. Wright Mills (eds.), *From Max Weber*. New York: Oxford University Press.

Welch, Claude E. (1984). "Human Rights as a Problem in Contemporary Africa." In Claude E. Welch and Ronald Meltzer (eds.), *Human Rights and Development in Africa*. Albany: State University of New York Press.

Wellman, Carl. (1985). *A Theory of Rights*. Totowa, N.J.: Rowman and Allanheld.

Whitehead, John C. (1988). "Third World Dilemma: More Debt or More Equity." *World Politics Annual Editions 88/89*, pp. 146–50.

Williams, Edward J., & Passe-Smith, John T. (1992). *The Unionization of the Maquiladora Industry: The Tamaulipan Case in National Context*. San Diego, Calif.: San Diego State University Press.

Woodward, Susan L. (1995). *Balkan Tragedy: Chaos and Dissolution After the Cold War*. Washington, D.C.: Brookings Institution.

Zimmerman, Robert F. (1993). *Dollars, Diplomacy and Dependency: Dilemmas of U.S. Economic Aid*. Boulder, Colo.: Lynne Rienner.

Zolberg, Aristide R., & Smith, Robert C. (1996). *Migration Systems in Comparative Perspective*. New York: International Center for Migration, Ethnicity and Citizenship.

Index

ABOUT THE AUTHOR

William H. Meyer is Associate Professor of Political Science at the University of Delaware. Among his earlier publications is *Transnational Media and Third World Development* (Greenwood, 1988).

3 5282 00510 4610

ISBN 0-275-96172-9

90000>

EAN

9 780275 961725

HARDCOVER BAR CODE